Fresh Start English

新发展英语

学习指南 2

顾　　问：王守仁
总 主 编：晨梅梅
主　　审：Brent Smith （加拿大）
本册主编：饶　辉
编　　者：（以姓氏笔画为序）
丁海燕　王原晴　文　昀　李晓梅
张　瑾　徐　楠　施荣根　秦志红
顾　萍

外语教学与研究出版社
FOREIGN LANGUAGE TEACHING AND RESEARCH PRESS
北京　BEIJING

图书在版编目(CIP)数据

新发展英语 = Fresh Start English：学习指南．2／晨梅梅总主编．— 北京：外语教学与研究出版社，2007.8

(新发展英语 = Fresh Start English)

ISBN 978-7-5600-6892-3

Ⅰ．新… Ⅱ．晨… Ⅲ．英语—教学参考资料 Ⅳ．H31

中国版本图书馆 CIP 数据核字 (2007) 第 130894 号

出 版 人：于春迟
项目负责：祝文杰
责任编辑：程　序
封面设计：王　薇
出版发行：外语教学与研究出版社
社　　址：北京市西三环北路 19 号 (100089)
网　　址：http://www.fltrp.com
印　　刷：北京双青印刷厂
开　　本：787×1092　1/16
印　　张：14.5
版　　次：2007 年 8 月第 1 版　2007 年 8 月第 1 次印刷
书　　号：ISBN 978-7-5600-6892-3
定　　价：17.90 元

*　　*　　*

前　言

《新发展英语》是一套专门为成人高等教育英语教学编写的教材，适用于各类高校的继续教育学院和成人高校中非英语专业的专升本、专转本、专接本、高升本学生，各类高校网络学院中远程教育非英语专业的本科学生，以及具有中级英语基础的人群。本教材在充分调研的基础上，遵循了高等学校中应用型人才的培养目标和高等继续教育的特点，重在巩固学生已经掌握的基础知识，并力图提高和拓展学生的英语实际应用能力。本着以应用为目的，以就业为导向，与社会需求、工作实际以及个人发展紧密联系的宗旨，本教材力求成为一套集可读性、趣味性、多元性、时代性和应用性为一体的新型成人本科综合实用英语教程。

本套教材共 4 级，供 4 个学期使用。每一级由主教材《新发展英语 综合教程》和配套辅助教材《新发展英语 学习指南》组成：

《新发展英语 综合教程》第 1 册起点约为 2,200 个单词，另学习新词汇约 500 个，着重巩固学生在本科阶段之前所学的英语基础知识。

《新发展英语 综合教程》第 2 册要求在巩固第 1 册的基础上再学习新词汇 500 个左右，并着重于进一步培养和提高学生的英语听、说、读、写、译五项基本技能。

《新发展英语 综合教程》第 3 册则要求在第 2 册基础上学习新词汇 500 个左右，并着重于进一步提高和发展学生的英语五项基本技能。

《新发展英语 综合教程》第 4 册的所有读写单元均以类型各异、题材丰富的应用文体为主（含读书报告、毕业论文、工作报告等）。除要求在第 3 册的基础上学习新词汇 500 个左右以外，第四册主要着眼于实用技能的拓展和应用，从而更好地与社会实践相结合。

为了更好地适应各类高校成人英语教学的实际需要，本套教材在编写框架上一改普通教材的传统结构，将主教材每册的 12 个单元分成 8 个读写单元和 4 个独立的听说单元，既可综合学习，全面展开，又可因时因地分开使用或选择学习，便于教学双方根据学习条件和课时量的多少各取所需，灵活使用。

与主教材配套的辅助教材《新发展英语 学习指南》与主教材各单元相呼应，读写单元配有课文翻译、语言点注释和所有练习的答案，并为学有余力的学生提供了泛读课文、相关背景资料和语言句法的讲解和配套练习。此外，听说单元还另配有文化背景资料和听说材料原文及参考情景交际对话，从而为教学双方提供最为方便和全面的学习参考。

由于全国各类高校的成人本科英语教学课时数相差很大，教学要求也相距甚远，教学条件和教学环境也各不相同，因此，编者建议，在使用本教材的时候，各校可根据本校教学单位的具体情况灵活掌握，可充分利用和发挥，也可压缩或选择使用。此外，由于本教材提供了较为详细的教学参考，因此在课堂教学时，建议教师可将一部分精力和时间放在组织小组讨论、角色表演等一些动脑、动手、动口等有利于语言表达和思维拓展的活动上。

本套教材由教育部高等学校大学外语教学指导委员会主任、南京大学外国语学院院长王守仁教授任顾问，由南京大学晨梅梅教授设计并任总主编。《学习指南》第2册由饶辉任主编，编者为（以姓氏笔画为序）：丁海燕、王原晴、文昀、顾萍、李晓梅、张瑾、施荣根、秦志红、徐楠。本教材在编写过程中得到了全国十多所高校的外国语学院、外语系、大学外语部以及继续教育学院或成人教育学院的大力支持。数十位高校一线的英语教师参与了编写工作。加拿大籍在华高校英语教师 Brent Smith 审阅了全书，出版社的编辑们为此倾注了许多心血，在此一并表示诚挚的谢意！

编者

2007年4月

Acknowledgments

We are deeply grateful to the authors and publishers of all the articles we use as the texts for this textbook. We apologize for the insufficient information in some cases due to our lack of resources. We intend to show every respect for intellectual property rights, and hope our pleading for the permission to use the related materials for teaching purposes will receive kind and generous consideration.

Unit 1

Extensive Reading

"Happiness Is..." by Susan Cheever from www.child.com/child/story.jhtml?storyid=/templatedata/child/story/data/happiness.xml.

Unit 2

Extensive Reading

"It Is Time to Let Go" by May Paron from *English Language Learning*, Issue No. 8, 2003. Foreign Language Teaching and Research Press.

Unit 4

Extensive Reading

"Give and Receive Highly-valued Compliments" by Steve Nakamoto from www.amazon.com/gp/richpub/syltguides/fullview/R1BTNRVCCDNNY4.

Unit 5

Extensive Reading

"Have You Hugged a Foreigner Today?" by Linell Davis from *Doing Culture: Cross-cultural Communication in Action*. Copyright © 1999 Foreign Language Teaching and Research Press.

Unit 7

Extensive Reading

"Say No to Western Fast Food" by U. J. Underwood from *An Integrated English Course 3* by Shi Zhikang. Copyright © 2005 Shanghai Foreign Language Education Press.

Unit 8

Extensive Reading

"Communications: Easier or More Difficult" by Michael Alvear from *College English*. Issue No. 2, 2002.

Unit 10

Extensive Reading

"Plagiarism for Dummies: Why Cheating Students Are Missing the Point of Education" by Paula Stiles from www2.associatedcontent.com/article/43206/ plagiarism_for_dummies_why_cheating.html.

Unit 11

Extensive Reading

"The Last Letter" from *Read and Think 3* by Ken Beatty. Copyright © 2005 Pearson Education Asia Limited and World Publishing Corporation.

Contents

UNIT 7 Happiness

Study Focus:

1. Understand this paradox (似非而是的论点): Fun does not bring happiness.
2. Learn to use the "more...than" structure.
3. Explain what happiness is.
4. Study the structure and features of paragraph writing.
5. Make some suggestions for living a happy life.

Part I Intensive Reading

课文译文

真正幸福的秘密

丹尼斯·普拉格

我住的地方有迪斯尼乐园、好莱坞和终年灿烂的阳光。你也许认为在这样一个迷人和充满乐趣的地方生活的人们会比别人更加幸福。如果这样的话，你就多多少少误解了幸福的本质。

很多聪明人把幸福等同于享乐。其实，享乐和幸福几乎或根本没有共同之处。享乐是我们在行为过程中的感受，幸福则是我们在行为结束后的感受。与享乐相比，它是一种更深刻、更持久的感受。

逛游乐场或看球赛，看电影或看电视，这些都是一些享乐性的活动，能帮助我们放松、暂时忘却烦恼，甚至还能让我们开怀大笑。但它们并不能带来幸福，因为活动结束时，它们的积极效果也会随之消失。

人们坚持认为充满乐趣、毫无痛苦的生活就等于幸福，这实际上却剥夺了他们获得真正幸福的机会。如果享乐和愉快等同于幸福，那么，痛苦必定等同于不幸福。但是事实恰恰相反：很多时候，能够带来幸福的事情往往都伴随着一定的痛苦。

结果，很多人都躲避那些实际上正是幸福之源的、需要付出艰苦努力的事情。他们害怕诸如结婚、抚养子女、成就事业、从事公益或慈善活动以及自我发展等不可避免会带来的痛苦。

问一个单身汉，为什么即使他觉得越来越不满足于约会却还是拒绝结婚。如果他是个诚实的人，他就会告诉你他害怕承诺。因为承诺实际上是相当痛苦的。单身生活充满了乐趣、冒险和兴奋。虽然婚姻生活也有这样的体验，但这些不是它最显著的特征。

同样，一对夫妇选择不要孩子是因为相对于略有痛苦的幸福，他们更喜欢没有痛苦的享乐。他们可以随时外出吃饭，到任何想去的地方旅游，愿意睡多晚就睡多晚。有小孩的夫妇如能睡上一晚的安稳觉或者能够有一个三天的假期他们就会感到非常幸运。我还没有见过哪位父母用“享乐”这个词来形容抚养孩子。

但是决定不生孩子的夫妇永远不会体验到拥抱孩子或夜里给孩子掖好被子时的愉悦心情。他们也永远不会知道看着孩子长大或与孙儿玩耍时所感受的那种欢乐。

当然，我也喜欢做那些享乐性的事情。我喜欢打短网拍墙球，喜欢和孩子（以及其他任何人）开玩笑；我的爱好也许太多了。

但这些形式的享乐并没有在真正的意义上给我带来幸福。更为艰苦的事情——写作、抚养孩子、与妻子加深感情、在世上行善等——会给我带来比享乐这最不持久的感觉更多的幸福。

理解和承认真正的幸福与享乐毫不相干是我们所能达到的最具有解放意义的认识之一。它解放时间：现在我们可以把更多的时间花在能真正增进我们的幸福的活动上。它解放金钱：购买无助于我们幸福的新车或时髦服装现在似乎已没有意义。另外它还把我们从嫉妒的心态中解放出来：我们现在明白，那些腰缠万贯、魅力十足的人，那些我们认定因为总是如此享乐所以肯定幸福的人，实际上也许一点都不幸福。

我们一旦懂得享乐并不带来幸福，我们就会开始一种截然不同的生活。其结果是真正地改变我们的生活。

Language Points of the Text

1. I live in the land of Disney, Hollywood and year-round sun. (*Para. 1*)

year-round: *adj.* existing, active, or continuous throughout the year “全年的；终年存在的，终年持续的”

Colorado is a year-round resort; there is fishing in the summer and skiing in the winter.

科罗拉多是个四季开放的胜地，那里夏天可以垂钓，冬天可以滑雪。

注意下列两词组的用法：

all-round（作定语）“全面的，多面的；全能的”

an all-round athlete 一名全能运动员

Measures should be taken to train the all-round ability of the college students.

应该采取措施对大学生进行全面能力的培养。

all the year round “整年”

John works all the year round, without a holiday.

约翰一年到头工作，没有一天假日。

2. If so, you have some mistaken ideas about the nature of happiness. (*Para. 1*)

mistaken ideas: wrong ideas 错误的观点

mistaken 作为形容词除修饰 idea, belief, view 等词外一般不用于名词前，但常和 be 动词连用做表语：

a. Many people have a mistaken belief that children should be asked to learn English as early as possible.

许多人误以为儿童应该尽可能早地学英语。

b. If I am not mistaken, you must bc from the south.

如果我没弄错的话，你肯定是南方人。

3. Many intelligent people equate happiness with fun. The truth is that fun and happiness have little or nothing in common. Fun is what we experience during the act. (*Para. 2*)

1) **equate...with...:** “将……等同于”

a. One should not equate passing examinations with being intelligent.

不能把通过考试与聪明等同起来。

b. Youth should not be equated with inexperience.

不应把年轻与没有经验等同起来。

2) **in common:** “共同”。在句中的结构为 have...in common（with somebody/something）

a. The newly married couples had very little in common.

这对新婚夫妇几乎没有共同之处。

b. I have a lot in common with my friend Andrew.

我与朋友安德鲁有很多共同点。

c. They have nothing in common in their teaching methods.

他们的教学方法毫无共同之处。

3) act 指具体的“举动、行为”，是短暂、个别的，强调动作结果。如：

He ran into the burning house and saved the child. That was really a brave act.

他冲进着火的房子救出小孩。那真是勇敢的行为。

4. But, they do not bring happiness, because their positive effects end when the fun ends. (*Para. 3*)

positive: *adj.* good or useful“好的，有用的；积极的，建设性的”

a. Don’t just make a negative criticism; give us some positive help.

别只是消极批评，给我们一些积极的帮助吧。

b. One secret of happiness is to hold a positive attitude towards life.

幸福的一个秘诀就是对生活持积极的态度。

5. The way people cling to the belief that a fun-filled, pain-free life equals happiness, actually diminishes their chances of ever attaining real happiness. (*Para. 4*)

The way 后面省略了 in which。people cling to the belief that... 为定语从句。

1) **chance:** *n.* possibility“可能性”

a. What is her chance (are her chances) of survival?

她生还的可能性有多大?

b. She has no chance of winning the match.

她不可能赢得比赛。

c. There is little chance of rain tomorrow.

明天下雨的可能性几乎没有。

d. Chances are (that) they have already arrived.

他们很可能已经到了。

2) **attain:** *vt.* to succeed in reaching a particular level or in getting something after trying for a long time“经长期努力后实现，获得，赢得”。近义词：obtain, gain

a. The black people in America attained freedom at last.

美国黑人终于获得了自由。

b. After three interviews she attained the position of student-council president.

她经过三次面试，赢得了学生会主席的职位。

6. But, in fact, the opposite is true: More times than not, things that lead to happiness involve some pain. (*Para. 4*)

1) **the opposite is true:** the reverse is true“情况正相反”

2) **more times than not:** more often than not, in most cases“多半，多数情况下”

3) **involve:** *v.*“包含，包括，需要”

a. Winning the game involves both skill and fortune.

赢得这场比赛既要技巧也要运气。

b. Learning a foreign language involves constant practice.

学外语需要不断实践。

7. As a result, many people avoid the very endeavors that are the source of true happiness. They fear the pain inevitably brought by such things as marriage, raising children, professional achievement, civil or charitable work, self-improvement. (*Para. 5*)

1) **endeavor:** *n.* effort “努力”（正式用语）

2) **source:** *n.* “来源”

For me, music is a great source of enjoyment.

对我而言，音乐是我快乐的一大源泉。

3) **raise:** *v.* to bring up “抚养”，多用于美国英语。

8. Ask a bachelor why he resists marriage even though he finds dating to be less and less satisfying. (*Para. 6*)

resist marriage: “拒绝结婚”

resist: *v.* “反对；抵抗，反抗；抵制，忍住”

a. I can never resist an ice-cream.

我一见冰淇淋就想吃。

b. When I heard the funny story, I could not resist laughing.

听见那个有趣的故事我不禁大笑起来。

c. the War of Resistance Against Japan 抗日战争

9. Marriage has such moments, but they are not its most distinguishing features. (*Para. 6*)

1) such moments 指代上文的 fun, adventure, excitement。

2) **distinguishing:** *adj.* “与众不同的，突出的”（在句中只作定语）。本词源于 distinguish “区别，区分，辨别”，另一形容词 distinguished 表示“杰出的、优秀的、受尊敬的”。

10. Similarly, couples who choose not to have children are deciding in favor of painless fun over painful happiness. (*Para. 7*)

...deciding in favor of painless fun over painful happiness: ...making a decision which prefers painless fun to painful happiness

in favor of: “赞成，主张”

a. Most people are not in favor of students getting married while studying in college.

多数人不赞成大学生在读书期间结婚。（句中作表语）

b. He refused a job in government in favor of a university appointment.

他拒绝了政府部门的工作而选择了大学里的一个职位。（句中作状语）

11. But these forms of fun do not contribute in any real way to my happiness. More difficult endeavors—writing, raising children, creating a deep relationship with my wife, trying to do good in the world—will bring me more happiness than can ever be found in fun, that least permanent of things. (*Para. 10*)

1) **contribute to:** to help to make something happen“有助于，促成，导致”

a. Fresh air and exercise contribute to good health.

新鲜空气和锻炼有助于健康。

b. Many factors contribute to this phenomenon.

诸多因素引起这一现象。

c. Her singing contributed greatly to the success of the party.

她的演唱对晚会的成功起了很大的作用。

2) **permanent:** *adj.* lasting“持久的，永久的”

比较 for ever, for good（副词短语）

3) ...will bring me more happiness than can ever be found in fun, that least permanent of things 中的 that least permanent of things 为 fun 的同位语。

...than can ever be found in fun 是一个省略结构，完整形式为：...than what can ever be found in fun.

12. Understanding and accepting that true happiness has nothing to do with fun is one of the most liberating realizations we can ever come to. (*Para. 11*)

1) **have nothing to do with:**“与……毫无关系”。类似的句型：have something to do with 与……有关

2) **come to:** to reach, to arrive at“达成（协议等），取得（结论等）”

come to a conclusion/an agreement/a decision

13. We now understand that all those rich and glamorous people who we were so sure are happy because they are always having so much fun actually may not be happy at all. (*Para. 11*)

注意本句的主要结构是 We now understand that all those rich and glamorous people... actually may not be happy at all。we were so sure...having so much fun 为定语从句。

14. The moment we understand that fun does not bring happiness, we begin to lead our lives differently. (*Para. 12*)

1) **the moment:** as soon as "一……就……"。类似的句型还有：The minute..., The instant... 等。

2) **life-transforming:** *adj.* "改变生活的"

Part II Text Comprehension (Key)

Reading Analysis

1. C 2. D 3. D 4. A 5. D

Information Recall and Summary

A.

1. He lives in the land of Disney and Hollywood where he can enjoy sunshine all the year round.
2. Happiness is equated with fun.
3. Fun is an emotion we experience during an act. Fun activities, such as going to an amusement park or a ballgame, watching a movie or television are the activities that help us relax, temporarily forget our problems, and even laugh.
4. He thinks that pain is not necessarily related to unhappiness and that in many cases things that lead to happiness involve some pain.
5. The difficult and painful endeavors such as marriage, raising children, professional achievement, religious commitment, civil or charitable work, and self-improvement are the source of true happiness.
6. Because they are afraid of making a commitment, which is very painful.
7. They will never experience the pleasure and joys in raising children.
8. Because it can save us time and money by freeing us from the activities which do not increase our happiness. We will realize wealth does not necessarily mean happiness and we will live a different, happy and new life.

B.

This passage is a discussion about the nature or real meaning of happiness. In view of some people's wrong ideas about happiness, the author maintains that fun and happiness are different and that fun activities cannot bring happiness. He illustrates with examples why many people choose not to do something that will lead to real happiness: They are afraid of pain and therefore prefer painless fun to painful happiness. Then he takes himself for example and argues that difficult things, not fun things, will bring him happiness. Finally, the author stresses the importance of a correct understanding of happiness. (100 words)

Information Organization

Topics	Supporting Details
Fun and happiness (Paras. 1-3)	You may think that people living in fun-filled places are happier than others. Many intelligent people think that fun equals happiness. The fact is that fun and happiness are different and fun activities do not bring happiness.
Pain and happiness (Paras. 4-10)	People think that fun and pleasure equal happiness and pain equals unhappiness. In fact, things that lead to happiness involve some pain. What many people do: avoid the painful and difficult endeavors. The reason: they fear pain and are afraid of making a commitment. Examples: a bachelor who resists marriage and couples who choose not to have children. The author's opinion: more difficult endeavors will bring more happiness.
The significance of a correct understanding of happiness (Paras. 11-12)	Liberating time and money; changing our outlook on happiness as well as our way of life.

Part III Skill Building (Key)

Word Forms

A.

1. care-free childhood
2. peace-loving people
3. time-consuming tasks
4. man-eating animals
5. a cotton-filled coat
6. a world-famous scientist
7. a state-owned company
8. home-made rice wine

B.

1. a. equals b. equality 2. a. liberty b. liberate
3. a. distinguish b. distinguished 4. a. contribution b. contributes

Vocabulary in Context

A.

1. d 2. e 3. g 4. h 5. c 6. a 7. b 8. f

B.

1. has nothing to do with what we are discussing
2. decided in favor of big companies over small ones
3. contributed to her failure in the exam

C.

1. A 2. D 3. C 4. D 5. A 6. B

D.

a. 1) action　2) act　3) action　4) activities

b. 1) source　2) source　3) origin　4) origin

Key Structures

A.

1. The way you have done your hair gives me a surprise.
2. The way many parents educate their children can be very bad for their development.
3. The way some young people deal with failures makes me think a lot.
4. The job needs more people than are provided because it is very difficult.
5. We often advise him not to drink more wine than is good for his health.
6. He never accepts more work than can be done.

B.

1. Many college students equate passing CET-4 with being good at English. The truth is that some high-scoring students in CET-4 cannot communicate with foreigners.
2. The moment she completed her studies in the junior college, she began to take undergraduate courses in a university.

Translation

A.

1. 娱乐性活动
2. 积极的影响
3. 慈善工作
4. raise children
5. more times than not
6. make a commitment

B.

1. B　2. A

Writing

A.

The following topic sentences are not effective and need some improvement:

This car is more than 20 years old.

I spent many summer vacations in Nanjing.

Mr. Smith is given a job.

These sentences simply tell the readers some facts, and they do not present the author's opinions or attitudes.

Improved versions:

My old car is my most valuable possession.

The summer vacation I spent in Nanjing was extremely depressing.

Mr. Smith is given a challenging job.

课文译文

幸福生活指南

彼得·凌

一天，我在书店里随便翻阅书刊时（这是我的习惯）看到一本有意思的小书，书名是《爱自己指南》。

书中用字母表的每一个字母代表一个鼓舞人心、催人奋进的词，对我们的生活具有指导意义。

凭借记忆并对书中的指导原则稍做修改，我得以总结出幸福生活的基础知识。

"A"代表懂得自己作为一个人的价值（acknowledging or appreciating your value as a person)，一个上苍赋予了自我意识、创造性想象力、良知、自立能力、意志力和多种智慧的人。

"B"代表相信自己（believing in yourself)，相信自己有能力利用自己的天赋过一种富有成效、意义深远的生活。

"C"代表关心自己和他人（caring about yourself and people)，满足自己在生活、学习、爱情和为后人留下点什么方面的基本需求，同时也要关心自己周围的人的类似的需求。

"D"代表胸怀大志（dreaming big dreams），追寻那似乎不可能实现但却给你指明方向的最异想天开的梦想。

"E"代表同情他人（empathizing with people），对别人的感受和想法表示理解。

"F"代表乐趣（fun），让自己享受生活，从自己所做的事和行事的方式中获得快乐。

"G" 代表慷慨给予（giving generously），给予他人你的时间、乐观的思想、关爱以及任何你能带给他人的东西。

"H"代表满意（happiness），对自己现在的状况和自己生活中的行为表示满意。

"I"代表想象（imagination），充分发挥想象力追寻梦想并寻找实现梦想的途径。

"J"代表快乐（joy），给你所遇到的人、一起生活或工作的人带去欢乐。

"K"代表知识（knowledge），不断学习并用自己的知识改善生活和社会。

"L"代表爱（love），无条件的爱，不仅指情感上或肉体上的爱，还有精神上的爱。

"M"代表激励（motivation），不仅约束自己、鞭策自己，而且还鼓励他人显露身手。

"N"代表友好（being nice），甚至对陌生人也要亲切友善。

"O"代表开明（openness），愿意接受他人、新观念以及一些荒谬但有趣的观点。

"P" 代表耐心（patience），管住自己，别太性急，按自然规律办事。

"Q"代表宁静（quiet），给自己的心片刻的安宁，找个清静的地方进行自查、反省，恢复活力。

"R"代表尊重（respect），尊重种族、宗教、文化、信仰和价值观的多样性。

"S" 代表微笑（smiling），那种甚至在绝望时刻也能自如微笑的能力。

"T"代表信任（trust），信任自己、亲戚、朋友和同事。

"U"代表团结（unity），与他人和平共处，尊重家人、朋友和同事的看法。

"V"代表胜利（victory），自己无论做什么，哪怕取得了再微不足道的成绩，也要加以奖赏和庆贺。

"W"代表惊奇（wonder），对人类、男人和女人、自己以及自然保持好奇之心。

"X"代表未知因素（"X" factor），寻找你自己身上和别人身上的特别之处，找出每个人的优势。

"Y"代表接受（saying yes to）有积极意义的挑战和冒险。

"Z"代表热情（zest），对生活的热情，对自己要做的事情的热情。

希望这些生活基础知识能成为你的生活指南。也许你可以用自己的话来表达使这些生活指南对你更有意义。

Reading Comprehension

1. F 2. T 3. F 4. F 5. F

Part V Extensive Reading

Happiness Is...

By Susan Cheever

1 "I'm not happy," my son said, as we stood in front of the ice-cream store one summer afternoon. We had just come from a birthday celebration, and the warm air felt good after the air-conditioned **chill** of the party. I gently guided my son away from the store. "Do you think an **ice-cream cone** would have made you happy?" I asked, **subtly** trying to indicate that an ice-cream cone after birthday cake wasn't something any **civilized** person would want. "Yes," he said, facing straight ahead. "An ice-cream cone would have made me happy."

2 "That's not happiness," I said. "What is happiness, then?" he asked. His question stopped me. Then I was able to find the word for the way my heart lifts sometimes when I'm just doing nothing with one of my children. "This, this is happiness," I said.

3 When Thomas Jefferson included "the **pursuit** of happiness" as a right in the Declaration of Independence, he was writing as one of the fathers of our country, but for real fathers and mothers, he has helped create centuries of **confusion**. What is happiness, **anyway**?

4 I remember how **passionately** I **wished for** things as a child and how furiously I believed that they would make me happy. When I was 5, I was **seized** by a desire for a baby grand piano. I had listened to a friend of my parents play **thrilling**, heart-stopping songs on his piano.

5 I wanted one so **badly**, my parents came to believe I must be some kind of piano **prodigy**. My mother **haunted auction** houses until she found a baby grand and won it on a low **bid**. The day I came home from first grade to find my piano

in our living room, I was delighted. I played a few **notes**, but when I realized how much effort it would take to **coax** pleasing sounds from the piano, I gave up. I **rarely** played after that.

6 I know that parents who try to make their children happy with toys and ice-cream cones and grand pianos have the best **intentions**, but they are **somehow** missing the point. Happiness doesn't come from desires being fulfilled; it comes from emotional needs being met. It comes from the **company** of those we love. Playing the piano might have made me happy—if I had been willing to spend the time it takes to learn—but having the piano didn't matter to me at all. Getting what we want is **gratification**; happiness is something else. Happiness is something that comes from **living through** desires—**thwarted** and **gratified**—and from finding a way to connect with the world and other people.

7 My children have had plenty of disappointments—I'm **divorced** from their father—yet they are happy. My 18-year-old daughter is happy partly because she has a sense of her own usefulness: She has helped me raise her brother. **Early on**, she discovered the cause and effect of study and good grades; she's now at Princeton. This makes her happy. My son is happy because he knows he has people who love him and support his talents. It's not the **acquisition** of a new book or a Lego set that makes him happy; it's the knowledge that he'll be allowed to **pursue** the interests **embodied** in those things. I make him happy by **honoring** his **passions**, not by gratifying them.

8 Thinking about it, I **associate** happiness with a feeling of satisfaction, a feeling I often get by being useful to someone else or by trying to find a way to **quiet** my mind. I believe happiness is the feeling of loving **balance** I have sometimes, on a late summer afternoon, walking down the street with one of my children—even though we didn't get an ice-cream cone. (633 words)

NEW WORDS

chill /tʃɪl/ *n.* 寒冷，寒气

cone /kəʊn/ *n.* 锥形物，圆锥体

ice-cream cone *n.* 冰淇淋蛋卷

subtly /'sʌtli/ *adv.* 巧妙地

civilized /'sɪvəlaɪzd/ *adj.* 文明的，有教养的

pursuit /pə'sjuːt/ *n.* the act of pursuing 追求

confusion /kən'fjuːʒən/ *n.* the act of confusing or the state of being confused 混乱

anyway /'eniweɪ/ *adv.* （加强问题的语气）到底，究竟

NEW WORDS

passionately /'pæʃənətli/ *adv.* 充满热情地

seize /siːz/ *vt.* to affect or take control of（情绪）支配，影响

thrilling /'θrɪlɪŋ/ *adj.* interesting and exciting 令人激动的

badly /'bædli/ *adv.* very much 非常

prodigy /'prɒdɪdʒi/ *n.* an unusually clever child 天才（特指神童）

haunt /hɔːnt/ *vt.* to visit often 常去

auction /'ɔːkʃən/ *n.* 拍卖

bid /bɪd/ *n.* an offer to pay a certain price for something esp. at an auction 出价，投标

note /nəʊt/ *n.* 音键，音调

coax /kəʊks/ *vt.* 哄，劝诱

rarely /'reəli/ *adv.* not often 很少

intention /ɪn'tenʃən/ *n.* plan, purpose 意图，目的

somehow /'sʌmhaʊ/ *adv.* for some reason that is not clear 不知何故

company /'kʌmpəni/ *n.* 陪伴

gratification /ˌgrætɪfɪ'keɪʃən/ *n.* satisfaction 满意

thwart /θwɔːt/ *vt.* 阻碍，反对

gratify /'grætɪfaɪ/ *vt.* to satisfy 使满足

divorce /dɪ'vɔːs/ *vt.* 与……离婚

acquisition /ˌækwɪ'zɪʃən/ *n.* 获得，取得

pursue /pə'sjuː/ *vt.* to carry out or follow something esp. interests, plan 追求

embody /ɪm'bɒdi/ *vt.* 体现

honor /'ɒnə(r)/ *vt.* to show respect for 尊重

passion /'pæʃən/ *n.* a very strong liking for something 酷爱

associate /ə'səʊʃieɪt/ *vt.* to connect in one's mind 把……联系在一起

quiet /'kwaɪət/ *vt.* to cause to become quiet 使平静，使安心

balance /'bæləns/ *n.* 平静、稳定的精神或心理状态；平衡

PHRASES & EXPRESSIONS

wish for 盼望，企求

live through 经历

early on 在初期，早先

PROPER NAMES

Princeton /'prɪnstən/ 普林斯顿，美国新泽西州中部一自治镇，是普林斯顿大学所在地

Lego /'legəʊ/ 乐高拼装玩具（商标名称）

Cultural Background

1. Susan Cheever

苏珊 · 奇弗，美国小说家。本文选自其所著 *As Good As I Could Be* 一书。

2. Thomas Jefferson

托马斯 · 杰斐逊（1743 年 4 月 13 日—1826 年 7 月 4 日），美国第三任总统（1801 年—1809 年）。他是《独立宣言》的起草者，与华盛顿、富兰克林等人一起被尊称为“美国之父”。

3. the Declaration of Independence

《独立宣言》，是一份于 1776 年 7 月 4 日由托马斯 · 杰斐逊起草，并由其他 13 个殖民地代表签署的最初声明美国从英国独立的文件。文件的开头部分提到追求幸福的权利：“We hold these truths to be self-evident, that all men are created equal, that they are endowed by their Creator with certain unalienable rights, that among these are life, liberty and the pursuit of happiness.”（我们认为下述真理是不言而喻的：人人生而平等，造物主赋予他们若干不可让与的权利，其中包括生存权、自由权和追求幸福的权利。）

课文译文

幸福是……

苏珊 · 奇弗

“我不觉得幸福，”一个夏日的午后当我们站在一家冰淇淋店门口的时候，儿子这样对我说道。我们刚刚参加完一个生日聚会出来，与屋里空调冷气的寒意相比，外面温暖的空气感觉很好。我轻轻地领着儿子从那家冰淇淋店门前走开。“你觉得给你买一个冰淇淋蛋卷就会使你感到幸福吗？”我问道，巧妙地向他暗示：吃完生日蛋糕后又要吃冰淇淋蛋卷并非优雅之举。“是的，”他回答道，面向前方。“如果买了冰淇淋蛋筒我会感到幸福的。”

“那不是幸福，”我说。“那什么是幸福呢？”他问道。他的问题令我一时语塞。不过后来我终于还是找到了回答他的措词，就是有时当我空闲时与我的某个孩子在一起的那种心情愉悦的感觉。“这，这就是幸福，”我回答道。

当托马斯 · 杰斐逊把“对幸福的追求”作为一种权利写入《独立宣言》时，他是我们国家的先父之一，而对于普通的父母们来说，他是持续了几个世纪的一场混乱的创始者。究竟什么是幸福？

我还记得我孩提时代曾经多么强烈地希望得到一些东西而又那么坚决地相信它们会使我幸福。我5岁时突然间想拥有一架小钢琴。因为我曾经听父母的一位朋友用他的钢琴弹奏出激动人心的、惊心动魄的乐曲。

我要一台小钢琴的愿望是如此的强烈，父母开始觉得我肯定具有某种钢琴神童的天赋。母亲经常往拍卖行跑，直到她发现了一台小钢琴并以低价成交。那时我读一年级，有一天放学回家，看见我的钢琴放在客厅里，心里很高兴。我弹了几个音符，但是当我意识到要用钢琴弹出动人的琴声需要付出多大努力时，我放弃了。从那以后几乎再也没有碰过它。

我知道那些用玩具、冰淇淋蛋卷以及大钢琴试图让孩子们幸福的父母们的意图是好的，但他们不知何故都没有抓住问题的关键。幸福并不在于愿望的实现，而在于情感需求的满足。幸福在于我们与我们所爱的人在一起。弹钢琴可能会使我感到幸福——如果当时我愿意花时间去学习弹钢琴的话——但拥有钢琴对我来说并不重要。获得我们想得到的是满意；而幸福则是其他的东西。幸福来源于愿望的经历过程——受到挫折以及得到满足——幸福来源于寻找与世界交流、与他人交流的途径。

我的孩子们有诸多的失望——我与他们的父亲离了婚——然而他们却感到幸福。我18岁的女儿感到幸福，部分原因是由于她有一种感觉，感到自己的作用。她一直帮我带她的弟弟。她很早就明白了学习和优良成绩之间的因果关系；现在她在普林斯顿上学，这让她感到很幸福。我的儿子感到幸福因为他知道有人爱他，知道有人培养他的才能。不是有了一本新书或得到一套乐高拼装玩具他就感到幸福；使他幸福的是他知道他会被允许继续发展自己在这些方面的兴趣。我是通过尊重他的爱好而不是满足他的需求来使他感到幸福的。

每每想到幸福，我总是把它与一种满足感联系在一起，通过使自己能够有助于他人或者通过努力设法平静自己的心态我就能常常得到这样的感觉。我认为幸福就是在一个夏日的午后与我的孩子在街上漫步时所产生的那种情感洋溢、心态稳定的感觉——即使我们没有买冰淇淋蛋卷。

Notes to the Text

1. "Do you think an ice-cream cone would have made you happy?" I asked, subtly trying to indicate that an ice-cream cone after birthday cake wasn't something any civilized person would want. (*Para. 1*)

   引号里的句子为虚拟语气，因为此刻母亲已经轻轻地将儿子从冰淇淋店领开，并没有为他买冰淇淋蛋卷。

2. Then I was able to find the word for the way my heart lifts sometimes when I'm just doing nothing with one of my children. (*Para. 2*)

   my heart lifts: "心里感到高兴"。

   不能望文生义，理解为"心（紧张得）提了起来"。lift 在这里表示"受到鼓舞；感到高兴"的意思。如：Their spirits lifted when help came. 当救援来到时，他们精神大振。作者没有具体说明 the word 的内容，只是说它是她用来表达自己与孩子在一起时愉快的心情的用语。

3. When Thomas Jefferson included "the pursuit of happiness" as a right in the Declaration of Independence, he was writing as one of the fathers of our country, but for real fathers and mothers, he has helped create centuries of confusion. (*Para. 3*)

   ...he has helped create centuries of confusion 是指杰斐逊在《独立宣言》中提到"追求幸福"，但对幸福的具体涵义并没有提到，以至造成几个世纪以来对于幸福涵义理解上众说纷纭的混乱局面。

4. It comes from the company of those we love. (*Para. 6*)

   company 在这里是"陪伴"的意思。本句含义：幸福在于我们与我们所爱的人在一起。这与本文第二段中 Then I was able to find the word for the way my heart lifts sometimes when I'm just doing nothing with one of my children. 和 "This, this is happiness," I said. 以及结尾段中的 I believe happiness is the feeling of loving balance I have sometimes, on a late summer afternoon, walking down the street with one of my children—even though we didn't get an ice-cream cone. 相呼应，表达的含义相同。

5. It's not the acquisition of a new book or a Lego set that makes him happy; it's the knowledge that he'll be allowed to pursue the interests embodied in those things. (*Para. 7*)

   句中有两个 It's...that... 强调句型。knowledge 在这里是"知道，得知，了解到"的意思。例如：The knowledge that the car might skid made Bill drive very slowly. 知道车轮可能会打滑，比尔将车开得很慢。Mike denied all knowledge of the murder. 迈克否认知道谋杀案的任何情况。

6. I believe happiness is the feeling of loving balance I have sometimes, on a late summer afternoon, walking down the street with one of my children—even though we didn't get an ice-cream cone. (*Para. 8*)

   balance: "心理、心态的平衡"。ice-cream cone 在本文开头已经提到，有象征的意义，象征并不能真正给人们带来幸福的"物质的需求和愿望"。除 ice-cream cone 之外，类似的具有象征作用的词还有不少，如：a baby grand piano, a new book, a Lego set 等。作者在文章再次提及 ice-cream cone，使文章首尾呼应，突出中心思想，增强了文章感染力。

Reading Comprehension

Choose the best option to complete each of the following statements.

1. The reason why the son was not happy is that __________.

   A. he didn't feel good because of the cold air in the room where the birthday party was held

   B. he could not eat ice-cream at the birthday party

   C. he was not allowed to eat the birthday cake

   D. his mother did not agree to buy him some ice-cream

2. Sometimes when the author is with one of her children without doing anything, she feels __________.

   A. happy　　B. relaxed

   C. empty　　D. nervous

3. The author writes about her childhood story in order to tell the readers __________.

   A. what happiness really means

   B. her parents' intentions in buying her the piano

   C. her thankfulness for what her parents did for her at that time

   D. her great regret for giving up learning to play the piano

4. Another possible title for this passage is __________.

   A. Happiness Is Having a Peaceful Mind

   B. Happiness Is a Matter of Feeling

   C. Happiness Is Being Together with the People You Love

   D. Happiness Is Being Useful to Others

Key

1. D　2. A　3. A　4. B

Vocabulary Study

Replace each of the underlined parts with the best choice given.

1. When I was 5, I was seized by a desire for a baby grand piano.

   A. arrested　　B. caught　　C. held　　D. taken

2. I wanted one <u>so badly</u>, my parents came to believe I must be some kind of piano prodigy.

A. so more　　B. not so well

C. so much　　D. so seriously

3. I know that parents who try to make their children happy with toys and ice-cream cones and grand pianos have the best intentions, but they are <u>somehow</u> missing the point.

A. in some way　　B. for some reason

C. somewhat　　D. somewhere

4. Happiness doesn't come from desires being fulfilled; it comes from emotional needs being <u>met</u>.

A. encountered　　B. agreed

C. experienced　　D. satisfied

5. It's not the acquisition of a new book or a Lego set that makes him happy; it's the knowledge that he'll be allowed to <u>pursue</u> the interests embodied in those things.

A. carry out　　B. run after

C. chase after　　D. search out

6. I make him happy by <u>honoring</u> his passions, not by gratifying them.

A. praising　　B. respecting

C. loving　　D. celebrating

Key

1. D　2. C　3. B　4. D　5. A　6. B

UNIT 2 Attitude

Study Focus:

1. Understand why it is unwise to save what is dear to you for a special occasion.
2. Practice using the "It's…that…" structure.
3. Explain why people should let go of（放弃）the negative things in life.
4. Learn how to write Telephone Messages.
5. Explain what is meant by "Change 'if only' to 'next time'".

Part I Intensive Reading

课文译文

每一天都是上帝赐予的礼物
——生活的原则

安·韦尔斯

姐夫打开姐姐衣柜最下面的抽屉，拿出一个用纸包着的东西。"这个，"他说，"不再是条什么衬裙了，现在只能当睡裙了。"他扔掉裹在外面的纸，把衬裙递给我。裙子做工精美，真丝质地，手工制作，镶着轻盈透明的花边。价格标签还在上面，数额可观。"我们第一次去纽约时简买的，少说也有八九年了。她还没舍得穿过，说要留到特别的日子穿。唉，我想现在是时候了。"他从我手中拿回衬裙，把它和床上我们要送到丧葬员那里的衣服放到一起。他的手在那柔软的衬裙上停了好一会儿，然后砰地关上抽屉，转身对我说："不要再把任何东西留到什么特别的时刻了。活着的每一天都是特别的。"

在整个葬礼中以及后来帮着姐夫和外甥女料理姐姐意外亡故后那些令人伤心的事务期间，我脑海中一直回响着他那番话。从姐姐家所在的那座中西部城市飞回加州的途中，我又想起那番话。我想到了姐姐从未见过、听过或做过的种种事情。想到了那些她虽然做了但却没有意识到有什么特别的事情。

我至今仍记得那番话，它改变了我的生活。我现在花更多的时间读书，而不是打扫卫生。我坐在露天平台上欣赏风景，而不再去操心园中的杂草。我花更多的时间和家人、朋友在一起，而不是去参加那些委员会会议。只要可能，生活应该是供人品味享受，而不是负累忍受的。我现在正努力认识这些时刻，并珍惜它们。

我不再“攒”任何东西。每当发生特别的事情，比如体重减了一磅，水池疏通了，第一朵山茶花开了，我们都把最好的瓷器和水晶器皿拿出来用。我要是高兴，就穿着漂亮的运动服去市场。我认为如果我看上去挺富有，我就能花上 28.49 美元买一小袋食品而不眨一下眼睛。我也不再把最好的香水留到特别聚会上用，五金店的店员、银行的出纳有和我那些参加聚会的朋友一样的能闻到香水的鼻子。

“有朝一日”、“总有一天”已不再是我使用的词汇。如果某件事值得看、听或做，我就会立即付诸行动。我不知道，如果姐姐当初知道大家都以为可以拥有的明天已不再属于自己了，她会做些什么。我猜她会给家人和几个好友打电话。也许会给从前的朋友打电话，为过去因鸡毛蒜皮的事引起的争吵道歉并重归于好。我想她会去吃她最喜欢的中国菜。但这只是我的猜测——我永远也不会知道了。

如果我知道自己时日不多，我会因那些还没有来得及做的小事感到气恼。我气恼，因为自己一再推迟看望好友，总想着改天再联系。我气恼，因为我还没写我打算要写的信——我想总有一天会写的。我会气恼和难过，因为我没有经常告诉丈夫和女儿我真心地爱着他们。

如今，我尽力不再耽搁、阻碍或保存能给我们的生活带来欢乐、为生活增添欢笑和光彩的东西。

每天清晨当我睁开双眼，我告诉自己今天是个特别的日子。每一天、每一分钟、每一次呼吸——真的都是上帝恩赐的礼物。

Language Points of the Text

1. My brother-in-law opened the bottom drawer of my sister's bureau and lifted out a tissue-wrapped package. (*Para. 1*)

brother-in-law 和 tissue-wrapped 为复合词。复合词是由两个或两个以上的词构成的新词，词与词之间有的用连字符连接，有的分开写，有的连在一起写。复合词的词性一般由最后一个构词成分的词性决定，重音落在第一个构词成分上，词义具有习语性质，许多复合词的意义不是其构成成分意义的总和。复合词的构成主要有以下几种情况：

noun + noun: chairperson, toothbrush

noun + verb + -ing: time-consuming (耗时的), air-conditioning (空调)

noun + verb + -ed: man-made (人造的), state-owned (国有的)

adjective + noun: shorthand (速记), deadline (截止日期)

adjective + noun + -ed: long-headed (精明的，敏锐的), red-eyed (红眼的，眼圈哭红的)

verb + noun: driveway (车道), breakneck (飞速惊险的)

adverb + noun: uptown (住宅区), downwind (顺风地；在下风处)

noun + verb: rainfall (降雨), waterfall (瀑布)

verb + adverb: breakup (破裂), knockout (击倒)

noun + adjective: carefree (快乐的；不需负责任的), lifelong (毕生的)

verb + -ing + noun: living room (起居室), drinking water (饮用水)

其他形式的复合词还有：go-between (中间人), father-in-law (岳父；公公), forget-me-not (勿忘我) 等。

2. "This," he said, "is not a slip. This is lingerie." (*Para. 1*)

slip: *n.*"无袖衬裙"，它的常用词义还有："小纸条（*n.*）；疏漏（*n.*）；滑倒（*vi.*）"

a. He wrote my address on a slip of paper.

他在一张纸条上记下我的地址。

b. He claimed that "recieve" was a slip of the pen for "receive".

他声称 recieve 是 receive 的笔误。

c. She slipped while she was getting out of the bath.

她从浴缸出来时滑倒了。

3. He discarded the tissue and handed me the slip. (*Para. 1*)

discard: *vt.* to get rid of something because you no longer need it"丢弃"

Some students discard objects because they don't know how to fix them.

有些学生丢弃东西是因为不会修理它们。

注意它与 abandon, desert 的区别：discard 指"扔掉无用或多余的具体物品"，用于人时，有强烈的轻蔑意味，用于思想、信仰时指"断然放弃"，如：

He discarded his illusions and regained his senses.

他抛弃了幻想，恢复了理智。

They were just using him, and were prepared to discard him if he no longer served their purpose.

他们只是在利用他，并准备在他不再有用时抛弃他。

abandon 和 desert 指"遗弃物品或人，或离弃某地"，abandon 含有"出于需要而不是很情愿地或通过逃避责任最终彻底放弃"的意思，如：

a. The stolen car was abandoned only five miles away.

被盗汽车被遗弃在仅 5 英里之外的地方。

b. After the war, many Londoners abandoned the city for good, starting a population decline.

战后，许多伦敦人永远离开了伦敦，导致该市人口开始下降。

desert 含有“故意背叛誓言、不履行职责和义务”，如：

a. He deserted his wife and child for another woman.

他为另一个女人抛弃了妻儿。

b. Many New Orleans police officers deserted the city in the days before the storm.

在暴风雨到来之前，新奥尔良许多警察都弃城而去。

4. The price tag with an astronomical figure on it was still attached. (*Para. 1*)

attach: *v.* to fasten or join one thing to another“缚，绑，系”

The little boy attached the balloon to his mother's dress.

小男孩把气球系在妈妈的连衣裙上。

attach 的常用搭配有：attach importance/significance/value/weight to“认为……重要”

Both her parents attach importance to education.

她父母亲都认为教育很重要。

5. Jan bought this the first time we went to New York, at least 8 or 9 years ago. (*Para. 1*)

1) 句中 the first time 引导时间状语从句，与其类似的词组还有 the last time, the（first/second/third...）day/week/year, the moment/minute/second“一……就”, immediately“一……就”，every time“每次”，(the) next time“下次”，例如：

a. Mary fell in love with Shanghai the first time she spent the Spring Festival in the city.

玛丽第一次在上海过春节时就爱上了这个城市。

b. Every time I listen to the song, I'll think of my sister.

每次我听到这首歌就会想起我的姐姐。

c. The military training program began the first day the students arrived.

学生们到的第一天就开始了军训。

d. His wife was sent to the operating room the moment we reached the hospital.

我们一到医院他的妻子就被送进了手术室。

2) time 后接定语从句时，引导词 that 或 at/in which 可以省略：

The first time (that 或 at/in which) I saw him was last year. 我头回见到他是去年。

3) 联想：for the first time“第一次”

A language selection menu will be displayed when you turn on the computer for the first time after purchase.

购买后第一次打开电脑时会出现语言选择菜单。

6. I remembered…and the days that followed when I helped him and my niece attend to all the sad chores that follow an unexpected death. (*Para. 2*)

1) that followed 和 when I helped him...an unexpected death 是双重关系分句，修饰先行词 the days.

She's the only girl I know who can play the piano.

她是我认识的唯一会弹钢琴的女孩。

还有一种双重关系分句，两个关系分句由并列连词连接：

We try our best to offer our guests unforgettable hours and days which they really enjoy and which they will always remember.

我们努力给客人提供难忘的时光，让他们觉得这段时间非常开心，难以忘怀。

联想：the following days, the days that follow, the days to come“随后的日子”

2) **attend to:** to deal with somebody or something“处理，对付某人或某事”

The doctor attended to the other patient before he got to my mother.

医生料理完另一个病人后才来给我妈看病。

3) 注意本句中时态的变化，remember，help 和第一个 follow 使用了过去时，是指当时作者在处理姐姐丧事时的行动和情况，而第二个 follow 用了现在时，指的是一般情况。又如：

The teacher said that gases expand when heated.

老师说气体加热会膨胀。（从句中 expand 用一般现在时表示是永恒真理。）

本段中 ...where my sister's family lives. 部分动词也用了一般现在时，表示作者姐姐的家人在作者写这篇文章时仍住在那里。又如：

He told me he works there as an editor.

他告诉我他在那儿当编辑。（现在时表示他现在仍在那里做编辑。）

7. I'm sitting on the deck and admiring the view without fussing about the weeds in the garden. (*Para. 3*)

1) **admire:** *vt.* to look at something or somebody you think is beautiful“欣赏”

We stopped and admired the beautiful campus.

我们停了下来，欣赏美丽的校园。

联想：admire somebody for something“因某事而钦佩某人”

He admired his father for his courage and selflessness.

他崇拜父亲，因为他勇敢无私。

2) **fuss about:** “（为小事）烦恼，过于忧虑”

a. Don’t fuss about an ordinary cold.

只是普通感冒，别大惊小怪。

b. His mother fussed about his spending habits.

他母亲非常担心他的花钱习惯。

联想：make a fuss of/over: “对……大惊小怪，对……过于关心”

a. Don’t make a big fuss over one low test grade.

别因为一次没考好就大惊小怪。

b. No one has ever made a fuss of me on my birthday.

从来没有人在我过生日时表现出特别的关心。

8. I’m trying to recognize these moments now and cherish them. (*Para. 3*)

1) **recognize:** *vt.* to identify from knowledge of appearance or characteristics “识别”

a. Doctors are trained to recognize the symptoms of different diseases.

培训医生识别不同疾病的症状。

b. They recognized the middle-aged man as a dangerous criminal.

他们认出这个中年男子是个危险的罪犯。

2) **cherish:** *vt.* to love, protect and care for somebody or something that is important to you “珍视”

Even though we went to college in different cities, I deeply cherished our friendship.

尽管我们不在同一座城市上大学，但我还是很珍惜我们的友谊。

9. …getting the sink unstopped… (*Para. 4*)

get something done: to do something or have it done for you “自己做或让别人做某事”

a. I shall be able to get the last chapter finished by tonight.

今晚我应该能完成最后一章。

b. Ms. Belfort got her office painted a bright yellow.

贝尔福特女士让人把办公室漆成鲜黄色。

get something/somebody doing/to do something: “使某物/人做……”

a. My brother managed to get my email working again.

我弟弟设法使我的电子邮件系统恢复了正常。

b. I couldn’t get my car to start this morning.

我今天早上没法把车子发动起来。

c. Another teacher got his students to write a formal letter first to find out what they knew.

另外一位老师让他的学生们先写封正式信件以了解他们知道些什么。

10. I wear my good blazer to the market if I feel like it. (*Para. 4*)

feel like something/doing something: to want something or want to do something“想要某物或做某事”

a. There are shops and bars in walking distance if you feel like a stroll.

如果你想逛逛，店铺和酒吧都不远，步行就能到。

b. I feel like having a nice cool glass of lemonade.

我很想来杯冰凉宜人的柠檬水。

11. My theory is if I look prosperous, I can shell out $28.49 for one small bag of groceries without wincing. (*Para. 4*)

1) **My theory is...:**“我的看法是……，我认为……”

My theory is every student counts and deserves the chance to succeed.

我认为每个学生都很重要，都应该有成功的机会。

2) **shell out:** to spend a lot of money on something“在……上花一大笔钱”

They've shelled out thousands of dollars for their kids' college education.

他们花了好多钱供孩子们读大学。

3) grocery“食品杂货店”；grocer's“食品杂货店”；

groceries“采购的食品杂货”；grocer“食品杂货商”

4) **wince:** *v.*“（因疼痛等）退缩，畏缩，脸部肌肉抽搐”

The boy winced as a sharp pain shot through his left leg.

左腿一阵剧痛疼得那个男孩龇牙咧嘴。

12. "Someday" and "one of these days" are losing their grip on my vocabulary. (*Para. 5*)

1) **someday:** *adv.* sometime in the future“有朝一日”，在英国英语中常分开写成 some day。

Someday I'll meet the right woman and we'll get married.

有朝一日我会碰到合适的女人，然后我们就结婚。

2) **one of these days:** at sometime in the future“总有一天”

You're going to get into serious trouble one of these days. 总有一天你要倒大霉的。

联想：one of those days: a day full of problems“倒霉的日子”

I'm sure everyone has one of those days and today was mine.

我相信人人都有不顺的时候，今天轮到我了。

3) **grip:** *n.* a firm strong hold“抓牢；控制”*v.* to hold something tightly“紧握，紧抓”

a. Emma immediately loosened her grip on my leg.

爱玛立即松开了抓住我的腿的手。

b. Both groups have a strong grip on their respective markets.

两家都牢牢掌控了各自的市场。

c. The baby gripped my finger with her tiny hand.

这个婴儿用她的小手紧紧抓住我的手指。

d. I was gripped by the film from the moment it started.

这部电影从一开始就把我深深吸引住了。

4) **vocabulary:** *n.* all the words used by a particular person or in a particular language or subject "词汇，词汇量"

a. She has a large vocabulary and loves crosswords.

她词汇量很大而且爱玩纵横字谜游戏。

b. The word "impossible" is not in/part of her vocabulary.

她的词汇里没有"不可能"这个词。

搭配：build up/develop/enlarge/enrich/extend/increase/widen one's vocabulary "扩大词汇量"；a huge/large vocabulary "丰富的词汇量"；a poor vocabulary "贫乏的词汇"

13. If it's worth seeing or hearing or doing, I want to see and hear and do it now. (*Para. 5*)

句中 it 指代值得看、听或做的事。

14. I'm not sure what my sister would have done had she known that she wouldn't be here for the tomorrow we all take for granted. (*Para. 5*)

1) I'm not sure 为主句，what my sister would have done had she known that...we all take for granted 作 sure 的宾语从句。在这个宾语从句中 what my sister would have done 为主句，had she known that she wouldn't be here for the tomorrow we all take for granted 是省略了 if 并倒装的非真实性条件状语从句，完整的状语从句是：if she had known that she wouldn't be here for the tomorrow we all take for granted。

a. She would have died that very night had it not been for her kid (if it had not been for her kid).

要不是她孩子，她那天晚上就死了。

b. Should the student not complete the work by the end of the next term (If the student is unable to complete the work by the end of the next term), a grade of F (fail) shall be assigned.

如果学生到下学期末还不能完成任务，就给不及格（F）。

2) **take something/somebody for granted:** 1) to assume something/somebody without question "视……为理所当然的"；2) to treat something or somebody with careless indifference "对……不重视，不关心"

a. Losing my job taught me never to take anything for granted.

失业使我懂得不能把任何事情都看成是理所当然的。

b. On the other hand, educational administrators should not take the teachers for granted.

另一方面，教育管理人员不应该把教师不当回事。

c. I'd always seen them together and just took it for granted that they were married.

我总是看到他们在一起，于是就想当然地认为他们已经结婚了。

15. It's those little things left undone that would make me angry if I knew that my hours were limited. (*Para. 6*)

该句使用了强调句型：It + is/was + 被强调的内容 + that/who 分句

a. When John's father passed away, it was his sister who supported him through school.

约翰的父亲去世后是他姐姐供他完成了学业。

b. It was that summer that I was diagnosed with lung cancer.

就在那年夏天我被诊断出了肺癌。

c. It was not until he was eighteen years old that he received his first pocket money.

直到 18 岁时他才拿到第一笔零花钱。

16. Angry because I hadn't written certain letters that I intended to write—one of these days. (*Para. 6*)

1) 本句中，主句部分的主语和谓语动词都被省略，完整句子为：I would be angry because I hadn't written certain letters that I intended to write—one of these days.

2) **intend:** *v.* to have as a plan or purpose“打算，计划”，常用句型有：

intend to do something“打算做某事”

intend doing something“打算做某事”

intend somebody to do something“打算要某人做某事”

be intended for“为……而准备的”

somebody intends that“某人打算……”

a. The teacher intended to have her class finish reading *Hamlet*.

老师打算让全班同学看完《哈姆雷特》。

b. Do you intend telling her what you think?

你打算告诉她你的想法吗？

c. Where did you intend your boyfriend to go?

你打算让你男朋友去哪里呢？

d. The party is really intended for new students so that they can meet each other.

这次聚会是专门为新生举办的，让他们可以彼此认识。

e. His parents intend that he shall take over their business.

他父母有意让他接管他们的公司。

3) **intention:** *n.* “意图，打算”，为普通词汇，指要采取的行动；

intent: *n.* “意图，目的”，为正式用语，主要用在法律和文学中，强调蓄意性。

a. We have no intention of giving up.

我们没有放弃的打算。

b. It is my intention to take a vacation next month.

我打算下个月去度假。

c. He's been charged with possessing a gun with intent to kill his wife.

他被指控持有枪支企图谋害妻子。

4) **intentional:** *adj.* “故意的，有意的”；**intended:** *adj.* “打算的，计划的”，一般只用于名词前

a. The murder was intentional and carried out for financial gain.

这是一起蓄意谋财害命案。

b. This rule has started to achieve the intended result and changed student behavior.

这个规定已开始达到预期效果，改变了学生的行为。

17. I'm trying very hard not to put off, hold back, or save anything that would add laughter and luster to our lives. (*Para. 7*)

1) **put off:** to delay doing something “推迟做……”

a. They had to put the wedding off because the bride's mother had an accident.

因新娘母亲出事，他们只好推迟了婚礼。

b. He can't put off going to the dentist any longer.

他再也不能拖着不去看牙医了。

c. Never put off until tomorrow what you can do today.

今日事，今日毕。

注意不要和 call off （取消）混淆。

The teacher called off the test.

老师取消了考试。

2) **hold back:** to delay something or somebody “推迟，耽搁；阻挡；抑制”

a. I can't hold the meal back for more than half an hour to wait for our guest.

我无法将用餐时间推迟半个多小时来等客人。

b. We started in good time but heavy rain on the road held us back.

我们是按时出发的，但路上大雨耽误了我们的行程。

c. His poor education is holding him back.

他没受过什么教育，这妨碍了他的发展。

d. She bit her lip to hold back the tears.

她咬着嘴唇强忍着眼泪。

3) **add...to...:** “给……增加……”

We added a few more students to the class.

我们给这个班级又增加了几个学生。

add fuel to the fire/flames “火上浇油”；add insult to injury “雪上加霜”

add to: to make a quality more extreme “加剧”

Her classmates' laughter only added to her embarrassment.

同学们的笑声使她更尴尬了。

add up to: “总计为；结果是”

a. The numbers added up to exactly 100.

这些数字总和正好是 100。

b. Their proposals do not add up to any real help for the poor.

他们的建议并没有给穷人任何实际的帮助。

Part II Text Comprehension (Key)

Reading Analysis

1. D 2. C 3. A 4. C 5. B

Information Recall and Summary

A.

1. It's an exquisite handmade silk slip trimmed with a cobweb of lace.
2. Because she was saving it for a special occasion.
3. He advised her not to save anything for a special occasion because every day she's alive is a special occasion.
4. His words have changed her life. Some examples of the changes are: she's reading more and dusting less; she's sitting on the deck and admiring the view without fussing about the weeds

in the garden; she's spending more time with her family and friends and less time in committee meetings.

5. Those little things that are left undone, for example, seeing good friends.
6. In the author's opinion, life should be a pattern of experience to savor, not to endure.

B.

The author's sister had saved her exquisite slip for a special occasion, only to end up wearing it at her own funeral. So her brother-in-law advised her not to save anything for a special time but to enjoy every day as a special moment. This advice has had quite an impact on the author and brought about a lot of changes in her life. To her, every day, every minute, every breath is now a gift from God. (76 words)

Information Organization

Event (Para. 1)	After her sister's unexpected death, the author's brother-in-law advised her not to <u>save anything for a special occasion but to live every day she's alive as a special occasion</u>.
Impact (Paras. 2-8)	The changes in the author's life after she took the advice: 1. She tries to recognize <u>the special moments</u> (for example, <u>spending more time with her family and friends</u>) in her life and cherish them. 2. She does not <u>save anything for a special occasion</u>. 3. <u>"Someday" and "one of these days" lose their grip</u> on her vocabulary. 4. Little things <u>left undone would make her angry if she knew her hours were limited</u>. 5. <u>To her, every day, every minute, every breath is now</u> a gift from God.

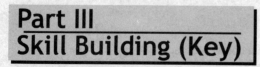

Part III Skill Building (Key)

Word Forms

A.

1. 提高，改善

2. 通风
3. 相似的人，同样的人
4. 支持
5. 见到，看到
6. 提及，提到
7. 完全地，彻底地
8. 行车，驾驶

B.

1) a. attached b. attached/attaches
2) a. live b. alive
3) a. attendant b. Attendance
4) a. intentional b. intention c. intend
5) a. laugh/laughter b. laughing

Vocabulary in Context

A.

1. e 2. a 3. b 4. c 5. f 6. d

B.

1. She always reminds her son of every detail that needs to be attended to.
2. George took for granted all that his parents did for him.
3. My sister worries and fusses about the smallest things.

C.

1. B 2. B 3. B 4. C 5. A

D.

a. 1) accident 2) accident 3) event 4) accident 5) incident
b. 1) worthwhile 2) worth 3) worthy 4) worth 5) worthy/worthwhile

Key Structures

A.

1. It was his students that showed him support.
2. It's *Scarlet Letter* that Professor Wang is reading in his office.
3. It's at the London Heathrow Airport that the detectives were waiting all morning.
4. The students were at ease, willing to contribute and participate without worrying about making mistakes.
5. US citizens can enter Japan as tourists and stay up to 90 days without applying for a visa.
6. She can almost walk down a flight of stairs without wincing in pain.

B.

1. My theory is if I can get through one day without smoking, I can get through every day without feeling awful.
2. I'm not sure what my neighbor would have done had he known that I had broken his window.

Translation

A.

1. 底层抽屉
2. 特殊的日子或场合
3. 欣赏风景
4. an astronomical figure
5. an unexpected death
6. a price tag

1. C 2. B

Practical Writing

Model 1

译文

电话留言记录

受话人：罗伯特先生

日期：2006年9月25日　　时间：上午10:30

打电话人：特赖恩先生　　单位：销售部

来电号码：021-33083488

留言内容：

特赖恩先生来电提醒您11月是他们商品销售的最佳季节，希望您回电告知是否可以提前发货。他将于9月28日出差，希望您今天下午5点前与他联系。

记录人：张岩

Model 2

译文

电话留言条

周一下午3:40

伦纳先生：

罗伯特·怀特刚打来电话，说他明天早上10点来找你商谈代理协议的事情，请你在我们的办公室等他。若时间不合适，请你给他回个电话。

杰克

Writing Exercise

Suggested samples for reference:

1.

Telephone Message

To: Mr. White

Date: 10 a.m., June 25, 2006

From: Mr. Johnson of Honeywer Co.

Message:

Mr. Johnson of Honeywer Co. will leave for Shanghai on business tomorrow. He wishes to cancel his appointment with you on the morning of June 27. He will contact you for another appointment when he gets back.

Message taken by: Helena (Secretary)

2.

Telephone Message

July 10

Fanny Zhao,

Peter Schulz called from Vienna, saying that they have to cancel the order No. 132. He hopes you can call him back between 9:00 and 11:00 tomorrow morning.

Sue Button

Part IV Fast Reading

课文译文

顿悟改变生活

无名氏

生活中没有比让人发生改变的顿悟更激动人心了——不仅仅是改变，而且是变得更好。当然，这样的时刻并不很多，但每个人都会有这样的时刻。这种顿悟有时来自书本，有时来自朋友。

那个寒冷的下午，我坐在曼哈顿的一家法国小餐馆里，心情非常沮丧，由于自己的一些失误，一项对我意义重大的研究失败了。

这时，一位老人从街对面走过来。他是心理医生，刚刚诊治完今天最后一位病人。老人快 80 岁了，但生活却很忙碌。他进了餐馆，坐到我身边，要了杯啤酒。“嗨，年轻人，”老人对我直言道，“有什么烦心事啊？”

我开始向他诉说自己的烦恼，我不为自己的失败责怪他人，我只怪自己。我讲完后，他放下杯子，说：“走吧，到我办公室去。”

“去你办公室？你忘了什么东西吗？”

“没有，”他轻声说，“我想让你听些东西，没什么别的事。”

我跟他到了办公室。他从架子上拿了一盘磁带，放进录音机里。他笑着说：“这盘磁带上有三个向我求助的人的简短录音。现在你注意听，找出在这三个病例里都出现过的一个两个字组成的词语。”

录音带里三个人的声音都不开心。首先说话的是个男的，显然生意上遭受了某种损失，他责怪自己没有很好地考虑未来。接着是个因她的寡母而终生未嫁的女人。她因几度错失良缘而自责不已。最后讲话的是位母亲，她十几岁的儿子惹上警察了，为此她不停地责怪自己。

“你注意到那个词语了吗？”他边说边关掉了录音机。“那几段录音中这个词语出现了六次。这是个很有害的词语。还没有找到吗？好吧，我写给你。”他写在纸上的两个字是“要是”。每天这位老人都要听他的病人重复这个词语几十次。

“要是我不那样做，或者干脆根本不做……”

“要是我更明智一点……”

老人解释说："问题是'要是'不能改变什么。它使人总想着做错的事。如果有了这种习惯，那就真的很麻烦了，你就不想再做更多的尝试了。你在餐馆里所说的就是这种典型的情况。"

我问道："那我该怎么办呢？"

"把'要是'改成'下次'，"老人说。

"下次？"

"是的，'下次'。这个词会帮你忘掉过去，从失败中吸取教训，奋勇向前，付诸行动。你自己试试吧。你会明白的。好了，年轻人，下课了。很高兴遇到你。你能帮我叫辆出租车吗？我该回家了。"

我们走出大楼，夜幕已在雨中降临了。我看见一辆出租车开过来，就赶紧跑上前去，但另外一个乘客抢在了我的前面上了出租车。

"哎呀，哎呀，"老人叹道，"要是我们早10秒钟下来就能赶上那辆车了。"

我笑起来，领会了他的暗示："下次我会跑得快一点。"

Reading Comprehension

Key

1. F　2. F　3. T　4. F　5. T

Part V
Extensive Reading

It Is Time to Let Go

By May Paron

1　The doctor's young **receptionist** asked the **sixtyish** patient, "Are you on Medicare?" "No, I'm not," he answered. "I'm still working, and I plan to retire when I'm one hundred and four." She laughed and asked him to take a seat. He and I were the only people in the waiting room, so I smiled at the man and said, "I liked your answer...and your spirit." "Thanks," he replied, "would you like to hear the story behind my statement?" "I'd love to," I agreed.

2　His name was John and he worked for a government **agency**. John **was**

responsible for approving **loan** applications for major home improvements. One day a woman called him and explained: "I need a loan to **convert** my heating **system** to gas, though I really don't mind the coal at all. It's those **darn** ashes—**lugging** them up from the **basement** all the time. I'm 104 now and I'm just so tired of carrying those ashes!" John was surprised at this **outpouring**, and a little **skeptical** of the woman's age claim, but the agency's **investigation revealed** that she was indeed 104 years old. Only now was she **rebelling** at the burden she'd borne for so many years.

3 After hearing John's story, I wondered if there wasn't a broader message here than just the remarkable **stamina** and **endurance** of an **extraordinary** woman. Picture the ashes as any heavy burden that one might carry inside for years, **unwilling** or unable to **release** feelings of anger, **resentment**, **envy**, or any other negative **connection** to the past. Happily, we don't have to shoulder this **emotional load** until we're 104, or even for another day, or even another moment.

4 By choosing to **let go of** the past, we can sweep out all the ashes that **weigh** us **down** and subtly affect every aspect of our health, our **relationships**, and our peace of mind.

5 My friend Jean was divorced after a thirty-year marriage that produced three daughters, one son and eight grandchildren. Because she had literally raised them **single-handedly**, Jean was hurt and angry that the children didn't **take her part** after the divorce. For months she refused to attend any family celebration to which her former husband Jim was also invited. When I reasoned that her children's **perception** of the relationship with and between the parents was probably altogether different from hers, she clung to the belief that she was right.

6 One day Jean called in tears. "Saturday is my granddaughter's birthday, and I really want to be with her, but I can't bring myself to face my former husband." "Jim isn't the problem," I said gently, "it's false pride. Instead of **holding on to** the painful past, which is over and done, let the feelings go and **get on with** your life. You're **depriving yourself of** the joy of sharing in these important occasions, while Jim feels free to experience them. Tell me, would you rather be right, or be happy?"

7 That must **have done the trick** because when Saturday arrived, Jean appeared at her daughter's home bearing her famous chocolate-chip **cookies** and a beautiful birthday cake.

8 How great it feels to let go! How **energizing**! And the more we practice the art of letting go of all **negativity**, the better able we become to devote our thoughts, our time, and our energy to living **joyfully** in the present, whatever age we happen to be.

(571 words)

NEW WORDS

receptionist /rɪ'sepʃənɪst/ *n.* an office worker employed chiefly to receive visitors and answer the telephone 接待员

sixtyish /'sɪkstɪʃ/ *adj.* 60岁左右的

agency /'eɪdʒənsi/ *n.* a department within a government or an international body that provides a particular service（政府或国际机构的）部，处

loan /ləʊn/ *n.* money that an organization such as a bank lends and somebody borrows 贷款

convert /kən'vɜːt/ *vt.* to change (something) into another form, substance, state, or product; to transform 使转变，使转化

system /'sɪstəm/ *n.* a device or set of devices powered by electricity 装置，设备

darn /dɑːn/ *adj.*（=damn）该死的，可恶的

lug /lʌg/ *v.* to pull or carry with force or effort 用力拖或拉等

basement /'beɪsmənt/ *n.* a story of a building, partly or wholly underground 地下室，地下层

outpouring /'aʊtˌpɔːrɪŋ/ *n.* a strong and sudden expression of feeling 倒出，泻出，涌出

skeptical /'skeptɪkəl/ *adj.* showing doubt 不相信的，表示怀疑的

investigate /ɪn'vestɪgeɪt/ *v.* to observe or inquire into in detail 调查，调查研究

investigation /ɪnˌvestɪ'geɪʃən/ *n.* the act or process of investigating 调查，调查研究

reveal /rɪ'viːl/ *vt.* 1) to make known 揭示，揭露；2) to display 展现

rebel /rɪ'bel/ *vi.* to resist or rise against some authority, control, or tradition 反抗，反对，不服从

stamina /'stæmɪnə/ *n.* 精力，耐力

endure /ɪn'djʊə(r)/ *v.* to bear 容忍，忍受

endurance /ɪn'djʊərəns/ *n.* the ability to continue doing something painful or unpleasant, esp. without complaining（忍）耐力

extraordinary /ɪk'strɔːdənəri/ *adj.* not normal or ordinary 非凡的，特别的，非常的

unwilling /ʌn'wɪlɪŋ/ *adj.* not willing; reluctant 不情愿的，不愿意的

release /rɪ'liːs/ *vt.* 1) to free from something that binds, fastens, or holds back; 放开，松开；2) to let go 释放

resentment /rɪ'zentmənt/ *n.* a feeling of anger or unhappiness about something that you think is unfair 怨恨，憎恨

envy /'envi/ *n.* jealousy 妒忌（的对象），羡慕（的目标）

connection /kə'nekʃən/ *n.* a relation between things or events 连接，关系

emotional /ɪ'məʊʃənəl/ *adj.* 感情的，情绪的

load /ləʊd/ *n.* something that is carried, as by a vehicle, person, or animal 负荷，负担

NEW WORDS

relationship /rɪ'leɪʃənʃɪp/ *n.* a relation between people 关系，联系

single-handedly /ˌsɪŋgl'hændɪdli/ *adv.* working or done without help 独立地，单独地

perception /pə'sepʃən/ *n.* a particular way of understanding or thinking about something 看法，观点

deprive /dɪ'praɪv/ *vt.* to take something away from 剥夺，使丧失

cookie /'kʊki/ *n.* 甜饼干，曲奇饼

energize /'enədʒaɪz/ *vt.* to give energy to 给予……能量或精力

energizing /'enədʒaɪzɪŋ/ *adj.* 使……精力充沛的，使有活力的

negativity /ˌnegə'tɪvəti/ *n.* the tendency to consider only the bad side of something or somebody 否定性，消极性

joyfully /'dʒɔɪfəli/ *adv.* happily 快乐地，高兴地

PHRASES & EXPRESSIONS

be responsible for 对……负责

let go of 松手，放手，放弃

weigh down 使……负重担，使……焦虑，压垮

take somebody's part 站在某人一边，支持某人

hold on to 紧紧抓住

get on with 继续干

deprive somebody of something 剥夺，夺去，使丧失

do the trick 起作用，达到目的，解决问题

PROPER NAMES

Medicare （美）老年医疗保健制度

Cultural Background

1. May Paron

   梅 · 派隆，美国作家，同时还从事精神心理方面的研究。

2. Medicare

   老年医疗保健制度，1965 年由当时的总统林登 · 约翰逊建立的一项政府医疗保险计划。根据该计划，美国政府为 65 岁及以上的老年人以及残疾人提供医疗费用减免。计划包括 A、B、C 三个部分：A 部分是住院治疗保险，支付病人住院期间的费用和一些随访的费用；B 部分支付部分医生服务费和门诊医疗保健费用；C 部分支付部分处方药费用。

课文译文

该放手时须放手

梅·派隆

诊所的年轻接待员问那个约摸60岁的病人："你享受政府的老年医疗保险吗？""没有，"病人说，"我还在上班呢，而且我打算干到104岁再退休。"接待员大笑，请他坐了下来。因为候诊室里只有我和他两个病人，我对他笑了笑，说道："我很欣赏你的回答，还有……你的精神。""谢谢，"他说，"你想听听这个回答背后的故事吗？""很想啊，"我应道。

他叫约翰，在政府部门工作，负责审批大型家居装修贷款申请。一天，一个妇人打来电话说："虽说我一点也不在乎烧煤供暖，但还是需要把贷款改成天然气的。这是因为那该死的煤灰——老是要把它们从地下室弄出来。我现在104岁了，搬运那些煤灰实在是让我厌烦透了！"这顿发泄使约翰感到愕然，对妇人所说的年龄也有些怀疑，但局里的调查显示该妇人的确是104岁。直到现在她才受不了已承受了这么多年的负担。

听了约翰讲的这个故事，我想它除了显示了一个非凡的妇人了不起的精力和耐力外，是否还有一个更广泛的含义？把那些煤灰想象成一个人在内心背负多年的重担，不愿或不能发泄自己的愤怒、憎恨和嫉妒的情绪，或者任何其他与过去有关的负面的东西。幸好，我们不必一直承担这种情感重负到104岁，哪怕多一天、多一刻都不必。

通过选择放手过去，我们就能清扫掉所有的"煤灰"。就是它们困扰着我们，微妙地影响我们的健康、我们的各种关系以及我们内心的安宁。

在结婚30年，有了三个女儿、一个儿子和八个孙子孙女之后，我的朋友琼离婚了。孩子们可以说是她一手拉扯大的，因此离婚后孩子们没有站在她这一边使她非常伤心和气愤。好几个月她都拒绝参加有前夫在场的任何家庭庆祝活动。我劝说她孩子们对父母与他们的关系以及父母之间关系的看法完全与她不同，但她却坚持认为她是对的。

一天，琼哭着打来电话："星期天是外孙女的生日，我很想和她在一起，但我无法使自己面对吉姆。""问题不是吉姆，"我轻声说，"问题是你的虚荣心。不要再死抓住痛苦的过去不放，那一切已结束了。忘了那些痛苦，开始你的新生活吧。你现在是在剥夺自己参与这些重要活动带来的快乐，而吉姆却自由自在地亲身体验这些重要时刻。告诉我，你是要正确还是要快乐？"

我的那番话肯定起作用了，因为星期六到来的时候，琼出现在她女儿的家中，还带来了她拿手的巧克力颗粒小甜饼和一个漂亮的生日蛋糕。

放手的感觉真棒！它让你觉得活力四射！对生活中的不愉快经历遗忘得越多，我们就越能将自己的思想、时间和精力用来享受此刻快乐的生活，不管我们是多大年纪。

Notes to the Text

1. The doctor's young receptionist asked the sixtyish patient, "Are you on Medicare?" (*Para. 1*)

   -ish 加在数字之后，表示“大约……之数的”、“……左右的”，如：Come at sevenish. 七点左右来。

2. John was surprised at this outpouring..." (*Para. 2*)

   this outpouring 指老妇人对 John 这个陌生人一口气讲了很多关于她自己的话，非常准确生动地表现了老妇人再也不愿承受已背负多年的负担的激动心情。

3. Only now was she rebelling at the burden she'd borne for so many years. (*Para. 2*)

   1) 本句为倒装句，突出强调了老妇人承受负担之久，到 104 岁高龄时才想起摆脱。

   2) only 位于句首并且修饰状语时要倒装：

   a. Only after we've lost everything are we free to do anything.
   我们只有在失去一切后才能有做任何事的自由。

   b. Only then did she realize she was speaking with the teacher himself!
   直到那时她才意识到自己是在和老师本人说话。

   注意：如果 only 不修饰状语，不用倒装：

   Only he managed to pass the exam. 只有他设法通过了考试。

4. Picture the ashes as any heavy burden that one might carry inside, unwilling or unable to… (*Para. 3*)

   这里 inside 指“在内心”，“在心中”，如：I felt inside that my life was about to change for the better. 我心里觉得自己要时来运转了。

5. Happily, we don't have to shoulder this emotional load until we're 104… (*Para. 3*)

   happily 为评注性状语，对整个句子进行说明或解释，表明说话人对所说话语的看法和态度。

   比较：I don't think he'll interview you personally. 我看他不会亲自接见你。(personally 为修饰性状语，修饰 interview)

   Personally, I don't think he'll interview you. 我个人认为他不会接见你。(personally 为评注性状语，表明所说的为说话人的个人意见。)

   因此，happily 在这里可理解为“幸亏”，“幸好” 。

6. And the more we practice the art of letting go of all negativity, the better able we become to devote…whatever age we happen to be. (*Para. 8*)

   本句由比较状语从句 the more…the better… 和由 whatever 引导的让步状语从句构成。

又如：

According to the study, the more motion, the longer the life.

根据这项研究发现，运动越多，寿命越长。

Whatever evidence you use, it is crucial to have the information the media, the public and the decision-makers want and understand.

不管你用什么来证明，关键是你的证据应是媒体、大众和决策者想要并能明白的。

7. 本文采用了夹叙夹议的方法：作者首先从自己听到的一则故事有感而发，指出人们应该选择放手过去；接着通过讲述自己朋友的经历来进一步说明放手过去的好处及重要性。文章语言朴实，贴近生活，娓娓道来，有理有据，令人信服。尤其是文中引用了不少人物对话，增强了文章的生活气息。最后一段感叹句的使用也增加了文章的感染力。

Reading Comprehension

Choose the best option to complete each statement and answer each question.

1. The word "burden" in the article means all of the following EXCEPT ________.

   A. ashes

   B. heating system

   C. negative feelings

   D. the painful past

2. According to the author, what prevented Jean from attending her granddaughter's birthday celebration was ________.

   A. her former husband

   B. her children's perception of the relationship with their parents

   C. her false pride

   D. her children's behavior after the divorce

3. The 104-year-old woman wanted to convert her heating system to gas because ________.

   A. gas is cheaper and safer than coal

   B. she had to carry the coal home by herself

   C. coal causes pollution

   D. she had to lug (用力拉) the ashes out of the basement

4. Which of the following is TRUE of John?

   A. He was the author's patient.

   B. He was not on Medicare because he was not 104 years old.

   C. He was with a government agency and in charge of loan application approval.

   D. He undertook an investigation into the 104-year-old woman's age claim.

5. The tone of the article is ________.

A. indifferent B. objective C. persuasive D. pessimistic

Key

1. B 2. C 3. D 4. C 5. C

Vocabulary Study

Replace each of the underlined parts with the best choice given.

1. John was responsible for <u>approving</u> loan applications for major home improvements.
   A. favoring B. authorizing
   C. appreciating D. denying
2. Happily, we don't have to shoulder this emotional <u>load</u> until we're 104, or even for another day, or even for another moment.
   A. pack B. goods
   C. burden D. freight
3. That must have <u>done the trick</u> because when Saturday arrived, Jean appeared at her daughter's home bearing her famous chocolate-chip cookies and a beautiful birthday cake.
   A. achieved the desired effect B. cheated fate
   C. made a joke D. played a trick
4. Because she had literally raised them single-handedly, Jean was hurt and angry that the children didn't <u>take her part</u> after the divorce.
   A. support her B. live with her
   C. do her share of the housework D. get involved in her divorce
5. By choosing to let go of the past, we can sweep out all <u>the ashes</u> that weigh us down and subtly affect every aspect of our health, our friendships, and our peace of mind.
   A. ruins B. bodily remains
   C. gray or black powder D. emotional burden
6. Picture the ashes as any heavy burden that one might carry inside for years, unwilling or unable to release feelings of anger, resentment, envy, or any other <u>negative</u> connection to the past.
   A. unpleasant B. pessimistic
   C. hostile D. contrary

Key

1. B 2. C 3. A 4. A 5. D 6. A

A. ruins B. fossils remains

Making Complaints and Expressing Dissatisfaction

Study Focus:

1. 含有 e 的字母组合 ure, ea, ei, ie 以及 ear 的发音
2. 如何表示抱怨、不满和表达歉意的回答

Part I Listening

Section A Phonetics

Key

1. A 2. D 3. D 4. B 5. C

Section B Short Conversations

Tapescripts

1. M: Janice! I'm sorry to say that you're late again!

   W: I'm awfully sorry I'm late.

   M: You're always late! What happened this time?

   W: Well, I was held up at the office and then got caught in a traffic jam.

   Q: What happened to Janice?

2. W: Yes, sir?

   M: Excuse me, but the meat is not fresh.

   W: I'm sorry, sir. I'll ask the manager to take care of this.

   M: No, I'll go to him myself.

   Q: Where does the dialogue happen?

3. W: Hello, this is Reception, Mr. Sun. You called us to report that there was something wrong with the toilet.

   M: Yes. I have never found a room with such poor facilities.

W: I'm terribly sorry about that. I'll check with the Maintenance Department. I assure you that they will come within minutes.

M: Would you? Oh, here they come. Thank you.

Q: What is the problem?

4. M: Good evening, madam. Is there anything I can do for you?

W: I'm afraid I have to complain about your restaurant service. I was badly treated by a rude waiter.

M: Sorry to hear that, madam. Thank you for bringing the matter to our attention. I'll contact the Food and Beverage Manager at once. I'm sure he'll deal with it.

W: Yes, please do.

Q: What does the lady complain about?

5. W: Why are you so angry with me? I told no one but Lily your secret!

M: Well, don't you know she is such a blabbermouth that no one trusts her? I bet everyone will know about my secret tomorrow!

W: Sorry for having caused you a lot of trouble.

M: I hope this will not happen again in the future.

Q: How does the man describe Lily?

Key

1. A　2. C　3. A　4. D　5. B

Section C Passages

Exercise One

Tapescript

Six Chinese who were flying from Amsterdam to Beijing were delayed at the airport from February 16 to 18, reported the *Beijing Morning Post*. KLM Royal Dutch Airlines gave each passenger an 800-euro traveller's check in compensation. But many feel they were discriminated against.

The airline has a different view. "Poor English handicapped the Chinese passengers from understanding an in-time communication with the airport," explained the employee from the Shanghai office of KLM Royal Dutch Airlines.

With so many people traveling by plane, delays and cancellations are unavoidable. If you have a problem, use these common requests to ensure that your complaint is dealt with properly.

Key

1) flying from 2) traveller's check 3) many feel 4) different view
5) the airport 6) Shanghai office 7) by plane 8) your complaint

Exercise Two

Tapescript

There was a survey about what people thought about traffic, petrol prices, and public car parks. In some car parks it now costs something like $5 to park a car for half an hour. The results show that 70% of the people surveyed complained about high petrol prices, and 60% want to see the traffic reduced. As well, 65% of those surveyed think car park charges are too high. Does that mean that there are 35% who actually think the charges are OK and would even be prepared to pay more, and another 30% who think petrol prices are OK? I mean that's absurd. I don't know anyone who doesn't think the price of petrol is too high.

Questions:

1. Which of the following is true about the survey?
2. How much do people pay for parking a car for half an hour?
3. What percentage of people complained about the high car park charges?
4. What does the author find absurd about the survey?
5. What is the author's attitude towards the high prices?

Key

1. C 2. A 3. A 4. D 5. A

Notes

1. Excuse me, but the meat is not fresh.
   这是一种比较有礼貌的投诉方式。当遇到不满意的事情和对待需要投诉时，礼貌的说法比较奏效。而且有趣的是，你可能先要说 SORRY，再提出你的投诉，这样显得更有教养和礼貌，你的问题也会得到更圆满的解决。又如，在商店里，收款员找错了钱，你可以说："Excuse me, I think you've given me the wrong change." 或者 "Sorry, I think this change is wrong. I gave you $20, not $10."
2. I'm terribly sorry about that.
   be/feel sorry about/for something："为某事感到遗憾或后悔"。如：Aren't you sorry

for/ about what you have done? 你难道对自己做的事不感到后悔? 若说 be/feel sorry for someone, 则表示“为某人感到惋惜”。如：I'm sorry for her. 真为她感到惋惜。

3. Tips for how to complain nicely and efficiently at the airport:

   a. Try to speak to someone on the spot. They might be able to sort out your problem right away. Be polite but firm. 试图当场跟机场工作人员说，也许他们会马上解决你的问题。但是要有礼貌，而且态度要坚决。

   b. Make a note of staff names, times and any other relevant information. With these facts, you'll have a better chance of getting redress (redress：“赔偿；救济”) 把机场工作人员的名字、时间以及其他相关信息记下来。有这些事实根据，你将更有机会获得赔偿。

   c. Wait in the ticketing line to ask for some sort of compensation: reimbursement (退款，补偿) for your ticket, ticket vouchers or a sum of money. Don' t be afraid to bargain (议价，交易) but don't be rude. 在售票处排队，要求某种赔偿——退票、赠券或一笔钱。别害怕讨价还价，但要有礼貌。

4. In some car parks it now costs something…park a car for half an hour. 在美国的公共停车场，特别是在商业区的停车场停车，费用会很高。比如：在曼哈顿—纽约市中心停车半小时，停车费是10美元。高昂的停车费使得很多美国人放弃了开私家车而改为乘火车或其他交通工具去商业区。

Part II Speaking

Section A Functional Language

➡ ***How to make a complaint:***

Suggested expressions

I'm sorry to say that…

Excuse me, but…

There was something wrong with…

I'm afraid I have to complain about…

I wish this would not happen in future.

➡ ***How to express dissatisfaction:***

Suggested expressions

You're always late.

Why are you so angry with…?

Well, don't you know…

➡ ***How to reply to complaints or dissatisfaction:***

Suggested expressions

I'm awfully sorry I'm late.

Sorry to hear that.

Thank you for bringing the matter to our attention.

Sorry for having caused you a lot of trouble.

I assure you that they will come within minutes.

Section B Dialogue

Key

1. A 2. C 3. B 4. A 5. D

Section C Situational Communication

Phase 1

Suggested samples

1. — Excuse me, but why do you always play my walkman without my permission?
   — I'm sorry. I thought you would not mind.
   — Well, I've had enough of it.
   — I do apologize. I assure you it won't happen again.
2. — Oh, dear!
   — What's wrong?
   — I can't say I feel happy about the hairstyle you've given me (or: I can't say I feel happy about the way you've cut my hair.)
   — Sorry, I'll redo your hair as soon as you would like. (or: I'm terribly sorry. Next time you come in I'll do your hair for free.)

Phase 2: Role play

Possible complaints and dissatisfaction and replies for reference

1. — Hello, I'm afraid I have to make a complaint. My plane was delayed two hours. I had a connecting flight (connection) leaving from Shanghai at 3p.m. Now I will miss it. Can you please book me on a later flight?

— I can’t tell you how sorry I am. I’ll do it at once.

2. — My teacher frowned at my essay. I have to rewrite part of it.

— Sorry to hear that.

3. — Waiter, the vegetable soup is cold. I can’t accept this. (or: This is unacceptable.)

— Oh, I’m terribly sorry, madam. Would you like me to take it back to the kitchen?

4. — I’m afraid I have to make a complaint. I’ve been trying to get through to the booking office for 20 minutes. But the line has been continuously busy. Why is it taking so long?

— Sorry for having caused you so much trouble.

5. — I can’t say I feel happy about what you have done to me.

— Sorry, I assure you I won’t do it again.

UNIT 4 Encouragement

Study Focus:

1. Understand why we should praise.
2. Learn to use the "As…, so…" structure.
3. Illustrate the effect of praise with one of your personal experiences.
4. Learn to develop a paragraph by listing or examples.
5. Explain the purpose of creating the Hello Day.

Part I Intensive Reading

课文译文

创造奇迹的话语

戈特弗里德 R. 冯克罗内伯格

"也许等我活到 100 岁的时候，我会习惯于别人对我做的每件事所采取的理所当然的态度，"一位家庭主妇向她的邻居吐露内心的秘密。"如果比尔偶尔能对我说几句好听的，他会让我的生活更加幸福。"

我们中很少有人意识到我们是多么需要鼓励，意识到我们必须时常感受赞扬的温暖，否则就会失去我们的自信。

我们所有的人都需要那种被人需要以及被人仰慕的感觉。但是除非我们听到别人的赞誉之辞，不然我们如何能够知道我们是被他人尊重的朋友或同事？

任何想改善与他人关系的人仅需表达一种赞同的理解就可以了。表达这种理解并使他人感到自己的重要性和价值的方式归结如下：经常在别人身上寻找你可羡慕和赞赏的东西并告知对方。

我们每个人都有自己的一幅心理图像，一种自我形象。为了获得比较满意的生活，这一自我形象必须是我们能够接受的、能够喜欢的。当我们对自我形象感到自豪时，我们会感到自信并会自由地展示自我，我们的表现处于最佳状态。而当我们对自我形象感到羞愧时，我们就会设法隐藏它而不是表达它。我们会变得不友好，难以相处。

一个被唤醒自尊的人的身上会出现奇迹。他会突然间更喜欢他人。他会更为善良，与周围的人更容易合作。赞扬是上光剂，有助于保持他的自我形象明亮闪光。

但这与你赞扬别人有何关系呢？关系多多。你有能力让奇迹在另外一个人身上出现。当你增强他自尊心的时候，你会使他喜欢你、想和你合作。

切斯特菲尔德爵士向他的儿子提出这样一条不同寻常的建议，要他效仿德尼韦奴瓦公爵："你会发现他是让人们先喜欢他们自己进而才喜欢上他的。"

诚意是赞扬时必不可少的。它会增强赞扬的效果。男人劳累一天下班回到家里，看见自己孩子的脸贴在窗户上期待着他时，那无声的赞美会滋润他的心田。

赞扬有助于消除日常交往中的磕磕绊绊。这一点在婚姻方面最为典型。然而也许正是在家庭中，赞扬的价值更不为人们重视。如果丈夫或妻子能注意在适当的时候说一句令人振奋的话，说明他（她）已经认识到幸福家庭生活最为重要的条件之一。

孩子们尤其渴望得到赞扬、安慰和欣赏。一位年轻母亲向她的牧师谈起一件令人心碎的事情："我的小儿子经常表现不好，我没办法只好责骂他。"但有一天他特别听话。那天晚上，我为他掖好被子下楼后听到他的哭声。我发现他头埋在枕头里。抽泣声中他问道："妈咪，难道我今天还不是一个好孩子吗？"

"那个问题像一把刀穿透了我的心，"那位母亲说道。"他做错事时我马上会去纠正他，但他表现很好时我却没有注意到。我安顿孩子睡觉时没有对他说一句表扬的话。"

别怕麻烦，从你孩子身上找出些可称赞的方面，你会发现他的能力和态度都会向好的方面发展。通过赞扬进行鼓励是让人们竭尽全力的最有效的方法。

正如艺术家们在向别人展示美的过程中会得到乐趣一样，任何掌握赞扬这门艺术的人都会发现它会给赞扬者和接受者带来同样多的祝福。这条谚语是有道理的："送人鲜花，手有余香。"

Language Points of the Text

1. "Maybe when I'm a hundred, I'll get used to having everything I do taken for granted," a young homemaker confided to her neighbor. "If Bill would compliment me once in a while, he'd make my life much happier." (*Para. 1*)

此处两句话都使用了强调的手法：第一句通过夸张 (when I'm a hundred) 强调"我永远也不会习惯于别人对我做的每件事所采取的理所当然的态度"；第二句通过虚拟语气句式强调"比尔从不称赞我，所以我的生活就不那么幸福"。

1) **take...for granted:** "认为……理所当然"（未意识到其重要性，也无感激的表示）

a. He never praises his wife: he just takes what she does for granted.

他从不赞扬妻子，认为她做的一切理应如此。

b. I used to take my washing machine for granted, but the other day when it suddenly stopped working, I started to realize how important it was.

以前我总是对洗衣机不以为然，但有一天洗衣机突然停止工作了，我才开始意识到它是多么的重要。

注意比较 take somebody/something for granted 与 take it for granted (that)... 的区别：后者表示“没有进行确认就相信”、“想当然地认为”的意思。例如：

The young girl took it for granted that the man would love her for ever.

这个年轻女子想当然地认为那男人会爱她一辈子。

2) **confide:** *vt.* to confess“吐露，透露”

句型为 confide...to..., confide that...，例如：

a. She confided her secret to her best friend.

她将秘密透露给她最要好的朋友。

b. The company's plans were confided only to the president and the directors.

公司的计划只让总裁和董事们知道。

c. He confided to his friends that he didn't have much hope for his marriage.

他向朋友们吐露他对自己的婚姻不抱多大的希望。

3) **compliment:** *v. & n.*“赞美，恭维”

常用句型：compliment somebody on something; pay a compliment (to) somebody on something/pay somebody a compliment on something“因为……而称赞，夸奖，恭维……”

a. Her guests complimented her on her cooking.

客人们夸奖她的烹饪技术。

b. We paid Nancy a compliment on her new dress.

我们称赞南希的新衣服。

4) **once in a while:** sometimes“有时，偶尔”

同义词组还有：now and then, from time to time, at times

2. Yet we must bask in the warmth of approval now and then or lose our self-confidence. (*Para. 2*)

本句可改写为：But we must be complimented or praised from time to time by others; otherwise we will lose our self-confidence.

1) **bask in:**“领略，享受，沐浴在……中”

I like to bask in the sunshine, while lying on the beach.

我喜欢躺在海滩上享受日光浴。

2) **approval:** *n.*“赞扬，赞许”

We all like others to show approval of what we do.

我们都喜欢别人对我们的行为表示赞许。

3. Anyone who wants to improve his relationships with others need only show a sympathetic understanding. The way to express this understanding and to give others the feeling of importance and worthiness boils down to this... (*Para. 4*)

1) **need only do something:** to only have to do something in order to do something else“只需……即可”

a. We need only look at the building to see how much money it will take to repair.

我们只要看一眼建筑物就会知道维修一下需要多少钱。

b. You need only show your student card to enter the Reading Room to read newspapers.

只要出示你的学生证就可以进阅览室读报。

2) **sympathetic:** *adj.*“赞同的，理解的，同情的”

a. Most people at the meeting were sympathetic to my suggestion.

会上多数人都赞同我的建议。

b. Everyone felt sympathetic towards the unfortunate family.

每个人都同情这个不幸的家庭。

3) **give others the feeling of importance and worthiness:** to make others feel that they are important and deserve to be respected“使他人感到自己的重要性和价值”

4) **boil down to:**“可归纳为，归结起来是”

a. Getting a good grade on your exam boils down to your studying hard.

考试成绩好可归结于你学习努力。

b. The whole matter boils down to a power struggle between the trade union and the directors.

整个事情可归结为工会和董事们之间的一场权力之争。

4. To find life reasonably satisfying, that self-image must be one we can live with, one we can like. (*Para. 5*)

1) **reasonably:** *adv.*“相当，颇；合乎情理地，通情达理地”

a. Given a job to do, you and I could live there and be reasonably happy.

假如有份工作，你我可以住在那儿而且会过得相当幸福。

b. He behaved very reasonably at the meeting.

在会上他表现得非常通情达理。

2) **live with:** “忍受，容忍，接受”

a. I don’t like the winter, but I have to live with it.

我不喜欢冬天，但我还得忍受。

b. In college, students must learn to live with different kinds of stress.

在大学里，学生们必须学会承受各种压力。

5. When we are proud of our self-image, we feel confident and free to be ourselves. We function at our best. When we are ashamed of our self-image, we attempt to hide it rather than express it. We become hostile and hard to get along with. (*Para. 5*)

1) **confident:** *adj.* “自信的，确信的”

a. The spokesman began to answer the reporters’ questions in a calm and confident voice.

发言人开始回答记者的问题，语气平静而自信。

b. We feel confident of/about the future of China’s education system.

我们对中国教育体制的未来充满信心。

c. She is confident that she will win the race.

她确信自己会在这次赛跑中获胜。

6. Praise is the polish that helps keep his self-image bright and sparkling. (*Para. 6*)

句中将 praise “赞扬” 比喻为 polish “上光剂，上光蜡”。

polish 做动词时意为 “磨光，擦光；使优美，润饰”。

a. You need to polish your English before you go to England.

你去英国前得把英语补一补。

b. He took out a copy of his speech and polished up a few lines.

他把演讲稿取出来润色了几处。

c. He polished his shoes with a new brush.

他用新刷子把鞋子擦亮。

7. What has this to do with your giving praise? A lot. You have the ability to perform that kind of miracle in another person. When you add to his self-esteem, you make him want to like you and to cooperate with you. (*Para. 7*)

1) **have /has to do with...:** “与……有关”

a. What does that have to do with what I have been saying?

那和我说的话有何关系？

b. I don’t know what it has to do with you.

我不知道它和你有什么关系。

常见搭配：have something/nothing/little to do with... “与……有些/没有/几乎没有关系”

a. He had little to do with the accident.

他与该事故无甚牵连。

b. I think this has nothing to do with your company, but has something to do with the local government.

我认为这事与你公司无关，但与当地政府有关。

2) **miracle:** *n.* “奇迹，令人惊奇的事”

a. The teacher told the lazy careless student that it'd be a miracle if he passed the examination.

老师对那个又懒又粗心的学生说，如果他能通过考试将是一个奇迹。

b. Doctors do their best to treat the sick, but they can't perform miracles.

医生尽其所能治病，但他们不可能创造奇迹。

常用搭配：work/perform a miracle/miracles “创造奇迹”；miracle drug “特效药，灵丹妙药”

3) **add to:** “增添”

a. The good news added to her excitement.

那个好消息令她更加兴奋不已。

b. The balloons added to the festival atmosphere of the city.

气球给城市增添了节日的气氛。

4) **self-esteem:** *n.* “自尊”

raise/lift/build (up) somebody's self-esteem “提高/增强自尊心”；low/poor self-esteem “自尊心不够”

My self-esteem was lifted by her warm smile.

她温暖的笑容增强了我的自尊心。

8. In a classic bit of advice, Lord Chesterfield suggested to his son that he follow the example of the Duke de Nivernois: “You will perceive that he makes people pleased with him by making them first pleased with themselves.” (*Para. 8*)

1) **a classic bit of advice:** a good/typical piece of advice “一条经典的/有名的/典型的建议”

Getting enough sleep at night is a good piece of advice to follow.

晚上要有充足的睡眠是一条应遵循的好建议。

2) **follow the example of/follow sb's example...:** “学习……的榜样，照……的样子”

a. He followed his brother's example and now runs a small hotel.

他学他哥哥的样子，现在开了一家小旅馆。

b. His politeness is a good example for others to follow.

他彬彬有礼，值得他人学习。

与 example 有关的搭配：

give/cite/provide an example“举例”；set/give an example to/for...“为……树立榜样”；

take (...) for example“以……为例”

3) **perceive:** *vt.*“认识到，意识到，理解；察觉，感知”

a. Finally he perceived his mistake.

最后他认识到自己的错误。

b. I perceived a change in his attitude to life.

我察觉到他的生活态度发生了变化。

c. Open a window, and different people may perceive the outside world differently.

打开一扇窗子，不同的人会对外部世界有不同的感知。

d. They perceived that the situation was getting worse and worse.

他们认识到形势在变得越来越糟。

9. Coming home after a hard day's work, the man who sees the faces of his children pressed against the window, watching for him, can water his soul with their silent but golden opinion. (*Para. 9*)

1) watching for him 做 faces 的补足语。此处表示“守候他或期待他”之意。

2) **golden opinion:** unspoken approval 指“孩子们对父亲无声的崇敬、赞誉之情”。

golden 修饰的常见词组：

golden opportunity“绝好的机会”；golden rule“金科玉律（重要规则）”；

golden mean“中庸之道”；golden wedding“金婚（结婚 50 周年）”

10. Praise helps rub off the sharp edges of daily contact. (*Para. 10*)

1) **rub off:**“擦掉”

a. Rub off the chalk marks on the blackboard.

把黑板上的粉笔字擦掉。

b. You should rub the graffiti (涂鸦) off the wall at once.

你应该立即将墙上的涂鸦擦掉。

这里 rub off 表示“磨去，磨掉”的意思。sharp edges 意指 hardships/stress“困难，压力”。

2) **contact:** *n.*“联系，接触，交往”；*vt.*“与……联系，与……接触”

a. There is little contact between neighbors in this community.

这个社区里邻里间几乎没有接触。

b. Please feel free to contact me if you have any difficulties.

如果有困难请尽管与我联系。

11. Yet it is perhaps in the home that the value of praise is less appreciated than elsewhere. The spouse who is alert to say the heartening thing at the right moment has learned one of the most important requirements for a happy family life. (*Para. 10*)

1) **appreciate:** *vt.* “重视，赏识；理解，意识到；感激，感谢”

a. He quit the job because his abilities were not fully appreciated by the employer.

他辞职不干了，因为他的能力没有得到老板的充分赏识。

b. I appreciate your difficulties but I cannot help.

我理解你的难处但我帮不上忙。

c. We really appreciate your inviting us to dinner.

非常感谢邀请我们赴宴。

2) **alert:** *adj.* “警觉的，注意的，留神的”

a. Tourists need to be alert to the dangers of traveling in the north of the country.

游客们在这个国家北部旅游时需要谨防危险。

b. A good hunting dog is alert to every sound and movement in the field.

好的猎犬对野外的任何响动都非常警觉。

12. “I had been quick to correct him when he did wrong, but when he had behaved, I hadn’t noticed. (*Para. 12*)

1) **do wrong:** “做坏事，犯过错”。常用于 do somebody wrong/do wrong to somebody “冤枉……，使……受冤枉”。

a. Parents all hope that their children will never do wrong.

父母们都希望自己的孩子永远不要做错事。

b. You do wrong to doctors when you say that they don’t try their best.

你说医生们没有尽全力是冤枉他们了。

2) **behave:** *v.* “行为得体，举止正确”

a. He is 30 now, and it’s time for him to start behaving.

他现在 30 岁了，是该举止像个样子的时候了。

b. Children are taught at home and at school to behave.

孩子们在家里和在学校都被教育要听话。

13. Take the trouble to find something to commend in your child, and you will discover that both his ability and attitude will improve. (*Para. 13*)

1) **take the trouble to do something:** to make a special effort to do something

“费神做……，不辞劳苦地去做……”

a. Please take the trouble to read the contract carefully.

请费心将合同认真读一下。

b. You needn't have taken the trouble to help us.

你本不必费事来帮我们。

联想：have trouble "有困难，有麻烦"；make trouble "制造麻烦"；take trouble "费事，费心"

2) **commend:** *vt.* "表扬、称赞；推荐"

a. We especially want to commend the efforts of Mr. Jefferson.

我们尤其想赞扬杰斐逊先生所做出的努力。

b. She commended this English novel to me as an extensive reading book.

她推荐这本英语小说给我作为泛读书籍。

14. As artists find joy in giving beauty to others, so anyone who masters the art of praising will find that it blesses the giver as much as the receiver. There is truth in the saying, "Flowers leave part of their fragrance in the hand that bestows them." ***(Para. 15)***

1) 句中 As..., so... 结构，意为"正如……一样；像……同样地……"（As it is true that..., it is equally true that...）。表示同等程度的对比关系，多用于书面语，有时可在 as 前加 just 以加强语气。

a. Just as he likes music, I like sports.

就像他爱好音乐一样，我爱好体育。

b. As the French love their wine, the English love their beer.

正如法国人喜欢葡萄酒那样，英国人喜欢啤酒。

2) **There is truth in...:** "……是对的（是有道理的）"

a. There is truth in what the teacher says, "You must act now before it is too late."

老师的话是有道理的："趁还来得及，你必须立刻行动起来。"

b. There is some truth in the proverb, "Laughter is the best medicine."

这个谚语有些道理："笑是最好的良药。"

3) **saying:** old saying, proverb "谚语，古语"

As the old saying goes, you can't judge a book by its cover.

古语云：人不可貌相，海水不可斗量。

Part II
Text Comprehension (Key)

Reading Analysis

1.C　2. C　3. A　4. C　5. B

Information Recall and Summary

A.

1. She was not happy enough because her husband took everything she did for granted and never complimented her.
2. The problem is that few of us realize it is very important that we should be encouraged or praised by others.
3. We can improve our relations with others by showing a sympathetic understanding, which is, always looking for something in others that we can admire and praise and tell them about it.
4. Praise helps keep our self-image bright and sparkling, and this will add to our self-esteem.
5. When we praise others, we must be sincere.
6. One of the most important requirements for a happy family life is that the spouse should give praise when necessary.
7. He wants to say that children are hungry for praise.
8. It means giving praise not only benefits the receiver, but also the giver.

B.

The passage starts with a dialogue between a young woman and her neighbor, which suggests that few people in our society are aware of the importance of encouragement. After that the author puts forward his argument that everyone needs encouragement and that everyone must learn to praise others. Then he explains why praise can work miracles to improve inter-person relationships. Positive and negative examples from daily life are also provided to further illustrate the effects of encouragement through giving praise. The passage concludes with a vivid comparison and an old saying, stressing that praise benefits the giver as well as the receiver.

(102 words)

Information Organization

Examples	Facts	Opinions
A young homemaker spoke her mind	She was unhappy because <u>her husband took everything she did for granted and never complimented her</u>.	Some people don't realize the importance of praise.
Lord Chesterfield made a suggestion	Duke de Nivernois makes people pleased with him by <u>making them first pleased with themselves</u>.	Praise benefits both the giver and the receiver.
A man coming home after a hard day's work had a nice feeling	His soul was watered <u>with his children's silent but golden opinion</u>.	Praise has a great effect.
A young mother told a heartbreaking incident.	Her little boy cried because <u>he was not praised</u> although he had been pretty good.	<u>Children</u> especially need praise.
Artists painting pictures	They <u>find joy</u> in giving beauty to others.	Praise benefits <u>the giver</u>.
People presenting flowers	Flowers leave part of their fragrance in <u>the hand that bestows them</u>.	Praise benefits <u>the giver as well as the receiver</u>.

Part III Skill Building (Key)

Word Forms

A.

1. self-service 自助
2. self-made 靠个人奋斗而获得成功的
3. self-centered 以自我为中心的
4. self-confident 自信的

5. self-taught 自学的
6. self-employed 自雇的
7. self-supporting 自给的
8. self-criticism 自我批评

B.

1. a. confidential b. confident
2. a. cooperate b. cooperative
3. a. ashamed b. shame
4. a. invaluable b. valuable
5. a. worthy b. worth

Vocabulary in Context

A.

1. d 2. f 3. g 4. a 5. h 6. b 7. c 8. e

B.

1. The whole discussion boils down to
2. You didn't take the trouble to consult the dictionary.
3. all his roommates do not get along with him

C.

1. D 2. C 3. A 4. C 5. A 6. B 7. D 8. A

D.

a. 1) classical 2) classic 3) classics 4) classic
b. 1) specially 2) especially 3) especially 4) specially

Key Structures

A.

1. Susan wants to quit rather than accept the new rules.

2. Many women like to go out to work rather than stay at home.
3. As the Americans like football, so the Englishmen like rugby.
4. Just as the Spring Festival is very important to the Chinese, so is Christmas Day very important to the Americans.

B.

1. Unless we start to save money in the bank now, how can we ensure that we will live a happy life when we are old?
2. Anyone who likes to book a table at a restaurant need only make a phone call.

Translation

A.

1. 偶尔
2. 受尊重的朋友
3. 心理图像
4. work miracles
5. daily contact
6. improve his relationships with others

B.

1. B 2. B

Writing

1

There are several reasons why I have chosen to study in Nanjing University. To begin with, the tuition here is quite reasonable, and this will lessen the economic pressure on my family. Secondly, the university is very close to my hometown, and it is convenient for me to go home from time to time to see my parents and friends. The most important reason is that Nanjing University is one of the key universities in China, in which I can meet many excellent professors and learn a lot of useful knowledge and skills for my future career.

2

There is an old saying in China: Practice makes perfect. This is true not only in our learning but also in other walks of life. For instance, when we study English, we have so much to learn such as grammar, vocabulary and writing. In order to learn them well, we need do more practice. We must read a lot, write a lot and listen a lot. Only after we have done more practice can we have a good command of it. Another case in point is typing. A good typist can type fast and accurately. But you would not be surprised at her performance if you know how much time she has spent practicing. Through practice, she has improved both her typing speed and accuracy.

Part IV Fast Reading

课文译文

问候日

鲍伯 · 珀克

“你好！我只是想告诉你，你做得很不错，把这个地方弄得挺干净的，”我对购物中心食品区的保洁工说。我想，我的一番话让他觉得很诧异。他抬起头来，过了好一会儿才说：“噢，谢谢。真的谢谢你的夸奖。”

我相信，他对我的赞美的确心存感激。

我一直都这样做。我会特意地去对某人说几句，或是在大家彼此无语时说点什么打破尴尬的沉默。很多人的工作一般都被认为是理所当然，人们对他们的付出或忽视，或避而不谈，或视而不见，毫无感激之情，而我却会对他们赞美一番。

昨天，我挑战自己，尽我所能在短时间内和尽量多的陌生人说话。我赞美他们，与他们聊天，或只是简单地说声“你好！”末了，我还会加上一句：“多谢了，朋友！”我是从比尔 · 考赤比的儿子那儿学来这一招的，他几年前在加利福尼亚被人杀死。比尔说，他的儿子总是以这种方式问候别人。

这样，我就创立了我自己命名的“问候日”。

这一主意源自我近来编写的一个故事《祝你一切如愿》。在故事中，我着重描述了自己与人说“再见”是多么的艰难。人们对故事的反应实在令人惊讶。有人写信给我，诉说错失机会与人道别的遗憾。有人在信中感谢我增强了他们这方面的意识。有人认同我的观点并承诺，不管何时与人说“再见”，他都会说上一句“祝你一切如愿”。

好多次，别人问我怎么会认识这么多可爱的人。原因很简单：见面我先说“你好”。

在故事的最后一行我写道："愿足够多的'你好'伴你走过最终的离别。"

我创立"问候日"，让最终的离别不再艰难，因为我知道有这么多的人曾经触动过我的生活。

第一天我在购物中心的挑战自我是成功的。称赞完保洁工手头的工作之后，我又走过去向卖比萨饼给我的那位女士夸奖她的比萨饼很棒，她登时笑容满面。花钱买午饭博她一笑，值！能多看一次她的笑脸，即使再花一回钱我也情愿。

接着，我去了报刊亭。边买口香糖边想着法子找点话讲。低头之际，我瞥见柜台上摆着一种草药能量棒，上面写着："有效的草药棒！"

我问报刊亭的摊主，我会不会买到无效的草药棒。他笑着答道："你知道，有的广告专家开着梅赛德斯奔驰，是因为他能想出诸如此类的奇妙的台词而获取丰厚的报酬。你我却都得干活过日子啊。"

我们俩都大笑。我说："多谢了，我的朋友！"接着我便走开了。我后来又观察了他一会儿，发现即便随后的四个顾客都没和他说话，但笑容仍一直挂在他的脸上。

在此，我向你提一个有挑战性的任务：每周选一天，宣布它为你的"问候日"。看看你能向多少人问好、能向多少人讲话、能夸奖多少人或者能启发多少人。当你完全适应这样的挑战后，再挑战自己在最短的时间内去和尽量多的人说话。

那么，你将形如市长，你将亮如明星。你会感觉浑身有使不完的力量。

Reading Comprehension (Skimming and Scanning)

Key

1. Y 2. N 3. Y 4. N 5. Y 6. N 7. NG
8. ignored or unappreciated 9. lost opportunities/lost chances
10. declare it their "Hello Day"

Part V Extensive Reading

Give and Receive Highly-valued Compliments

Steve Nakamoto

1 As a **former** public speaking **instructor** for Dale Carnegie & **Associates**, I had

the task of complimenting my students after they made a 2-minute talk in front of our class. During the students' talk, I would **search for** something in their story that I admired, respected, liked, enjoyed, or appreciated. By **consciously focusing on** the good in the other person, I was able to give a **sincere** and highly-valued compliment by finding a **positive** quality and **backing** it **up** with **evidence** in their talk.

2 I've found that you can give honest and sincere compliment in your personal and **professional** lives just as easily as I did as an instructor for Dale Carnegie & Associates. Here are some ways to help you get better at giving and receiving compliments so that you can begin building stronger relationships with other people in your own life:

1) GIVE COMPLIMENTS IMMEDIATELY: If you respond quickly with a sincere compliment, the other person is not likely to feel that you are being **premeditated** and **manipulative**.

2) SPEAK IN SIMPLE TERMS: If your compliment is too complicated, it can sound premeditated or designed to **shift** the focus off of the **recipient** and onto you, the giver. If the compliment is too **over-the-top**, then the receiver may feel uncomfortable with the compliment and doubt its **authenticity** or **suspect** your **motive**.

3) FIND THE MORE **UNIQUE** COMPLIMENT: The rule of **thumb** here is that the rarer the compliment, the more valuable it is. So that means don't state the obvious. Tell the other person something that they feel is underappreciated or misunderstood about them in order to have a more highly-valued compliment.

4) MAKE IT A PUBLIC COMPLIMENT: If the situation is present, feel free to make your compliment **in the presence of** others. This will have a more powerful effect on the receiver than just giving your compliment **in private**.

5) TRY PUTTING IT IN WRITING: Sometimes a message of support or appreciation in writing on a card or **memo** may have a more powerful and lasting effect on the recipient. You never know how many times a person may re-read and re-experience the joy of well-chosen words of kindness in the **privacy** of their own home.

6) FIND A WIDE **ARRAY** OF GOOD THINGS TO SAY: Look for compliments in either: 1) **Appearance**, 2) Actions, 3) **Possessions**, 4) Character **traits**, or

5) **Refined** style or good tastes. There are plenty of good things to compliment a person on, if you know where to look.

7) PASS ALONG GOOD NEWS: A **third-party** compliment is when you pass along good news from another source. You can tell how other people have been impressed by an **individual**. By being **specific** and giving details, you can give the gift of a subtle sincere compliment even if you're not the original source.

8) ACCEPT COMPLIMENTS LIKE A GIFT: When another person takes the time to compliment you, don't **toss** it back in their face. Instead, be a **gracious** acceptor of the gift by simply making eye contact, smiling, and saying "Thank you".

9) BECOME A SINCERE PERSON: It is hard to make sincere compliments when you're not a sincere person. The greatest benefit to giving compliments is that it starts retraining you to focus on the good in other people. When you start to change your mental and emotional habits for the good, you start changing your entire life for the good.

3 Giving and receiving compliments is one of the simplest, yet most effective ways to build your relationships with other people. It is also one of the most powerful mental and emotional shifts that any person can make for themselves in order to **change** their lives **for the better**. (618 words)

NEW WORDS

former /'fɔːmə(r)/ *adj.* 以前的；*n.* (the) 前者

instructor /ɪn'strʌktə(r)/ *n.* person who instructs 教师；指导者；大学讲师

associate /ə'səʊʃiət/ *n.* (协会的) 会员

consciously /'kɒnʃəsli/ *adv.* 有意识地；有意地

sincere /sɪn'sɪə(r)/ *adj.* (of feelings, behavior) real, true, or honest; genuine 诚挚的，真诚的

positive /'pɒzətɪv/ *adj.* definite; sure; leaving no room for doubt 肯定的，积极的

evidence /'evɪdəns/ *n.* anything that gives reason for believing something 根据，证据

professional /prə'feʃənəl/ *adj.* of a profession; doing or practising something as a full-time occupation or for payment or to make a living 职业的，专业的

premeditate /ˌpriː 'medɪteɪt/ *v.* to consider, plan (something) in advance 预谋，预先计划

manipulative /mə'nɪpjələtɪv/ *adj.* managing or controling (somebody or something) cleverly, esp. by using one's influence or unfair methods 操纵的，控制的

shift /ʃɪft/ *n.* change of place or character; substitution of one thing for another 转换，转变，替换

NEW WORDS

recipient /rɪ'sɪpiənt/ *n.* person who receives something 接受者

over-the-top /ˌəʊvəðə'tɒp/ *adj.* excessive; too much 过度的，过于夸张的

authenticity /ˌɔːθen'tɪsəti/ *n.* genuineness; quality of being authentic 真实性，可靠性，准确性

suspect /sə'spekt/ *vt.* to feel doubt about 怀疑，疑有 /'sʌspekt/ *n.* 嫌疑犯，可疑分子

motive /'məʊtɪv/ *n.* something that causes somebody to act 动机，目的

unique /juː'niːk/ *adj.* being the only one of its type 独特的，唯一的，独一无二的

thumb /θʌm/ *n.* 拇指

presence /'prezəns/ *n.* the fact or state of being present; attendance 在场，出席

memo /'meməʊ/ *n.* (memorandum) note or record for future use 备忘录；便条

privacy /'prɪvəsi/ *n.* state of being away from others, alone and undisturbed 独处，清静

array /ə'reɪ/ *n.* 1) 排列；2) 一群

appearance /ə'pɪərəns/ *n.* 1) 外观，外貌；2) 出现，露面

possession /pə'zeʃən/ *n.* something one owns (常用复数) 所有物

trait /treɪt/ *n.* distinguishing quality or characteristic 特征，特点，特性

refine /rɪ'faɪn/ *vt.* 1) to make or become pure 提炼，精制，提纯；2) to improve 使精美，改进

third-party /ˌθɜːd'pɑːti/ *n.* 第三方

individual /ˌɪndɪ'vɪdʒuəl/ *n.* any one human being 个人，个体；*adj.* 个别的，单独的

specific /spə'sɪfɪk/ *adj.* 1) detailed or precise 明确的，具体的；2) relating to one particular thing, etc., not general 特定的，特有的

toss /tɒs/ *vt.* to throw up into or through the air 扔，抛，掷

gracious /'ɡreɪʃəs/ *adj.* (of persons and their behaviors) pleasant; kind; agreeable 有礼貌的，和蔼的

PHRASES & EXPRESSIONS

search for 寻找，搜查

focus on （注意力、研究、讨论等）集中

back up 支持

in the presence of 当……的面；在……在场的情况下

in private 在私下，秘密地

change...for the better 使……向好的方面改变

课文译文

真诚赞美，接受赞美

史蒂夫·拉卡莫托

作为一个曾在戴尔·卡耐基协会工作过的演讲教师，我有一个任务：在我的学生面对全班做完一个两分钟的演讲后赞扬他们。学生们演讲时，我会在他们的演讲词中寻找一些我所钦佩、尊敬、喜欢、欣赏或者赏识的东西。在有意识地关注他人的优点后，我能够发现其中好的一面并以他们在演讲中的表现加以佐证，由此来表达诚挚而宝贵的赞美。

我发现，你能够和曾经作为戴尔·卡耐基协会教师的我一样，在你的个人生活和职业生涯中轻松地进行诚实而真挚的赞美。这里有一些方法有助于你更加有效地赞美他人和接受赞美，从而使你能在自己的生活中开始与他人建立更加牢固的关系：

1. 立刻赞美：如果你反应迅速，真诚地赞美，别人就不会觉得你是有所预谋或企图摆布他人。
2. 言简意赅：如果你的赞美过于复杂，听起来像是预先策划或设计好的，目的是为了把注意力从被赞美者身上转移到你，也就是赞美者的身上。如果赞美过于夸张，那么被赞美者就会感觉不自在，并且会怀疑其真实性，或者怀疑你的动机。
3. 独特的赞美：根据经验，赞美的方式越是与众不同就越有价值。所以，这就意味着不要去说那些显而易见的东西。和对方说他们感觉未受赏识或受到误解的东西，使赞美显得更加宝贵。
4. 公开赞美：如果情况许可，尽可能当面赞美他人。这比你在私下里赞美要有效得多。
5. 试试写信赞美：有时，写在卡片或者便条上的表示支持或欣赏的话语可能会对被赞美者产生更强烈、更持久的影响。你不知道一个人会悄悄地在家里多少次反复阅读和回味那些精心挑选的赞美之词。
6. 大量赞美：从以下这些方面寻找可以赞美的东西：1）外表，2）行为，3）物品，4）性格特点，5）高雅的风度或良好的品位。如果你知道从哪些方面去寻找，你就会发现一个人身上有许多事情可以加以赞美。
7. 传递赞美：第三方的赞美是指由你传递的来自他人的赞美。你可以告知某人有人对他的印象是多么的深刻。通过具体而详尽的描述，你就能送出一个含蓄而诚挚的赞美之礼，哪怕你并不是礼物的原主人。
8. 像接受礼物一样接受赞美：当别人花时间来赞美你时，别把它迎面扔回。相反，用眼神交流、微笑，说“谢谢你”，礼貌地接受赞美之礼。

9. 做一个真诚的人：当你自己都不是一个真诚的人时，就很难真诚地赞美他人。赞美他人的最大好处在于它开始重新培养你关注他人优点的习惯。当你开始向好的方面改变你的心理和情感习惯时，你也开始向好的方面改变你的整个生活。

赞美和接受赞美是一种最简单但却是最有效的与他人建立关系的方法之一。它也是为了使生活向着更好的方面发展，任何人都能独立做出的最重要的心理和情感改变之一。

Notes to the text

1. During the students' talk, I would search for something in their story that I admired, respected, liked, enjoyed or appreciated. (*Para.1*)
   本句中的 would 用于描述过去的习惯或例行的活动。would 与 used to 的区别为：would 强调过去某种特定情况下的动作，是完全过去的事情，与现在没有联系；would 只表示重复的动作，不表示状态。used to 强调过去的习惯性动作或状态，但如今已不存在，与现在的情况形成对比，既可表示过去持续的状态，也可表示过去重复的行为。
   When Smith was pursuing his bachelor's degree in college, he would read deep into the night.
   当史密斯在大学攻读学士学位时，他常常阅读至深夜。(过去习惯)
   Man used to think that the earth was flat.
   过去人们常认为地球是扁平的。(过去持续的状态，但现在人们不这样认为了)

2. The rule of thumb here is that the rarer the compliment, the more valuable it is. (*Para. 2*)
   rule of thumb: “根据经验估计，(根据实际经验的)粗略的计算方法或做法”。过去曾经用拇指尖到第一关节的长度为尺度量东西，故有此说法。
   John's house was burglarized last night. The rule of thumb is that he should report the case to the police immediately, but he didn't.
   约翰的家昨夜被盗了。根据一般的经验，他应该立刻向警方报案，但他没有。
   As a rule of thumb, you'll pay £10 a month for each £100 you borrow.
   根据经验估计，你每月要为所借的每 100 英镑支付 10 英镑。

3. So that means don't state the obvious. Tell the other person something that they feel is underappreciated or misunderstood about them in order to have a more highly-valued compliment. (*Para. 2*)

state the obvious:“说些显而易见的话”。that 引导定语从句，修饰其前的 something。they feel 为插入语。

The dean is improving the plan, so tell him anything you feel is helpful.

系主任正在润色计划，告诉他你们觉得有益的任何建议。

4. You never know how many times a person may re-read and re-experience the joy of well-chosen words of kindness in the privacy of their own home. (*Para. 2*)

You never know: 与 God knows 或 Who knows 意思相同。

a. God knows where he has gone.

谁知道他去哪里了。

b. You never know whether the news in the newspaper is true or false.

谁知道报纸上登的消息是真还是假。

c. Who knows how the young film star has become so popular overnight.

谁知道这位年轻的电影明星是如何一夜成名的。

5. A third-party compliment is when you pass along good news from another source. (*Para. 2*)

party: *n.*“(合同、诉讼等中的)一方”

the two parties to a marriage contract“婚约的双方当事人”

third-party: someone who is not one of the two main people involved in an agreement or legal case, but who is affected by it in some way“第三方”

a. Our military ties threaten no third party.

我们的军事关系不威胁任何第三方。

男女关系的“第三者”可译为 the third person, the other man or the other woman.

b. Their marriage has broken just because of the other man.

正是因为第三者插足，他们的婚姻破裂了。

6. The greatest benefit to giving compliments is that it starts retraining you to focus on the good in other people. (*Para. 2*)

the good:“优点；好处；益处”

a. What's the good of doing that?

做那事有什么好处?

b. exchange the bad for the good

以恶易善

7. It is also one of the most powerful mental and emotional shifts that any person can make for themselves in order to change their lives for the better. (*Para. 3*)

make shift(s):“设法；尽量想办法”

We must make shift(s) for our kids to receive a better education.

我们必须设法让我们的孩子们接受较好的教育。

for the better:“转好”

His health changed for the better.

他的身体状况有所好转。

相似的结构：for the worse“变坏，恶化”

The patient took a turn for the worse.

该患者病情恶化了。

联想：change from bad to worse“每况愈下；愈来愈坏”

Things are going from bad to worse nowadays.

现在，情况变得愈来愈坏。

Reading Comprehension

Choose the best option to complete each statement and answer each question.

1. From the passage, we see that __________.

   A. the author tries to persuade us to give and receive highly-valued compliments

   B. the author tells us how to give and receive highly-valued compliments

   C. the author thinks it is greatly significant to give and receive highly-valued compliments

   D. the author offers us some different ways to give and receive highly-valued compliments

2. If you compliment others sincerely and quickly, __________.

   A. it's likely that you are welcome

   B. you are possibly considered having everything planned beforehand

   C. you are probably thought to be manipulative

   D. you are possibly considered being purehearted

3. According to the author, which of the following statements is TRUE?

   A. Compliments are supposed to be conveyed in simple terms.

   B. Compliments should be made in private.

   C. Compliments must be in a written form.

   D. Compliments have to be original.

4. According to the passage, which of the following is NOT TRUE?

   A. Sincere compliments are profitable to the persons who give them.

   B. Sincere compliments are advantageous to the persons who receive them.

   C. Sincere compliments are beneficial to the persons who give and receive them.

   D. Sincere compliments are instructive to the persons who give and receive them.

5. The tone of this passage is __________.

A. neutral B. instructive C. critical D. ironical

Key

1. C 2. A 3. A 4. C 5. B

Vocabulary Study

Replace each of the underlined parts with the best choice given.

1. By consciously focusing on the good in the other person, I was able to give a sincere and highly-valued compliment by finding a <u>positive</u> quality and backing it up with evidence in their talk.

A. good B. useful

C. confident D. sure

2. If the compliment is too over-the-top, then the receiver may feel uncomfortable with the compliment and doubt its authenticity or suspect your <u>motive</u>.

A. incentive B. motion

C. objective D. object

3. Find the <u>unique</u> compliment.

A. familiar B. sole

C. similar D. particular

4. By being specific and giving details, you can give the gift of a <u>subtle</u> sincere compliment even if you're not the original source.

A. considerate B. delicate

C. moderate D. dedicated

5. When another person takes the time to compliment you, don't toss it back in their face. Instead, be a <u>gracious</u> acceptor of the gift by simply making eye contact, smiling, and saying "Thank you".

A. rough B. distinct

C. polite D. genuine

6. It is also one of the most powerful mental and emotional <u>shifts</u> that any person can make for themselves in order to change their lives for the better.

A. approaches B. changes

C. solutions D. suspicions

Key

1. A 2. A 3. D 4. B 5. C 6. B

UNIT 5 Cultural Difference

Study Focus:

1. Learn to define（下定义）culture shock.
2. Grasp the following structure: Once..., it's much harder to...
3. Explain the importance of hugging a foreigner.
4. Learn how to write interoffice memos.
5. Understand the statement: Let's get together.

Part I Intensive Reading

课文译文

出国工作的关键：克服"文化冲击"

杰夫·楚

与你所想的不同，在国外生活最困难的既不是寻找住处，也不是学习当地语言，而是怎样克服"文化冲击"。"文化冲击"不是一系列随机的事件，它通常有五个发展阶段。

第一个阶段：蜜月期

在国外生活的头一两个月就像是度蜜月一样，周围的一切都是新的，你为之兴奋、着迷，一切都像在梦中一样，你很庆幸自己做出了出国工作的决定。但谁都知道，蜜月总有结束时。

第二个阶段：排斥期

很快，新环境让人感到新鲜、兴奋、着迷的光彩开始褪去。你不得不回到现实，真正开始在国外工作和生活。你会突然发现自己的做事方式——在工作或其他方面——在新环境下不适用。你要买东西的时候商店不开门，因为电视节目和电影都使用另一种语言，所以闲暇时间没有娱乐。如果你的麻烦日益增多而没有人帮助你，你会觉得当地人根本不能理解你的难处或对你漠不关心。这随之会引发"文化冲击"的一种必然情绪：对新环境的敌视。你开始讨厌所在国以及一切与之有关的东西。

第三个阶段：逃避期

一旦你开始排斥所在国的文化，要想改变你的态度会很困难。你或许可以再试一试，乐观地面对一切并改变你的态度；或者选择容易的办法，即减少与人接触。如果是后者，你在新环境下的失败迹象非常明显：你拒绝继续学习当地的语言，拒绝与当地人交朋友，并对当地的文化不再有任何兴趣。最糟糕的是，你开始认为人们会仅仅因为你是外国人而欺诈你。走上这条路会导致你最终被孤立起来，因为人们能感觉到你的敌意而开始避免与你接触。

第四个阶段：接纳期

如果你能成功跨越第三个阶段，克服“文化冲击”就容易得多了。某一天，你会发现自己也能微笑面对起初一些让你非常难过的事。一旦如此，说明你已经开始适应。随着你对当地的语言和风俗越来越适应，你的自尊心和自信心会慢慢恢复。你对新家的感觉会从最初的勉强接受转变为由衷的喜爱。你会最终理解这不是国内好还是国外好的问题：生活有很多不同的方式，它们没有优劣之分。

第五个阶段：回归期

很多时候，正当情况开始好转时，你可能发现工作即将结束，该收拾行李回国了。大多数人会想，回国多好呀，可以回到熟悉的环境，回到朋友、家人以及所有你喜欢、珍惜的东西旁边。但是重新适应国内的环境比大多数人想象的要困难得多。当你慢慢迫使自己喜欢在国外的新家时，你可能不得不逐渐改变一些根深蒂固的观念，以接纳新的价值观和生活方式。一旦接受了新的习惯和生活方式，你很难再回到原来的生活。你可能还需要花相当长的一段时间来重新熟悉自己国家的文化。

Language Points of the Text

1. Contrary to what you may think, the hardest part of living abroad isn't finding a place to stay or learning the language. (*Para. 1*)

1) **contrary to:** “相反的，对抗的”

a. His opinion is contrary to mine.

他的意见与我的意见相反。

b. Contrary to his doctor's advice, he began to smoke again.

他不听医生的建议，又开始吸烟了。

2) **abroad:** *adv*. “在（到）国外”

go abroad “出国”；live abroad “在国外生活”；return from abroad “从国外回来”；home and abroad “国内外”

a. The experts from home and abroad attended the international conference held in Beijing.

国内外专家参加了在北京举行的这次国际会议。

b. Studying abroad may have advantages as well as disadvantages.

出国留学有利有弊。

拼写容易混淆的词：

aboard: *adv. & prep.* “上船，上车，上飞机”

2. Culture shock does not happen as a series of random events. It usually evolves over a series of five stages. (*Para. 1*)

1) **a series of:** “一系列，一连串”

A series of lectures on genetic engineering are delivered in this medical college.

这所医学院举行了一系列关于遗传工程的讲座。

2) **random:** *adj.* “任意的，随机的” *n.* “随机”

a. The dean asked some random students to join in a discussion.

院长任选几个学生参加讨论。

at random “随机地，胡乱地”

b. When he buys the lottery tickets he likes to choose numbers at random.

他买彩票时喜欢随机选号。

3) **event:** *n.* “事件，大事；比赛项目”

a. The novel narrates the great events of the 1940s.

这部小说叙述了 20 世纪 40 年代的那些大事。

b. Finishing first in eight events, Jim Thorpe beat the whole New Mexico team.

吉姆 · 索普一人打败整个新墨西哥队，在八个项目中获得第一。

与 event 相关的短语：

at all events “不管怎样，无论如何”；in any event “不管怎样，无论如何”；in the event of (that) “万一，假若”

4) **evolve:** *v.* “（使）进化，（使）演化；（使）发展，（使）演变”

a. Hygiene has evolved into preventive medicine.

卫生学已逐步发展成为预防科学。

b. The British political system has evolved over several centuries.

英国的政治体系是经过几个世纪逐步形成的。

3. The first couple of months of living abroad are typically a honeymoon period when everything is new, exciting, and fascinating. (*Para. 2*)

1) **couple of:** “一对，两个；几个”

The president visited the special industrial zone couple of days ago.

总统几天前参观了这个特殊工业区。

a couple of：“一对，一双” a couple of players 一对选手

2) **fascinate:** *v.* “迷住，强烈地吸引住”

The children were fascinated by the toys in the shop windows.

孩子们被商店橱窗里的玩具深深吸引住了。

fascinating: *adj.* “吸引人的，迷人的”

a. What a fascinating shop window!

多么吸引人的商店橱窗呀！

b. It is fascinating and encouraging to observe the development of this immense progress.

看到如此巨大的进步令人着迷，使人振奋。

4. Soon enough, the sheen rubs off the new, exciting, and fascinating experiences and you have to come back down from the clouds and actually live and work in this place. (*Para. 3*)

1) soon 这里作副词，表示“不久，很快”（注意各种不同位置，通常放在句末或放在主要动词前，有时放在句首）

Soon it would be filled with college students.

很快这里就会挤满了大学生。

enough 这里作副词，修饰副词 soon，表示“够……”（紧跟所修饰的词）。soon enough 本处译为“很快，够快”。例如：He didn't work hard enough and so he failed the CET-4 exam. 他学习不够努力，所以没有通过四级考试。

2) **sheen:** *n.* 光辉，光泽

a. There was a sheen of tears in her eyes.

她的眼里闪着泪花。

b. The setting sun gave a beautiful sheen to the lake.

落日给湖面增添了美丽的光泽。

5. Suddenly you'll start to discover that your ways of doing things—professionally and otherwise—just don't work in the new environment. (*Para. 3*)

1) otherwise 是个常用词，也是一个多义词。在不同的语境中，otherwise 的含义和用法有很大的差异：

otherwise 用作连词，意思为“否则；要不然”

a. I was on business trip that day, otherwise I would have taken part in the press conference.

那天我出差，否则我会去参加记者招待会的。

b. Seize the chance, otherwise you will regret it.

抓住机会，要不然你会后悔的。

otherwise 用作副词，意为“在其他方面”，“不（是）这样的”或“另外；别样”。

a. This story sounds reasonable, but the facts are otherwise.

这个故事听起来很合理，但事实并不是这样的。

b. He evidently thinks otherwise.

他显然有不同的想法。

c. The rent is high, but otherwise the house is satisfactory.

房租是贵了点，可这房子在别的方面倒令人满意。

otherwise 组成的短语：

and otherwise “等等；及其他”（本课文用法）

a. We bought sugar, tea, eggs and otherwise.

我们买了糖、茶叶、鸡蛋等等。

b. In secondary schools， students learn Chinese, mathematics, English and otherwise.

学生们在中学里学习语文、数学、英语等等。

2) **work:** *v.* “（想法、计划等）行得通，有效，起作用”

It is no good trying that method, because it won’t work.

使用那个方法没好处，因为它行不通。

6. As your troubles add up and no one wants to lend a hand to help, you start thinking the locals are either incapable of understanding your problems or just don’t care. (*Para. 3*)

1) 本文中 as your troubles add up 意思是“当你的麻烦越来越多”。词组 add up 意思是“增加，添加，合计”

a. The evidence adds up to a case of murder.

所有的证据都说明这是一起谋杀案。

b. The money he spent added up to 1,000 *yuan*.

所花费用总计达 1,000 元。

2) **lend a hand:** “给与，提供帮助”

We didn’t know you were in trouble at that time, otherwise we would have lent you a hand.

我们当时不知道你遇到了困难，要不然我们会帮助你的。

7. This in turn triggers the emotion that is one of the surest signs of culture shock: hostility to the new environment. (*Para. 3*)

1) **in turn:** "反过来"

Theory is based on practice and in turn serves practice.

理论建立在实践的基础上，反过来又为实践服务。

与 turn 有关的短语：

by turns 意为"轮流，交替"

They laughed and cried by turns.

他们一会哭，一会笑。

take turns 意为"轮流做某事，替换"

The three men took turns driving so one would not be too tired.

这三个人轮流开车，这样就不会有人太疲劳。

2) **trigger:** *vt.* "激发起，引起"

a. The election of the new president triggered an armed clash.

新总统的当选引起了武装冲突。

b. The story reported in the local newspaper triggered a heated discussion on ethics.

当地报纸上的报道引发了关于伦理的热烈讨论。

3) **sign:** *n.* "符号，征兆，迹象"

a. The weather shows no signs of getting better.

天气没有好转的迹象。

b. Mary developed signs of flu after she visited an old friend in the hospital.

从医院看望一个老朋友回来后，玛丽出现了流感的症状。

4) **hostility:** *n.* "敌意，敌对"

He displayed traditional Arab hostility toward the West.

他表现出阿拉伯人对西方的传统敌意。

8. Once you start rejecting your host culture, it's much harder to recast your attitude. (*Para. 4*)

1) **reject:** *vt.* "抵制，拒绝"

Nancy rejected Peter's offer of help.

南希拒绝了皮特提供的帮助。

辨析 decline, refuse, reject

refuse, reject, decline 都有"拒绝"的意思，decline 多指"有礼貌地谢绝，婉辞"，一般只表示通过话语来拒绝。如：I'm afraid I must decline your invitation. 恐怕我得谢绝你的邀请。refuse 比 decline 语气重，通常指"直接并且态度坚决地拒绝"，如：He refused to accept this advice. 他不肯接受这一意见。reject 比 refuse 语气还要重，一般指“不容置疑地断然拒绝”，并常含有“驳回”的意思，如：His application was rejected. 他的申请被驳回了。另外 refuse, reject 不一定非要通过话语，如：The horse refused the apple/rejected the apple. 这匹马拒绝吃那个苹果。但不用 declined the apple。

2) host 意为“主人，东道主”，可以构成如 host country “东道国”，host family “接待家庭”等词组。本文 host culture 可译为“所在国文化”或“新到国家的文化”。

3) **recast:** *vt.*“彻底改动；重做”

The Labor Party has to recast its political image to fit the times.

工党不得不改变政治形象以适应时代。

9. You can either decide to try again—approach everything again with a smile on your face and change your attitude—or you can take the easy road and just withdraw further into your shell. (*Para. 4*)

1) **approach:** *v.*“走近，靠近，接近，快到”

Miss Linda was not easily approached by men.

男人不容易接近琳达小姐。

2) take the easy road 意为“选择好走的道路，选择容易的事做”。

3) withdraw further into one's shell 这个短语是 come out of one's shell 的相反用法，come out of one's shell 意思是“(在社交场合) 不再羞怯，开始对人友善并愿意交谈，开始活跃起来”。例如：He has to know you for a long time before he really begins to come out of his shell. 他非得认识你很长时间之后才会真正愿意和你攀谈。

4) **withdraw:** *v.*“使撤退，使退出；从银行取钱”

a. His name was withdrawn from the list of Nobel Prize nominees.

他的名字从诺贝尔奖候选人名单上消失了。

b. He withdrew from newspaper work to devote all his time to writing.

他退出新闻工作以便将他所有时间用于写作。

c. She withdrew 500 dollars from the bank in order to buy a new mobile phone.

为了买部新手机，她从银行取出了 500 美元。

10. And worst of all, you begin to believe that people are out to swindle you just because you are a foreigner. (*Para. 4*)

1) **worst of all:**“最坏的部分，最坏的情况，最糟糕的是”

Worst of all, not one of us knew the way.

最糟的是，我们当中没有一个人认识路。

类似的短语还有：best of all“首先，第一，最……”；first of all“第一，首先”

2) **swindle:** *v.* (out of) to cheat (someone), esp. so as to get money illegally“向某人骗取（尤指钱财），诈骗（某人的）钱财”

Mary swindled him out of his life savings.

玛丽骗走了他一生的积蓄。

11. Following this path will inevitably increase your isolation because people will sense the antagonism and begin to avoid you. (*Para. 4*)

1) **isolation:** *n.*“隔离，孤立，脱离”

the isolation of the slums from the rest of the city

贫民区和城市其他地区的隔离

2) **sense:** *vt.*“觉得，意识到”

The horse sensed the danger and stopped.

马感觉到了危险，停了下来。

12. If you can make it through Stage 3, the road to getting over culture shock typically gets smoother. (*Para. 5*)

1) **make it:**“做成，完成，成功，达到目的”

a. After years as an unsuccessful businessman Mr. Nixon has finally made it.

在经历了多年生意不景气之后，尼克松先生最后成功了。

b. They will never make it across the desert.

他们将永远不能穿越那个沙漠了。

2) **get over:**“克服（困难等），从……恢复过来”

a. Leo got over his illness very slowly.

利奥慢慢地从病中恢复了。

b. Fred didn't remarry; he never got over the shock of losing Jane.

弗雷德没有再婚，他永远不能从失去珍妮所受的打击中恢复过来。

13. Your affection for your new home will grow from reluctant acceptance to genuine fondness. (*Para. 5*)

1) **affection:** *n.*“深挚的感情，爱情”

Sally had a great affection for the town where she grew up.

萨莉对她从小生活的城市怀有深挚的感情。

2) **reluctant:** *adj.* unwilling, and therefore perhaps slow to act“勉强的，不愿的”（可作定语和表语）

a. He gave a reluctant promise.

他勉强答应下来了。

b. Everyone was reluctant to leave the party.

每个人都不愿意离开晚会。

3) **genuine:** *adj.*“真正的”

a. Is the necklace genuine gold?

项链是真金的吗？

b. The sofa is made of genuine leather.

沙发是真皮的。

辨析 genuine, real, true, authentic

real 一般指实体或表里一致的事物。This is a real diamond. 这块钻石是真货。

true 指 real 所表示的真实，但要先有一个判断真实与否的准绳，如某种模式、型号、类型或专门定义。例如：a true Christian 一个虔诚的基督教徒；The whale is not a true fish, but a mammal. 鲸实际上不是鱼，而是一种哺乳动物。

genuine 是最常用的词，适用于任何果真具有所指的来源、作者或性质的东西。例如：a genuine oil painting by Rembrandt 伦勃朗油画的真迹；a genuine bargain 真正的便宜货。

authentic 常可与 genuine 交换使用，但 authentic 强调有正式证据或文件证明，表明某东西是真的，而 genuine 只确定某东西不是假的或伪造的。例如：an authentic antique 一件真古董；The geologists declared the fragment to be an authentic specimen of a rare fossil. 地质学家宣称这件碎片是一种稀有化石的真实样品。

拼写容易混淆的词：genius *n.*“天才（不可数），天赋”；generous *adj.*“慷慨大方的”

14. You'll finally understand that it's not a matter of whether here is better than there... (*Para. 5*)

a matter of:“一个……问题”

It was a matter of life and death for the Red Army soldiers.

对于红军战士来说，这是生死存亡的问题。

It is not a matter of..., it's a matter of...“这不是一个……问题，而是一个……问题”

I take this seriously. It's not a matter of money; it is a matter of principle.

我是认真的，这不是一个金钱的问题，这是一个原则问题。

15. Many times, it's just about the time where things begin to jell that you may realize that your assignment is ending and the time has come to pack up and return home. (*Para. 6*)

1) Many times, it's just about the time...begin to 本文意为“很多次，正当……时候……”的句型。

Many times, it's just about the time where doctors begin to find a new medicine to fight against the virus that they may realize that another new virus has emerged.

很多时候，正当医生们开始发明一种新药去消灭某种病毒时，他们会发现又有另一种病毒出现了。

容易混淆的词组：

It's high/about time that... 表示“到了该……的时候了，现在该……了”，that 从句后应接虚拟语气结构，动词常用过去式。

a. It is about time (that) we ordered the dinner.

到了我们订餐的时间了。

b. It is high time (that) the government took some measures to control pollution.

到了政府采取一些措施去治理环境污染的时候了。

2) **jell:** *v.* (of ideas, thoughts, etc.) to take a clear shape“（意见、想法等）定形，成形”

I found the film confusing—there were a lot of different ideas that didn't really jell.

我觉得这部片子内容很混乱，许多不同观点都不够清楚。

3) **pack up:**“收拾衣服，收拾工具”

The company will probably pack up and move south.

这家公司可能就要收拾家当南迁了。

16. Most start thinking about how nice it will be to return to familiar surroundings, back to friends and family and all the things you love and cherish. (*Para. 6*)

cherish: *v.* to value“珍爱”

a. I greatly cherish the close relationship between our two cities. I also greatly value the position we enjoy as one of your most important trading partners.

我非常珍视我们两座城市之间的密切关系，我也非常重视我们作为你们最重要的贸易伙伴之一所享有的地位。

b. We Chinese cherish freedom and independence.

我们中国人都珍视自由和独立。

17. When you slowly forced yourself to like and love your new home abroad, you probably had to gradually deconstruct your long-held beliefs to make room for values and ways of life. (*Para. 6*)

1) **deconstruct your long-held beliefs:**“放弃一些长期坚守的信仰”

deconstruct: *v.*“解构，分解，破坏”

de- 用于动词和名词之前，表示“否定，与之相反”

It took 10 minutes to deconstruct a complicated sentence in the exam.

分析试题中的一个难句用了 10 分钟。

2) **make room for:** “留出空间，让地方”

a. We'll make room for you in the back of the car.

我们将在车后座给你留出位子。

b. This desk takes up a lot of room.

这张课桌很占地方。

18. It will also take you quite some time to reacquaint yourself with your home culture. (*Para. 6*)

1) **reacquaint with:** to have met socially again “与……再次相识”

It was difficult enough for Lisa to reacquaint herself with campus life after she had left the school for so many years due to financial reasons.

由于经济原因辍学多年之后，对于莉萨来说，重新熟悉校园生活是相当困难的。

2) home culture 这里和上文提到的 host culture “新到国家的文化”相对应，指“自己祖国的文化”。

Part II Text Comprehension (Key)

Reading Analysis

1. B 2. B 3. A 4. A 5. D

Information Recall and Summary

A.

1. The first couple of months of living abroad is called the honeymoon period. It is a period when everything is new, exciting, and fascinating.
2. The surest sign of culture shock in the rejection stage is hostility to the new environment.
3. You can withdraw further into your shell and increase your isolation. The people will sense your antagonism and begin to avoid you.
4. Your affection for your new home will grow from reluctant acceptance to genuine fondness.
5. It will take you quite some time to reacquaint yourself with your home culture. You probably had to gradually deconstruct your long-held beliefs to make room for new values and ways of

life. You adopted new habits and a new lifestyle and it can be difficult to go back to your old life.

B.

This passage discusses, in the second person, some facts and explanations about culture shock which happens when you are working in a foreign country. Culture shock involves five different stages in which culture differences affect your emotions, habits, attitudes, values and lifestyles. Some suggestions are also given in the passage to help you survive culture shock to adapt to the different cultures both at home and abroad. (67 words)

Information Organization

Topics	Supporting Details
The Honeymoon Period (Para. 2)	The honeymoon period is the first couple of months of living abroad. During this stage, everything is new, exciting, and fascinating.
The Rejection Stage (Para. 3)	During the rejection stage, You start to discover that your ways of doing things just don't work in the new environment.
The Regression Stage (Para. 4)	During the regression stage, you refuse to continue learning the local language, make friends among the locals, or take any interest in the local culture. And worst of all, you begin to believe that people are out to swindle you just because you are a foreigner.
The Acceptance Stage (Para. 5)	When you can make it through the acceptance stage, you begin to become more comfortable with the local language and customs, your self-esteem and self-confidence will return. You'll finally understand that it's not a matter of whether here is better than there: There are different ways to live your life and no way is really better than another.
The Re-entry Stage (Para. 6)	When you slowly forced yourself to like your new home abroad, you probably had to gradually deconstruct your long-held beliefs to make room for values and ways of life. It will also take you quite some time to reacquaint yourself with your home culture.

Part III Skill Building (Key)

Word Forms

A.

1. defrost 除霜
2. devalue 贬值
3. deforestation 砍伐森林
4. decolorize 使漂白，褪色
5. inaccurate 不精确的，不准确的
6. inadequate 不充足的，不适当的
7. inappropriate 不恰当的，不相宜的
8. independent 不依赖的，独立的

B.

1. a. typical b. type c. typically
2. a. professional b. profession c. professionally
3. a. capability b. capable c. incapable
4. a. recovered b. discovered c. uncovered
5. a. acceptance b. accept c. acceptable

Vocabulary in Context

A.

1. h 2. e 3. a 4. c 5. b 6. d 7. f 8. g

B.

1. He lent me a hand translating the paper into English.
2. As a female teacher, you must get over your shyness.

C.

1. a 2. c 3. b 4. d 5. a 6. c 7. d 8. a

D.

a. 1) hostility　　2) hospitality　　3) hostility　　4) host

b. 1) adjust　　2) adapt　　3) adopt　　4) adjust

Key Structures

A.

1. Contrary to what I thought, he has proved to be very successful.
2. Contrary to my expectation, she failed the examination.
3. Once you object to a man, it's much harder to revise your attitude towards him.
4. Once her mind is made up on any subject, it's much harder to influence her.

B.

1. They in turn kept an eye on the vase that is the most valuable antique of the display.
2. But worst of all, I began to believe that I had no chance to see David again just because I was not accepted by the college in Britain.

Translation

A.

1. 文化冲击
2. 东道国
3. lend a hand
4. genuine fondness
5. random events
6. long-held beliefs

B.

1. C　　2. B

Practical Writing

Model 1

译文

备忘录

收件人：各位代表

发件人：销售代表Sue Button

日期：　2005年2月20日

事由：　订购再生纸

现在所有的代表都应使用再生纸。大家可以填写特别订购单（见所附样单），按以往手续订购。在填表时请注意填全下列信息：

1. 写明页数，而不是包数；

2. 若提前一个月订购，可享受打折；

3. 每笔订购需另计邮费和运费。

所用纸张的颜色，各代表可自行选择，一旦选定，请勿更改。

Model 2

译文

备忘录

收件人：斯蒂芬·鲍尔

发件人：丹·史密斯

日期：　2006 年12月16日

事由：迁址

鉴于我公司的迅速发展，原来的办公楼难以满足业务的要求。我们在市中心新建了另一幢大楼，我们将于12月20日迁往新楼。新办公室将于12月27日开始使用。我们的新地址和传真号码如下：

地址：加拿大温哥华市盘敦威大道20号詹姆森建筑有限公司

传真：287998

Writing Exercise

Suggested samples for reference:

1.

Memo

To: All (staff & students)

From: Mr. Lawson (president's office)

Date: April 28, 2006

Re: Summer hours

Summer is drawing near. Due to the longer daylight savings time, we need to prolong the working hours. As of May 1, afternoon classes will start at 14:00 (the morning schedule will remain the same); the school bus leaves at 17:00; the power supply in the teaching building & students' dorm will remain working until 11:00p.m. The logistics departments are to make arrangements for their office hours in light of this new schedule.

If you have any questions, please consult the president's office.

2.

Memo

To: All employees

From: Brian Aponte

Date: November 18, 2006

Subject: fitness center

The board of directors approved the project of setting up a fitness center during their meeting yesterday.

The project will begin immediately and should be completed within 90 days. An employee representative from each division will be appointed to determine the type of equipment and the programs that will be made available.

We are happy to be able to provide a facility to contribute to the physical fitness of all our employees. Your representative on the task force will contact you soon for your suggestions.

Part IV Fast Reading

课文译文

不要对外国人说“让我们聚聚吧”

阿特 · 巴赤沃德

在美国与外国人交往的麻烦在于他们总是从字面上理解美国人说的每句话。

我有一位法国朋友名叫迈克。前几天我在街上遇到他，在平常的闲聊之后我说：“有时间给我来电话。”

第二天他果真打来电话。

“你好！”他说，“我是迈克。你说过让我给你打电话。”

“我说过吗？”

“对，难道你不记得了吗？昨天我们在宾夕法尼亚大街聊天时你对我说的。”

“我的意思并不是要你立即就打电话。那不过是一种说再见的方式而已。”

“那么你是不想在电话里和我聊聊了？”

“说实话，我真的没什么可说的。”

“但是你让我给你去电话的。”

“瞧，目前我正忙得不可开交。有时间我们一起吃午饭吧。”

“我很乐意，什么时间？”

“我暂时决定不了。不如你喊我吧！”

两天之后，我听到路边有人在喊我的名字。我打开办公室的窗户，看见迈克在下面。

“你到底在那儿喊什么？”我冲他叫道。

“是你说的，我想吃午饭的时候就喊你，今天怎么样？”

“今天我忙着呢。”

“既然你忙成这样，为什么还告诉我想吃午饭就喊你？”

“当美国人说：‘改天我们一起吃午饭’，他未必就是那个意思，那只是个玩笑话，当不得真。你们法国人说‘Au revoir’，德国人说‘Auf wiedersehen’，西班牙人说‘Hasta manana’，而我们美国人则说‘让我们一起吃午饭’。在我们国家，这相当于说‘别给我打电话，我会给你去电话的’。”

迈克说："我并不想打扰你。"

"你并没有打扰我。我会让你明白的。我们看看有没有时间,这两天抽空一起喝一杯。"

"那太好了,"迈克说。

第二天，我正汗流浃背地忙着一个专栏。这时候，迈克探进头来。

"什么事？"

"我只是查看一下你是否想喝一杯。"

"你没看到我正忙着吗？"

"现在我是看到了，但是在查看之前我是无法知道的。"

"你都快让我发疯了。我之所以对你说'我们改天一起喝一杯'是因为我想让你不要在窗下喊我。"

"你只需要告诉我。你不想见到我就行了，"迈克受伤地说道，"而不是让我来找你，你再次失约。"

我感觉糟透了。"你是对的。我很抱歉如此对你。在美国，我们习惯于在彼此分手的时候约定不久再次见面，而没有人会当真以为对方会遵守这个约定。如果和街上遇到的每个人都吃午饭，我们什么事情也别想做成了。"

"我明白，"迈克说，"但是如果你改变主意的话，你有我的名片，随时可以打电话给我。"

"我没有你的名片，迈克。这你又不懂了。当美国人互相交换名片以后，通常一到家他们就将名片扔掉了。"

Reading Comprehension

Key

1. It is just a nice way to say good-bye.
2. It means " Don't call me, I'll call you."
3. The exact meaning of the sentence is: I wanted you to stop hollering under my window.
4. After Americans exchange business cards with each other, they usually throw them away when they get home.
5. The trouble with foreigners is that they take everything Americans say literally.

Part V Extensive Reading

Have You Hugged a Foreigner Today?

Linell Davis

1 Probably not.

2 If you are a typical Chinese you do not hug anyone in public. (Well, maybe you put your arm around your sweetheart's waist as you **stroll** down the street.) Go to any airport or train station and you will see scenes of greeting and good-bye with all the feelings expressed in the face and the eyes and in the **practical** things loved ones do for one another. It is unlikely that someone will put their arms around the returning or departing dear one and **squeeze**.

3 How much more unlikely that you would hug a foreigner? A foreigner is a *wai guo ren*, a person outside the wall. Not much hugging goes on inside the wall, inside the **intimacy** of the family home, and people outside are dealt with much more formally than people inside. Sure, you might welcome a guest to your home or office and that guest would be given the best hospitality you can offer. You would show the sincerity of your welcome by performing many **rituals** such as giving the guest your undivided attention and paying compliments that carry the message that the guest is great and you are humble. Most foreigners are treated as **honored guests**. You don't hug an honored guest.

4 But you should.

5 The question "Have you hugged a foreigner today?" is not really a question. It is a suggestion, a play on the popular American slogan "Have you hugged your kids today?" That was never meant to be a question but a reminder to parents to physically demonstrate their affection for their children every day. Parents should get closer to their children. They should let them know in a very concrete way that they are loved.

6 So when I say, "Have you hugged a foreigner today?" I am not asking you a question. I am advising you to reduce the social distance between you and the Westerners you meet. I am not suggesting that you put your arms around the Westerners you know, but I am suggesting that you **put aside** your home culture rules of politeness that say you should show your sincerity by being humble and

deferential. Instead show your sincerity by standing tall, looking the person in the eye, saying your name in a clear strong voice and giving the person a firm handshake. Don't ruin it by being **tentative** with your grasp. Reach out and hug that hand. Take as much of the hand as you can get hold of and squeeze.

7 By doing this you show that you consider yourself equal to the person you are meeting.

8 In the West people of different social statuses communicate in a way that tries to reduce the status differences. A **high-ranking** person will convey the message "I am just like you." Similarly, a lower-ranking person will communicate in a way that sends the message, "I am just as **capable** as you are."

9 In China it is considered polite to stress your low position and the other person's higher status, greater accomplishments or finer virtue. A Westerner on the receiving end of such behavior is likely to interpret this as a lack of self-confidence, as a sign that you are unsure of yourself and probably inexperienced in the present social or business situation. They are likely to take your word for it that you are unworthy, that your **humility** is a reliable message about your self-confidence or ability. Your sincere effort to be polite can **backfire** if the Westerner interprets your weak handshake as meaning that you are not worth paying attention to.

10 So, hug a foreigner today. (600 words)

NEW WORDS

stroll /strəʊl/ *v.* to walk a short distance slowly or lazily, esp. for pleasure 散步，溜达，漫步

practical /'præktɪkəl/ *adj.* effective or convenient in actual use 实用的

squeeze /skwiː z/ *v.* to hold tightly 紧握，拥抱

intimacy /'ɪntɪməsi/ *n.* the state of being intimate 亲密，亲切

ritual /'rɪtjuəl/ *n.* one or more ceremonies or customary acts which are often repeated in the same form 仪式，例行习惯

deferential /ˌdefə'renʃəl/ *adj.* 恭敬的，顺从的

tentative /'tentətɪv/ *adj.* done without confidence; hesitant 踌躇的，犹豫的

high-ranking /ˌhaɪ'ræŋkɪŋ/ *adj.* 地位高的

capable /'keɪpəbl/ *adj.* having the power, skill, or other qualities needed to do (something) 有能力的，有本领的

humility /hjuː'mɪləti/ *n.* the quality of being humble; lack of pride 谦逊，谦恭

backfire /ˌbæk'faɪə(r)/ *vi.* 发生意外，产生事与愿违的结果

PHRASES & EXPRESSIONS

honored guest 尊贵的客人

put aside 搁在一边

Cultural Background

Linell Davis

里那 · 戴维斯是一位在中国执教多年、对东方文化有着浓厚兴趣的美籍专家。在多年旅居中国的生涯中，Linell Davis 从观念、思维、习俗、人际交往等方面入手著书立说，比较中美两个民族在宏观文化之下其微观文化的巨大差异，并通过大量详实的材料佐证了他多年来对中国微观文化的感悟与思索。

课文译文

你今天拥抱外国人了吗?

里那 · 戴维斯

也许没有。

如果你是典型的中国人，你不会在公共场所拥抱任何人。(哦，也许你在街上散步时会搂着你爱人的腰)。 到任何机场或火车站，你可以看见人们打招呼或道别时，真情在脸上和眼中流露，或是相爱的人们为彼此做一些实际事情。但人们不会伸手去紧拥他们归来和离别的亲人。

拥抱外国人对于你是多么不可能? 外国人是国外的人，一个局外人。 即使在家庭内部，人们也很少拥抱，对待外人则更多规矩。当然，你也许把一个客人接到家里或办公室，那个客人也许会受到最好的款待。你也许会以很多礼仪来表现你真诚的欢迎，如给予你的客人不分彼此的关心及表现出客尊主卑。大多数外国人都被当作贵宾。你不会去拥抱一下贵宾。

不过，你应该去拥抱你的客人。

“你今天拥抱外国人了吗? ” 不是一个问句而是一个建议，模仿的是美国流行语“你今天拥抱你的孩子们了吗? ” 这句话也决不是一个问句，而是提醒父母，每天以拥抱的方式表示对孩子的爱。父母应该与他们的孩子更亲近，应该以非常具体的方式让孩子知道父母爱他们。

因此当我说：“你今天拥抱外国人了吗?” 我不是在向你提问。我是在建议缩短你和所遇到的外国人的距离。我不是在建议你张开臂膀拥抱你已认识的外国人，而是在建议把自己国家以谦恭表示诚意的礼节暂放一边。相反你要站直，凝视对方的眼睛，清晰响亮地介绍自己的名字，用力握对方的手来表示真诚。不要让犹豫不决的握手增加了社交距离。伸出手去握住对方的手，并尽力紧紧握住。

这样做表示你认为自己和对方是平等的。

在西方不同社会地位的人们在交流时尽力缩小社会地位的差距。地位高的一方会传递这样的信息："我和你地位一样。"同样，地位低的一方也会传递这样的信息："我和你一样能干。"

在中国表示礼貌的方式是强调自己地位低而对方地位高以及成就卓著或品德高尚。西方人对于接收到的此类行为的信息会理解为缺乏自信，即一种你对自己没把握，或目前没有社交和商业经验的表现。他们很可能会把你的话当真，即你没有价值，你的自谦是对你自信心和能力的真实反映。如果对方把你无力的握手理解为你不值得受重视，那你真诚表示礼貌的努力就会事与愿违。

因此，今天就拥抱一个外国人吧。

Notes to the Text

1. It is unlikely that someone will put their arms around the returning or departing dear one and squeeze. (*Para. 2*)

   1) 句型 It is unlikely that 表示"看起来不太可能发生，没有……倾向的，不太可能的"。

   It's unlikely that Donna will attend the meeting.

   唐娜出席会议的可能性不大。

   2) squeeze: *v.* "紧握，拥抱；挤压，挤车"

   a. My mother squeezed me tightly on the morning I left home to go to college.

   我离家上大学的那天上午，母亲紧紧地拥抱我。

   b. Mr. Johnson squeezed himself into a crowded bus on rush hour.

   约翰逊先生在上下班高峰时间挤进一辆拥挤的公交车。

2. Similarly, a lower-ranking person will communicate in a way that sends the message, "I am just as capable as you are." (*Para. 8*)

   1) similarly: *adv.* "相似的，类似的"

   Girls wear fashionable clothes; similarly, some birds have bright feathers.

   女孩穿时装，同样，有些鸟类有着鲜艳的羽毛。

2) convey: *v.* “传递，传达，表达，转达（思想、情感、信息等）”
convey the message 传递信息；convey the feelings 表达感情；
convey the ideas 表达想法；convey best wishes 表达祝愿

3. A Westerner on the receiving end of such behavior is likely to interpret this as a lack of self-confidence, as a sign that you are unsure of yourself and probably inexperienced in the present social or business situation. (*Para. 9*)
interpret... as...: *v.* “把……理解为；解释，阐明”
I interpreted his silence as a refusal.
我把他的沉默理解为拒绝。
辨析 interpret 和 translate:
这两个词都有“翻译”的意思，interpret 一般指口译；translate 既可指口译也可指笔译。

4. Your sincere effort to be polite can backfire if the Westerner interprets your weak handshake as meaning that you are not worth paying attention to. (*Para. 9*)
1) backfire: *vi.* “发生意外，产生事与愿违的结果”
The plan may backfire on you.
这个计划可能会对你产生适得其反的结果。
2) be worth doing: “值得”，be worth 后可接名词或动名词。
His suggestion is worth considering.
他的建议值得考虑。

Reading Comprehension

Choose the best option to complete each statement and answer each question.

1. If you are a typical Chinese and go to any airport or train station, you will see scenes of greeting and good-bye with all the feelings expressed ________.
A. by exchanging hugs in public
B. in the face and the eyes
C. by saying “I love you”
D. through mobile phones

2. Why don’t you hug a foreigner according to the text?
A. Because a foreigner is a dangerous person.
B. Because a foreigner has some infectious disease.
C. Because a foreigner is a *wai guo ren*, a person outside the wall.

D. Because we Chinese don't like foreigners.

3. In the West , people of different social statuses communicate in a way that ________.

A. the high-ranking person will convey the message "I am superior to you"

B. tries to reduce the status differences

C. the lower ranking person will communicate in a way that sends the message "I am inferior to you"

D. tries to reduce the gender differences

4. In China it is considered polite to ________.

A. stress your high position and other person's lower status

B. hug in public

C. stress your low position and other person's higher status, greater accomplishments or finer virtue

D. exchange greetings loudly in public

5. Which of the following is the reason why we should hug a foreigner?

A. It will reduce the social distance between you and the Westerners.

B. It will bring us financial benefits.

C. It will narrow the gap of social statuses between you and the Westerners.

D. It will show our dignity.

Key

1. B 2. C 3. B 4. C 5. A

Vocabulary Study

Replace each of the underlined parts with the best choice given.

1. It is unlikely that someone will put their arms around the returning or departing dear one and squeeze.

A. press B. shake

C. kiss D. hug

2. Sure, you might welcome a guest to your home or office and that guest would be given the best hospitality you can offer.

A. welcome B. likeness

C. care D. treatment

3. That was never meant to be a question but a reminder to parents to physically demonstrate their affection for their children every day.

A. determine B. show

C. design D. illustrate

4. I am not suggesting that you put your arms around the Westerners you know, but I am suggesting that you put aside your home culture rules of politeness that say you should show your sincerity by being humble and deferential.

A. pay no attention to B. put back

C. set up D. pay back

5. In the West people of different social statuses communicate in a way that tries to reduce the status differences.

A. exchange information B. respect women

C. love children D. celebrate holidays

Key

1. D 2. A 3. B 4. A 5. A

Making Offers and Giving Responses

Study Focus:

1. 字母组合 ew, eu, au, augh 以及 aw 的发音
2. 如何表达提供以及如何回答（表示接受/表示拒绝）

Part I Listening

Section A Phonetics

Key

1. D　2. A　3. C　4. C　5. A

Section B Short Conversations

Tapescript

1. W: What would you like to drink, sir?

   M: I'd like to have a beer and a glass of water.

   W: With ice?

   M: Yes, thank you.

   Q: What does the man want to have?

2. M: What about going to the cinema with me tonight?

   W: In all fairness, I can't go out with you tonight, as I haven't got any money.

   M: I can lend you some.

   W: No, thanks.

   Q: What can be inferred from the dialogue?

3. M: Excuse me.

   W: Yes?

   M: I'm looking for Mr. Smith's office. Do you know where it is?

   W: I'm sorry, I don't know, but the guard over there should know.

   Q: Where does the man want to go?

4. W: Hi there! My name's Helen. You're new around here, huh?

M: Yes. My name's Andrew. I came to this college a couple of weeks ago.

W: Well, if there's anything I can do for you, let me know.

M: Thanks, I appreciate that!

Q: Where does the conversation probably take place?

5. M: Can I help you?

W: Yes, please. I want that red bag.

M: OK. Here you go.

W: Thanks.

Q: What's the relationship between the two speakers?

Key

1. C 2. A 3. B 4. B 5. D

Section C Passages

Exercise One

Tapescript

The university has a dedicated Careers Service, which offers advice and support on searching for work, obtaining work experience, choosing a career, employer information and further study. They hold extensive careers information and vacancy listings in their well-equipped information room. In addition, a wide range of employers regularly visit the Careers Service to recruit new graduates and there are skills workshops throughout the year.

Key

1) offers advice 2) work experience 3) further study 4) careers information

5) In addition 6) regularly visit 7) new graduates 8) throughout

Exercise Two

Tapescript

I went into a room where four men were seated at a large table. One of them rose and walked round to shake hands with me. He introduced himself and then pointed at a chair, in which I seated myself. After asking me briefly about my place of birth and my working experience, they began to question me carefully on marketing. Now I was pleased, for it was a familiar subject to me. They asked me many questions, the years of study and work helped me greatly, and I knew I was doing well. When it was over, Mr. Robert, who had welcomed me, said: "Well, now, we are completely satisfied with your replies and we feel sure that, in terms of qualifications, ability and experience, you are well suited to the post we have in mind. But if we employ you, it means we must place you in a position over a number of our English employees; many of them have been with us for a long time. So I'm afraid, we will not be able to offer you the job."

I felt suddenly weak, and I was quite unable to think. Yet somehow I managed to leave the office, realizing that it was totally because of my black skin.

Questions:

1. What kind of meeting did the speaker have with the four men?
2. Which of the following statements is NOT true?
3. What happened to the speaker in the end?
4. According to the passage, why was the man rejected?
5. What can you infer from this passage?

Key

1. A　　2. D　　3. C　　4. C　　5. B

Notes

1. Yes?“什么事?”

   这个 Yes 用升调说出来，在口语中有一个用法就是表示“什么事”，比如说你的好朋友叫你的名字，最简单的回答方式就是，Yes?“什么事啊?”当然你也可以说：What's up? 另外，有时候去买东西或去图书馆借书，服务人员看到你站在柜台前面，他会问你：May/Can I help you? 不过同样地，他们也会用 Yes?，就是问你：“有什么事吗?”

2. Hi there!“喂!”

   这是外国人在口语中常用的表达方式。there 在这里用作感叹词，用于表示安慰或各种感情。语意随情境、表达方式的改变而改变。如：

   There! Do you feel better now? 怎么样，你好些了吗?

   There, there. Stop crying. 好了，好了，别哭了。

   There now! 你看！(用以显示说话者讲过的话是对的。)

   There, there! 好啦，好啦！(表示安慰。)

   So there! 这就是我最后的决定（最后的话）；你看，事情就是这样！

   You had him there. 这下你把他制住了。

3. Here you go.

   指的是一件事情还在进行之中．例如店员正把你买的东西交付给你，他会说：Here you

go. 反之，如果东西已经到了你手上，他则会说：There you go.

4. equal opportunity “均等机会”

这是商界用语。指对雇员或申请就业者在种族、肤色、宗教、信仰、性别、年龄等方面不加歧视的做法。

Part II Speaking

Section A Functional Language

➡ ***How to offer help:***

Suggested expressions

Yes?

Can I help you?

What would you like to drink?

I can lend you some.

If there's anything I can do for you, let me know.

➡ ***How to accept offers of help:***

Suggested expressions

Yes, please.

Yes, thank you.

Thanks, I appreciate that!

➡ ***How to decline offers of help:***

Suggested expressions

No, thanks.

Section B dialogue

Key

1. C 2. A 3. D 4. A 5. C

Section C Situational Communication

Phase 1

Suggested samples

1. — Hey, why so upset?
   — I have to fininsh my PPT but I'm afraid I can't do well. You know I'm not good at operating the computer.
   — Oh, would you like me to do something for you?
   — I'd appreciate it if you could.
2. — Hi, what's up?
   — I'm doing some cleaning. I'm on duty today.
   — Is there anything I can do?
   — Not really. Thank you all the same.

Phase 2

Possible offers and replies for reference

1. — Yes? Can I help you?
   — I want to borrow a book for English test.
2. — Let me help you with the bike.
   — It's all right, I can do it myself.
3. — Don't worry. If there's anything I can do, I'd be (only too) happy to help.
   — I'd appreciate it if you could/would.
4. — Well, there's a bank just round the corner. I can show you where it is.
   — Thank you very much. That's very kind of you.
5. — Yes, madam. Can I help you?
   — Yes, please. Yesterday my daughter bought this shirt from this shop. I'd like to change it as it is too small. Here, I've got the receipt.

UNIT 7 Food

Study Focus:

1. Study the difference in attitudes toward food between an American and a Chinese.
2. Practice using the "No wonder (that)…" structure.
3. Understand the author's attitude toward Western fast food.
4. Learn how to develop a paragraph by cause and effect.
5. Read about the typical Chinese cuisines.

Part I Intensive Reading

课文译文

一个外国人眼中的中国饮食文化

莫大伟

十年前，我开始与一位来自四川、性格开朗的中年访问学者学中文。他当时就住在我波斯顿的公寓楼内。他非常健谈，我们的中文课经常离题，长时间去谈论中国文化的方方面面。他最初教我写的两个汉字是“人口”，我至今仍清晰地记得，当时他指着纸上的字说道：“瞧，‘人口’！因为中国有十多亿人要养活，这个词就很自然地把‘口’看作最重要的部分。由此我们可以推论中国人的性格——食为先。”

随着对中国和中国人民越来越多的了解，我发现他的观点非常准确，中国人不仅经常想着食物，而且实际上可以说对此十分痴迷，因此中国文化经常表现出食文化的特点。

中国人对食物从不草率从事。

1988 年我去北京出差，参加一次中国宴席时，第一次直接接触了中国的食文化。虽然在美国我经常吃中餐，但是我还是难以想象中国宴席是多么的绝妙和奢侈。

头六七道菜就占满整张桌子，而且还要碟子摞碟子地摆放。当时，在我这个深受美国教育的人看来，这第一批食物肯定就是要上的所有菜肴，所以我迫不及待地大吃起来，菜肴丰富的品种和上乘的质量让我眼花缭乱。而我周围的中国客人却完全是另外一种反应。

他们对每道菜只尝上一两口就放下筷子继续聊天。“他们一定不饿，”我不以为然地想着，继续享用我的盛宴。

然而让我吃惊的是，很快越来越多的菜肴不断堆上早已像小山一样的桌子，另外还有两三个汤、各种小菜、点心等精致好吃的食物，看样子足够所有人民解放军吃的。难怪其他客人只尝上一两口，他们深知头几道菜不过是庞大的美食冰山的一角，而我在最初的十五钟后就已经吃得饱饱的，以至于只好坐在那儿傻呆呆地瞧着服务员一道接一道地把菜肴端上桌来。

几年以后，我还是不习惯中国人在外面吃饭时的这种习惯，而且以一个美国人的眼光来看，中国人点菜有一条潜规则：至少要多点一道菜，“适可而不止”。这种浪费行径近来在中国也一直遭受批评。有人提出点菜要适量，至少要把剩菜打包带回家。然而这种根深蒂固的倾向仍然残留：对主人来说，提供的饭菜要多得让客人吃不完才好。

当然，在美国却大不一样，而且两者差异相当明显。几年前我在中国报纸上读到一篇文章，觉得非常有意思。这篇文章讲述了一个中国代表团参加白宫举办的国宴的事情，文章中登出了这次宴会的完整菜单以供读者娱乐——这是一份典型的白宫宴会菜单，只有一个肉类主菜，两三道烹饪精美的蔬菜，一份好看的甜点和咖啡。文章编辑显然认为这样的招待相当可笑，几乎是一个荒谬的玩笑。在美国政府所在地举办的这次官方宴会如果放在中国则可能被看作是一种侮辱，因为在他们看来，国宴上如此少的食物只能相当于一份午夜的点心。

Language Points of the Text

1. A foreigner Encounters Chinese Food Culture (*Title*)

encounter: *vt.* 1) to meet with“遭遇，遇到（困难，危险）”；2) to run into“意外地遇见，偶然碰到”（不用进行时）

a. I expect to encounter many difficulties in the course of this job.
我预料在做这件工作的过程中会遇到许多困难。

b. She encountered a friend on the plane.
她意外地在飞机上遇见了一个朋友。

n.（常接 with）“遭遇，冲突”

an encounter with new ideas 与新思想的冲突

my encounter with a lion 我与狮子的一次遭遇

2. I first began to learn Chinese ten years ago from a cheerful middle-aged visiting scholar from Sichuan, who was living at the time in my apartment building in Boston. (*Para. 1*)

1) who 引导非限制性定语从句，修饰 scholar。

2) **at the time:** “那时候”

I told you at the time that I thought you were stupid.

那会儿我告诉你我认为你很蠢。

联想：at a time “每次”；at one time “一度，过去曾经”；at all times “在任何时候，经常”；at any time “随时”；at times “有时”

3. He was a great talker, and often our lessons would turn into lengthy digressions on various aspects of Chinese culture. (*Para. 1*)

aspect: *n.* “（问题，事物等的）方面”

a. We should study every aspect of a subject.

我们应该研究问题的每一个方面。

b. A leader should consider a problem in all its aspects.

领导要考虑问题的方方面面。

4. The very first two Chinese characters he taught me to write were the characters in the word for “population”, *renkou*. (*Para. 1*)

1) he taught me to write 是定语从句，修饰 characters。

2) **very:** *adv.* “最，极”，最高级前或 first, last 之前加 very 起加强语气的作用。

a. The very first thing you must do is ring the police.

你必须做的第一件事是打电话给警察。

b. They arrived only at the very last moment.

他们在最后一刻才到。

c. This cake ought to be good, because I used the very best butter.

这蛋糕应该很好吃，因为我用了最好的奶油。

比较第七段中 ...hosted at the **very** seat of the American government..., 此处 very *(adj.)* 应表示“真正的，恰好的”。

例如：He is the very man I am looking for. 他正是我要找的人。

5. And this can give you an important clue to the Chinese personality: Food is never far from our minds. (*Para. 1*)

1) **clue:** *n.* “线索，提示”（后接 to）

The police had no clue to his identity.

警察没有关于他身份的线索。

2) **personality:** *n.* “个性，人格”

a. He has a strong personality.

他有坚强的性格。

b. Her personality, not her beauty, made her popular.

不是她的美丽而是她的性格使她受人喜爱。

3) **far from:** “远离；远非，一点也不”（常接名词，形容词或动名词）

a. They had rented a villa not far from the Holiday Inn.

他们租了一座离假日宾馆不远的别墅。

b. I am far from pleased with your behavior.

对你的行为我很不满意。

c. She realized this was far from the truth (being true).

她意识到这绝非事实。

6. Chinese people not only think a lot about food, they are virtually obsessed with it. (*Para. 2*)

1) **virtually:** *adv.* almost, very nearly “实际上，基本上”

a. He was virtually penniless.

他基本上身无分文。

b. My book is virtually finished; I've only a few changes to make in the writing.

我的书基本写好了，仅有几处要改动一下。

2) **be obsessed with/by:** “迷住，困扰”

a. She is obsessed with the desire to become a great scientist.

她一心一意想成为大科学家。

b. She is obsessed by the fear of death.

她为死亡的恐惧所困扰。

7. The result is that Chinese culture is often characterized as a *shi wenhua*, "food culture". Chinese people do not kid around when it comes to food. (*Para. 2*)

1) **be characterized as:** “刻画为，描写为；叙述为”

a. The author characterized the central figure as a weak and incompetent person.

作者把故事主人公描绘成一个软弱无能的人。

b. The treaty was characterized as a major breakthrough for Chinese-Russian energy cooperation.

这条约被称为中俄能源合作的一大突破。

be characterized by = be characteristic/typical of; feature“以……为特征”

a. An elephant is characterized by its long trunk.

长鼻子是大象的特征。

b. The education system there is characterized by its emphasis on success in exams.

重视通过考试是那里教育制度的特点。

另两个词 typical, feature 也可表示“以……为特征”，例如：

a. The painting is fairly typical of his early work.

这幅画是他较为典型的早期作品。

b. Advanced level dialogues feature more complex sentence types.

高级对话是以更多的复合句型为特点的。

2) **kid around (with somebody):**“和某人开玩笑”，多用于口语

Don't take notice of him; he's just kidding around.

别理他，他只是在开玩笑。

8. My first direct exposure to this aspect of China came when I attended a Chinese banquet during a trip to Beijing in 1988. (*Para. 3*)

exposure: *n.*“暴露”，与动词 expose 一样，多与介词 to 连用。

a. Too much exposure to X-rays can cause skin burns, cancer or other damage to the body.

过多接触 X 射线会导致皮肤烧伤、癌症，以及对人体的其他伤害。

b. It's important to expose children to more important books.

让儿童多读一些好书是很重要的。

9. In the United States I had eaten Chinese food often, but I could not have imagined how fabulous and extravagant a real Chinese banquet could be. (*Para. 3*)

1) 这里用过去完成时 had eaten，表明在参加 1988 年中国宴席之前经常吃中餐，表示“过去的过去”的时间概念。

2) could not have done 常用来表示从现在或过去看来过去不可能发生的事。这里表明在参加这次中国宴席之前，很难想象中国宴席有多么的绝妙和奢侈。

a. They couldn't have left so soon.

他们不可能那么早就走了。

b. “You do realize that you were driving at 100 mph, don't you?”

“No, officer, I couldn't have been. This car can't do more than 80.”

“你意识到你正以每小时 100 英里的速度行驶吗？”

“不，警官，我不可能行驶得那么快。这辆车跑不到 80 英里以上。”

10. The first six or seven dishes seemed to fill the table to overflowing, with plates precariously wedged one on top of another. (*Para. 4*)

1）with plates precariously wedged one on top of another 这里是with复合结构，作伴随状语，

a. **With my heart beating fast**, I watched the man climbing the steep rock.

我看着那人攀爬陡峭的悬崖，心中怦怦直跳。

With my heart beating fast = and my heart beat fast，作伴随状语。with 复合结构除用名词 + 分词形式外，还可以名词（代词）+ 形容词，名词（代词）+ 介词短语，名词（代词）+ 副词，或名词（代词）+ 不定式等形式。

b. **With eyes red**, she told me the whole story.

她眼睛红红地告诉了我整个故事。

c. **With the sun up**, they continued their journey.

太阳冉冉升起，他们继续自己的旅程。

d. He couldn't sleep well, **with her in danger**.

她身处危险之中，令他难以入眠。

e. He knew that she could and would succeed **with him to help her**.

他知道有他的帮助，她能，也一定会成功的。

2）**on (the) top of:** "在……的上面"

She laid her hands on top of his.

她把手放在他手上。

11. With my American-bred expectations, I assumed this vast first wave of food was surely the total number of dishes to be served, and I dug in greedily, dazzled by the variety and sheer quantity. (*Para. 4*)

1) **expectation:** *n.* [U] "希望，期望"

a. There is every expectation of a cold winter.

极有可能冬天会很冷。

b. He has little expectation of passing the exam.

他考试及格的可能性很小。

[pl.] "预期的事物，期望"

a. She had high expectations of what university had to offer.

她对大学所提供的一切抱有很高的期望。

beyond (all) expectation(s) "出乎意料地"

come up to; live up to; meet the expectation(s) of parents "不辜负父母的期望"

2) **assume:** *v.* to suppose, presume “假定，（无根据地）认为”

a. I assume his honesty (that he is honest).

我认为他是诚实的。

b. We must assume he is innocent until he is proven guilty.

在证明他有罪之前，我们必须假定他无罪。

3) **variety:** *n.* “变化，多样”

a. We demand more variety in our food.

我们要求增加食物品种。

a variety of: “种种，各种”

b. Nowadays, people in the city enjoy a variety of music.

如今城里人享受各种各样的音乐。

辨析：**variety/diversity**

这两个词均能表示“多种多样,多样性,种种”的意思。variety 可表示形式或性质的不同，多指不同种类的相关事物或同一大类中的不同事物。diversity 着重性质、形式或品质的全然不同。试比较：

a. A teacher has a wide variety of duties.

教师有多方面的职责。

b. A person who has traveled widely has a diversity of interests.

一个游历广泛的人会有许多不同的兴趣。

4) **sheer:** *adj.*（作定语）“完全的，纯粹的；陡峭的，垂直的”

a. He won by sheer luck.

他全靠运气取胜。

b. Such behavior is sheer foolishness.

那种表现愚蠢透顶。

c. sheer cliff 悬崖

5) **quantity:** *n.* “量，数量”

a. Natural gas was discovered in large quantities beneath the North Sea.

在北海海底发现大量天然气。

b. He lost a great/small quantity of blood.

他流失了大/少量的血。

以 quantity 为主语的句子中，其谓语动词的数与 quantity 本身的单复数一致，而与其所修饰的名词的数无关：quantities of + 可数名词复数/不可数名词 + 复数动词谓语。例如：Quantities of food were on the table. 桌上有丰盛的食物。

6) dazzled by the variety and sheer quantity 是过去分词短语作伴随状语，相当于一个并列句：

I dug in greedily, and I was dazzled by the variety and sheer quantity.

12. No wonder my fellow guests had merely sampled a few bites of each dish; they knew very well that these first few items were just the tip of a titanic culinary iceberg. (*Para. 5*)

1) **no (little, small) wonder:**“难怪，不足为奇”。它是 It’s no/small/little wonder that 句型的省略形式，连词 that 常省略。

a. The Browns dislike large, noisy crowds. Small wonder they didn’t go to the fair.

布朗夫妇不喜欢人多嘈杂，难怪他们没去集市。

b. It’s no wonder you’ve got a headache, since you drank so much last night.

你昨晚喝了那么多，难怪要头疼了。

2) **fellow:** *adj.*（用作定语）“同伴的，同事的”

fellow students 同学（同学之间的称呼）；fellow teacher 同事 （教师之间的称呼）

3) **item:** *n.*“（尤指清单上、一群或一组事物中的）一项，一件，一条；（节目、新闻等的）一条，一则”

a. The first item she bought was an alarm clock.

她买的第一样东西是闹钟。

b. a list of household items

家庭用品项目清单

c. the first item on the program

节目单上第一个节目

d. There is an item on the kidnapping in today’s newspaper.

今天报纸上有一则关于这次绑架的消息。

4) **tip:** *n.*

① tip of the iceberg“（事物）外表的一小部分，端倪”

The official statistics on drug addition are only the tip of the iceberg; the real figures may be much bigger.

官方对吸毒的统计数字仅显示了全部情况的一小部分，实际数量要大得多。

② on the tip of one’s tongue“就在嘴边，差点说出”

What was his name? It is on the tip of my tongue, but I just can’t remember.

他叫什么名字？就在我嘴边，却一下子想不起来。

③“忠告，指点，经验，窍门”

He gave her some tips about the care of her new car.

他对她就如何保养新车提出了几点建议。

13. I, however, was so stuffed after the first fifteen minutes that I could only watch in a bloated stupor as the remainder of the banquet took its course. (*Para. 5*)

1) 句中用了 so...that... 句型，可理解为“我是如此之饱以至于只能……”。

2) **stuff:** *v.* “填满，塞满”，此处表示 eat too much，通常只接物作宾语，不接人作宾语；crowd 和 pack 既可接人也可接物。

a. I was so stuffed after Christmas dinner that I could barely get out of my chair.

圣诞大餐我吃得太饱，胃胀得几乎站不起身来。

b. The room is crowded/packed with people/furniture.

房间里挤满了人/堆满了家具。

3) **remainder:** *n.* 此处指“宴席上的其他菜肴”；the remainder 作句子的主语时，谓语的单复数由其所指代的名词的单复数所决定。

a. Twenty students in the class are boys and the remainder are girls.

班上有 20 个男生，其余的都是女生。

b. The remainder of the wine is enough for me.

剩余的酒足够我喝了。

4) **take its course:** “（事物）自然发展（至结束），听其自然”

We have to let the illness take its course.

这个病我们只能听其自然。

14. …and it also seems from my American perspective that Chinese people have an implicit rule of ordering at least one dish too many. (*Para. 6*)

1) **perspective:** *n.* “（观察事物的）视角，观点”，相当于outlook, view。

a. We can view the situation from a new perspective.

我们可以从新的视角看待形势。

b. The battle is of great significance when viewed in the perspective of the progress of the war.

从战争进展的视角来看，这场战斗意义重大。

比较下列两个易混淆单词的用法：

respective “各自的”，后面总是连接复数名词，如：

After the meeting, the classes went to their respective rooms.

会后各班都回到了各自的教室。

prospective “未来的，可能的”，如：a prospective buyer for the house 有可能买房的主顾

2) **implicit rule:** “潜规则”

3) **one…too many:** “多余的一个……，不需要的一个……”

Don’t pay attention to him. He has drunk one glass of wine too many.

别管他，他多喝了一杯。

15. The wastefulness of this practice has been criticized in China recently, and some advocate ordering more sensible quantities, or at least taking the leftovers home in a "doggie bag", but there remains a deeply-ingrained tendency on the part of a host to provide much more than the guests could possibly eat. (*Para. 6*)

1) **practice:** *n.* "习惯，常规"

It's a dangerous practice to get off a bus before it stops.

公共汽车未停稳就下车是很危险的做法。

an international practice 国际惯例；local practices 当地的风俗；doctor's practice 医生执业

2) **sensible:** *n.* "明智的，合理的"

a. She is sensible with her money.

她花钱很明智。

b. He was fully sensible of his own shortcomings.

他完全知道自己的缺点。

易混淆的词：sensitive (to/ about) "(对……) 敏感的"；sentimental "感情上的，易动感情的"

a. Don't mention she's put on weight — she is very sensitive about it.

不要说她胖了——她对此非常敏感。

b. She kept all the old photographs for sentimental reasons.

她保存所有的旧照片是出于感情上的原因。

3) 饭菜打包一般用饭盒（lunch box），而作者却用 doggie bag，而且把这个词用引号括起来，似有调侃之意。因为很多人以给狗吃为借口索取 doggie bag，实际上是带回家自己吃的。作者认为即使带给狗吃也不应该浪费剩饭菜。

4) 这里 ordering 和 taking 做 advocate 的并列宾语。

5) there + remain/exist/live/lie/stand/enter/appear/come/follow… 是含非 be 动词的存在句型，以突出主语的力量。

a. There remains nothing more to be done?

再没有别的办法了？

b. In the garden there stood a statue.

花园里有座雕像。

c. There followed an uncomfortable silence.

接着是一阵难以忍受的沉默。

6) **on the part of somebody (on somebody's part):** "就某人而言；代表某人，某人所做的"

a. It was a mistake on the part of Mr. Jones to sign the contract without reading it.

不先看合同就签字是琼斯的错。

b. This requires great efforts on the part of the students as well as the teachers.

这需要老师和学生的共同努力。

7) much more than…could/can… 相当于 cannot， 意为“简直不，无法，难以”，这里用肯定的形式表示否定的意义，译时要译出否定含义。

a. The beauty of the park is more than words can describe.

这公园美得无法用语言形容。

b. This is more than I can tell you, sir.

这一点我是不能告诉你的，先生。

c. He loves her more than the words can say.

他对她的爱难以言表。

16. This is not the case in America, of course, and the difference can be very striking. (*Para. 7*)

1) **be the case:** to be true “是事实，是实情”

a. If that is the case, then I'll be very disappointed.

如果那是真的，我将非常失望。

b. That was found to be the case in/with many third-world countries.

人们发现那种情况在许多第三世界国家都存在。

2) **striking:** *adj.*“引人注目的，容貌出众的”

a. She was a girl of striking beauty.

她是个容貌出众的女孩。

b. There are striking similarities between the two books.

这两本书有不少非常相似的地方。

17. The complete menu for the dinner was included in the newspaper article for the amusement of readers—it was a typical White House banquet menu, featuring only one main meat dish, a couple of haute cuisine vegetable dishes, a fancy dessert and coffee. (*Para. 7*)

1) 破折号后面 it was a typical White House banquet menu… 作第一个 menu 的同位语，补充说明菜单的内容；featuring only one main meat dish, … 是分词短语作定语。

2) **fancy:**

adj.“别致的，花色的，根据想象的”

a very fancy pair of shoes 一双式样别致的鞋

fancy excuses 不着边际的借口

v. imagine“想象”

接 v-ing　Fancy meeting you here. 想不到在这儿见到你。

接宾语 + 不定式或 as　I don't fancy him to be/as an actor. 我想象不出他是个演员。

接 that 从句　Can you fancy that she is a scholar? 你能想象得到她竟是位学者吗?

18. The paper's editors clearly viewed such an offering as rather laughable, almost a ridiculous joke. (*Para. 7*)

view…as…: 把……看作……, 课文中还出现了 pick out…as；perceive…as。类似的表达还有: consider…as；regard…as；take…as；think of…as； treat…as。

19. This official dinner, hosted at the very seat of the American government, would have been considered an insult in the Chinese context, where such a minuscule meal would be perceived as the equivalent of a midnight snack! (*Para. 7*)

1) 此句中 would have been considered 为虚拟语气，假定放在中国将会出现的结果。例如：Your vacation time would have been wisely used to study, had it not been for the TV. 要不是这台电视，你假期的时间就可以很好地用来学习了。

2) **context:** *n.* the general conditions in which an event, action, etc. takes place“(事件发生的) 前后情况，背景；上下文，语境”

a. Guess the meaning of the word from its context.

由上下文猜这个词的意义。

b. The negotiation should be regarded within the context of this new situation.

应该在新形势的背景中认识这次谈判。

3) where 引导的是非限制性定语从句，修饰 Chinese context。

Part II Text Comprehension (Key)

Reading Analysis

1. C　2. D　3. A　4. C　5. B

Information Recall and Summary

A.

1. A cheerful middle-aged visiting scholar from Sichuan.

2. Food is never far from our minds.
3. Chinese people do not kid around when it comes to food.
4. He dug in greedily, dazzled by the variety and sheer quantity.
5. They seemed merely to take a bite or two of each dish and then put their chopsticks down, continuing to chat.
6. Surprised. Because more dishes soon were piled on top of the already mountainous stack.
7. Ordering at least one dish too many.
8. An insult. Because in China such a minuscule meal would be perceived as the equivalent of a midnight snack.

B.

This passage describes Chinese food culture from the point of view of an American. In his eyes, Chinese people not only think a lot about food, but they are virtually obsessed with it. Then the author describes from his own experience how fabulous and extravagant a real Chinese banquet could be. Even years later, he is still not accustomed to this aspect of dining out in China. Finally, he compares American food culture with Chinese food culture, and points out that the difference between the two can be very striking. (88 words)

Information Organization

Topics	Supporting Details
What did the author think of Chinese food culture? (Paras. 1-2)	Food is never far from our minds. Result: Chinese culture is often characterized as a *shi wenhua*, "food culture".
Author's first direct exposure to Chinese food culture. (Paras. 3-5)	My reaction: I dug in greedily after six or seven dishes were served. Chinese guests' reaction: They seemed merely to take a bite or two of each dish and then put their chopsticks down, continuing to chat. Reason: With my American-bred expectations, I assumed this vast first wave of food was surely the total number of dishes to be served. Result: I could only watch in a bloated stupor when more dishes were served.

(*to be continued*)

(*continued*)

Topics	Supporting Details
What did the author think of this aspect of dining out in China? (Para. 6)	He was not accustomed to it.
The food culture difference between America and China. (Para. 7)	A typical White House banquet menu would have been considered an insult in the Chinese context.

Part III Skill Building (Key)

Word Forms

A.

1. historian
2. employee/employer
3. speaker
4. beggar
5. American
6. liar
7. Chinese
8. actress/actor
9. novelist
10. engineer
11. creator
12. mountaineer

B.

1. a. personality b. personal 2. a. quality b. quantity
3. a. sensible b. sensitive 4. a. fancy b. fantastic

Vocabulary in Context

A.

1. c 2. g 3. e 4. h 5. a 6. b 7. f 8. d

B.

1. Far from taking my advice

2. There must be some misunderstanding on her part.
3. is characterized as one of the greatest pieces of engineering work

C.

1. C 2. D 3. A 4. A 5. C 6. A

D.

a. 1) assume 2) suppose 3) suppose 4) assumed 5) supposed
b. 1) precise 2) accurate 3) exact 4) accurate 5) exact

Key Structures

A.

1. No wonder you can't sleep when you eat so much.
2. No wonder you've got a headache since you drank so much last night.
3. No wonder he has taken ill considering that he has been overworking for years.
4. She thought she was hurt but it wasn't the case.
5. It is simply not the case that educational standards have fallen.
6. Is it the case that you've lost all your money?

B.

1. In England she had bought some chinaware, but she could not have imagined how elegant and beautiful the real chinaware could be.
2. There remains a growing tendency on the part of those estate agents to price the houses higher than the ordinary people could possibly accept.

Translation

A.

1. 访问学者
2. 冰山一角
3. 国宴
4. Chinese character
5. implicit rule
6. striking difference

B.

1. C　　2. B

Writing

Exercise

Nowadays the market is flooded with fake commodities. This phenomenon is due to several factors. **First**, some manufacturers are money-oriented. To their mind, producing fake products is a short cut toward getting rich. **On the other hand**, some consumers have the wrong idea that inferior goods can be used equally but they are much cheaper. **A third contributing cause is** the law, much of which cannot punish severely those who manufacture fake products. All these contribute to the wide spread of fake products.

课文译文

食在中国

弗雷德 · 盖尔

食堂

在中国，我们经常到外教餐厅吃午餐，尽管有些老师更喜欢自己做饭。这里食物不差，但也不是特别好。我们通常要一两个荤菜和几个素菜。我们常常会在前一天点好要吃的菜，然后付给他们钱。在这里，你可以看到馄饨汤、炒猪肉丝、豆腐。在中国的不同地方，你可以吃到不同的菜肴。而中国学生一般都在食堂享用那些缺乏吸引力的菜。

中餐快速指南：

- 东北菜（吉林、黑龙江省）是与美国菜最相似的，多牛肉、土豆、炖菜、谷类、面包。在吉林的朝鲜族餐厅常可以吃到狗肉。
- 广东菜以它的各式点心以及食用各种奇怪的动物而著名。
- 四川、湖南、湖北菜通常放辣椒，味道极辣（如宫爆鸡丁）。
- 上海菜偏甜，味略淡。
- 重庆火锅在北京和其他地区都很流行。它可能很辣，可很有趣味。
- 西安有一条非常棒的街，在那儿你可以吃到各种穆斯林食品，多是牛肉、羊肉（无猪肉、啤酒)。北京和其他大多数北方城市都有穆斯林餐厅和穆斯林居民区。你到处可以看到小贩沿街叫卖羊肉串。

- 沿海城市将为您提供各种海鲜，包括你从不知道其存在的动物。

餐馆

中国有不同价位的各式餐馆。你可以在露天或便宜的餐馆里花16元就吃得很好（不到2美元)，而在一次商务旅行中我们招待中国主人的一顿宴席则花了8,000元（将近1,000美元)。餐厅通常有块开阔的地方，就像我们习惯的那样摆上很多桌子，但他们在后面还有许多小包间。他们常用圆桌，菜肴摆在桌子中间的圆转盘上，这样人人都可以够到。每个人面前放一个小盘子，然后用筷子或勺子取食自己想吃的食物。

通常喝点啤酒，但你也可以点可乐、雪碧、果汁、豆浆、酸奶等，许多中国主人常会劝你喝白酒。在正式宴会上每个人都要向大家敬酒，说完“干杯”后把杯里的东西喝完。

快餐现在很流行，多数大城市都有麦当劳与肯德基。你还可以找到A&W(另一种汉堡包连锁店)、加州牛肉面、必胜客和TGIFridays。我最近去了一家比萨饼自助餐厅，味道不错。

Reading Comprehension

Key

1. T 2. T 3. F 4. T 5. F

Part V Extensive Reading

Say No to Western Fast Food

U. J. Underwood

1 With the **advent** of fast food **chains** from the West such as McDonald's, Kentucky Fried Chicken and Pizza Hut, the Chinese are being introduced to a **diet** that **markedly** increases the death rate from certain diseases in any population.

2 The main **killers** in North America, the **degenerative** diseases such as heart attack and **stroke** as well as **colon cancer**, will become a way of death, not life, in China if the Chinese do not act quickly and compete with these health destroying

food chains.

3 Scientific studies from all over the world show that a diet high in animal foods such as **pork**, **beef**, chicken, **dairy** products **undermines** one's health. **Deposits** of animal fat cling to the walls of **arteries**, **blocking** the supply to various organs. This causes diseases in almost every organ, but **in particular** it damages two of the most **vital** ones, the heart and the brain. Unfortunately, Western fast food belongs to this kind of diet.

4 Compare these problems with the excellent health one may enjoy if one **consumes** good Chinese food. The cook goes out every day, **procures** great-tasting, fresh vegetables, then cooks them for just a few minutes so that their **nutritional** value is **preserved** and quickly **serves** them, in a most **artistic** and **elegant fashion**. Please cling to your traditional ways of eating. They are far **superior** to those of the West.

5 Certainly the fast food chains make lots of money, but who wants to fill the pockets of a foreign food chain that **proceeds** to ruin the health of the Chinese people?

6 How the Chinese can **patronize** these fast food places when Chinese cook such **delectable** food, not just in this country but over the entire world, is **beyond** my comprehension.

7 **Cholesterol**, the dangerous fat-like substance, is found in all animal food, even in the milk now more frequently appearing in China. The white flour used in hamburger **buns** and pizza **dough** has had most of the **vitamins** and **minerals** removed, yet it is called "**enriched**" white flour. Of the dairy products, cow's cheese is one of the worst **offenders**. It **plugs up** the **bowels**, contributing to many diseases of the colon, including colon cancer, the second largest killer of all cancers in the West. Yet cancer of the colon is still rare in China, because the Chinese diet is rich in **fiber**, which helps prevent cancer of the colon.

8 Western restaurants are clean and tastefully **decorated**. Moreover, these restaurants also do indeed have "good service and an inviting dining atmosphere." However, Chinese food chains could do **likewise** if they would organize themselves as the Western chains do.

9 The lessons in management and **décor** are the only ones worth learning from

the **invasion** of this country by the Western fast food chains. In other words, only imitate the style of the restaurants, not the content of the food or the menus **in any way, shape or form**.

10 Do not let the desire for money destroy the wonderful tradition that China has established in producing **absolutely fantastic tasty** as well as **healthy** food.

(509 words)

New Words

advent /'ædvent/ *n.* the arrival or coming of (an important event, period, person, etc.) (重要事件、时期、人等）到来，来临

chain /tʃeɪn/ *n.* connected shops 连锁店

diet /daɪət/ *n.* the food usually eaten by a person or an animal 饮食，食物

markedly /'mɑːkɪdli/ *adv.* noticeably 显著地

killer /'kɪlə(r)/ *n.* a thing that kills 致人死亡的食物

degenerative /dɪ'dʒenərətɪv/ *adj.* 衰退的，退化的

stroke /strəʊk/ *n.* 中风

colon /'kəʊlɒn/ *n.* 结肠

cancer /'kænsə(r)/ *n.* 癌症

pork /pɔːk/ *n.* 猪肉

beef /biː f/ *n.* 牛肉

dairy /'deəri/ *adj.* 牛奶的，乳品的

undermine /ˌʌndə'maɪn/ *vt.* to weaken or destroy by stages 逐渐损坏

deposit /dɪ'pɒzɪt/ *n.* 沉积物，沉积层；沉淀

artery /'ɑːtəri/ *n.* 动脉

block /blɒk/ *v.* to be in the way of 阻塞

vital /'vaɪtəl/ *adj.* of the greatest importance 重要的

consume /kən'sjuːm/ *v.* to eat or drink 吃或喝

procure /prə'kjʊə(r)/ *v.* to obtain 获得

nutritional /njuː'trɪʃənəl/ *adj.* 有营养的

preserve /prɪ'zɜːv/ *v.* to keep 保持

serve /sɜːv/ *v.* to give food to 端菜，上菜

artistic /ɑː'tɪstɪk/ *adj.* 艺术的，精巧的

elegant /'elɪgənt/ *adj.* beautiful and well made 精致的

fashion /'fæʃən/ *n.* manner 姿态，方式

superior /suː'pɪəriə(r)/ *adj.* good or better in quality or value 比……好的，比……优越的

proceed /'prəʊ'siːd/ *vi.* to continue after stopping 继续进行

patronize /'pætrənaɪz/ *vt.* 光顾

delectable /dɪ'lektəbl/ *adj.* very pleasing, delightful 赏心悦目的

beyond /bi'ɒnd/ *prep.* out of the reach of, much more than 超出……范围，为……所不能及

cholesterol /kə'lestərɒl/ *n.* 胆固醇

bun /bʌn/ *n.* a small round bread 小而圆的面包

dough /dəʊ/ *n.* 生面团

vitamin /'vɪtəmɪn/ *n.* 维生素

mineral /'mɪnərəl/ *n.* 矿物质

enriched /ɪn'rɪtʃt/ *adj.* 强化的，给食物添加

NEW WORDS

维生素和矿物质的

offender /ə'fendə(r)/ *n.* 冒犯者，使人不快的东西

bowel /baʊəl/ *n.* 肠（尤指人肠），结肠

fiber /'faɪbə(r)/ *n.* 纤维

decorate /'dekəreɪt/ *v.* 装修；装饰

likewise /'laɪkwaɪz/ *adv.* in the same way 同样地

décor /'dekɔː(r)/ *n.* 装饰

invasion /ɪn'veɪʒən/ *n.* the spread of something usu. harmful 侵犯，侵害

absolutely /ˌæbsə'luːtli/ *adv.* completely 完全地

fantastic /fæn'tæstɪk/ *adj.* very great, remarkable 极好的，极出色的

tasty /'teɪsti/ *adj.* delicious 美味的

healthy /'helθi/ *adj.* 健康的

PHRASES & EXPRESSIONS

in particular 特别，尤其

plug up 堵塞

in any way, shape or form 以任何形式

PROPER NAMES

McDonald's 麦当劳

Kentucky Fried Chicken 肯德基

Pizza Hut 必胜客

课文译文

对西方快餐说不

U. J. 安德伍德

随着麦当劳、肯德基、必胜客等西方快餐连锁店的涌入，中国人正被引入这样一种饮食：它在任何国家都会导致某些疾病，从而使死亡率显著上升。

中国人如果不迅速作出反应，与这些破坏健康的食品连锁店竞争，那么在北美洲导致诸如心脏病、中风和结肠癌等变性疾病的主要元凶，将会在中国变成一种死亡方式而不是一种生活方式。

世界各地的科学研究表明：饮食中如果含有较高的动物类食品，诸如猪肉、牛肉、鸡肉和奶制品，会逐渐损害人的健康。沉积的动物脂肪附着在动脉壁上，从而阻塞了各个器官的血液供应，几乎所有的器官都会由此产生疾病，尤其对人类最重要的两个器官——心

脏和大脑产生伤害。不幸的是，西方快餐就属于这类饮食。

把这些问题与健康相比，你就会觉得享用中国美食是一种享受。厨师每天出去买回美味新鲜的蔬菜，只烹饪几分钟以保留它们的营养价值，然后摆放得精巧别致，端上桌来。请保持你们传统的饮食方式，它们比西式的好得多。

当然这种快餐连锁店赢利很多，可是谁又想向这个继续摧毁中国人健康的外国食品连锁店的口袋里装钱呢？

我百思不得其解：中国人烹饪出如此赏心悦目的菜肴，又怎么会光顾这些快餐店呢？而且不仅在中国，全世界都是如此。

在所有动物类食品中，甚至在越来越多中国人饮用的牛奶中都发现含有胆固醇——危险的脂肪类物质。汉堡包、比萨饼中使用的白面粉，被去除了绝大部分的维生素和矿物质，却被称作"富强"白面粉。奶制品中奶酪是最坏的东西，它堵塞结肠，导致许多结肠方面的疾病，包括结肠癌——西方癌症第二大杀手。然而结肠癌在中国还很少，因为中国饮食中富含纤维，可以帮助防止结肠癌的发生。

西方餐馆很干净，装修雅致，而且这些餐馆有着优质的服务和诱人的就餐环境，但是中国食品连锁店，如果像西方连锁店一样组织起来的话，也可以做到这一点。

西方快餐连锁店对这个国家的侵害中，唯一值得学习的是他们管理和装饰方面的经验，换句话说，只模仿西方餐馆的模式，不要模仿食物的内容和任何形式的菜单。

不要让获取金钱的欲望，破坏了中国长期以来建立的烹制美味、健康食物的优良传统。

Notes to the Text

1. …the Chinese are being introduced to a diet that markedly increases the death rate from certain diseases in any population. (*Para.1*)

   diet 这里指 particular foods，后面由关系代词 that 引导的一个定语从句表示这些饮食会引起某些疾病，从而最终使死亡率显著上升。in any population 这里指 in any country，意指这种饮食在各个国家都会出现此种结果。

2. The main killers in North America, the degenerative diseases such as heart attack and stroke as well as colon cancer… (*Para. 2*)

   1) the main killer: the main causes of death 这里作者把致命的疾病形象地比作"杀手"。

   2) the degenerative diseases 作 killers 的同位语。

3) as well as 为并列连词，相当于 and，或 and also。

a. John can speak Chinese as well as French. = John can speak both Chinese and French.

约翰会说法语也会说汉语。

b. You helped him as well as me. = You helped both him and me.

你帮助了我也帮助了他。

3. Scientific studies from all over the world show that a diet high in animal foods such as pork, beef, chicken, dairy products undermines one's health. (*Para. 3*)

此句中谓语动词 show 后面是由连词 that 引导的一个宾语从句，在该宾语从句中，diet 是主语，undermines 是谓语动词，high in animal foods... 是形容词词组后置，修饰主语 diet，作者向我们叙述了什么样的饮食会损害我们的健康。

4. Deposits of animal fat cling to the walls of arteries, blocking the supply to various organs. (*Para. 3*)

blocking the supply to various organs 是分词短语作结果状语，表明"动物脂肪附着在动脉壁上，从而阻塞了各个器官的血液供应"。

5. Compare these problems with the excellent health one may enjoy if one consumes good Chinese food. (*Para. 4*)

注意比较 compare A with B 和 compare A to B 之间的区别，前者表示 A 与 B 相比较，后者表示把 A 比作 B。

a. compare New York with London

比较纽约和伦敦

b. compare the world to a stage

把世界比作舞台

6. Please cling to your traditional ways of eating. (*Para. 4*)

= Please keep your tradition in your eating habits.

请保持传统的饮食方式。

7. They are far superior to those of the West. (*Para. 4*)

形容词 superior 表示"比……优越/好"，但无比较级，要表示两者进行比较时不用 than，而用 to。

a. Your knowledge of history is much/far superior to mine.

你掌握的历史知识比我多得多。

far 可用于修饰形容词或副词比较级或最高级，以加强其程度。

b. The food was far better than I expected.
食物比我想象的好得多。
c. You have in the proper sense far more imagination than I have.
按本来的意义上说，你的想象力比我丰富得多。

8. How the Chinese can patronize these fast food places when Chinese cook such delectable food, …, is beyond my comprehension. (*Para. 6*)
1) fast food places = places where fast food is served
2) how 引导一个主语从句，is beyond my comprehension 是谓语。这里指作者对此现象难以理解：中国人烹饪出如此赏心悦目的菜肴，又怎么会光顾这些快餐店呢？

9. Cholesterol, the dangerous fat-like substance, is found in all animal food, even in the milk now more frequently appearing in China. (*Para. 7*)
the dangerous fat-like substance 作 cholesterol 的同位语，more frequently appearing in China 作 milk 的定语。

10. It plugs up the bowels, contributing to many diseases of the colon, including cancer, the second largest killer of all cancers in the West. (*Para. 7*)
contributing to many diseases of the colon, … 是分词短语作结果状语，the second largest killer 作 cancer (of colon) 的同位语。

11. However, Chinese food chains could do likewise if they would organize themselves as the Western chains do. (*Para. 8*)
likewise: *adv.* “同样地，照样地”
a. This is how I do it. I want you to do likewise.
我是这样做的，我要你照我这样做。
b. She made all of her dresses with long sleeves, and I made mine likewise.
她做的衣服都是长袖的，我做的衣服和她的一样。

Reading Comprehension

Choose the best option to complete each statement and answer each question.

1. What is the author's attitude toward Western fast food?
A. Angry. B. Indifferent. C. Positive. D. Negative.

2. The word "patronize" in Paragraph 6 means ___________.
A. visit B. be a customer C. like D. refuse to come

3. What relative merits (优点) does Chinese food have?

A. Nutritional value. B. Delicious taste. C. Artistic presentation. D. All of the above.

4. What should we NOT learn from the western restaurants according to the text?

A. Good service and inviting atmosphere. B. Quality of the food.

C. Management. D. Decoration.

5. What food is beneficial to our health according to the text?

A. Dairy products. B. Animal food. C. Fresh vegetables. D. Refined food.

Key

1. D 2. B 3. D 4. B 5. C

Vocabulary Study

Replace each of the underlined parts with the best choice given.

1. The Chinese are being introduced to a diet that markedly increases the death rate from certain diseases in any population.

A. noticeably B. clearly C. largely D. attractively

2. This causes diseases in almost every organ, but in particular it damages two of the most vital ones, the heart and the brain.

A. specially/great B. especially/important

C. particularly/convenient D. typically/attractively

3. Compare these problems with the excellent health one may enjoy if one consumes good Chinese food.

A. eats B. swallows C. buys D. uses

4. The white flour used in hamburger buns and pizza dough has had most of the vitamins and minerals removed.

A. cleaned up B. cleared up C. taken away D. taken off

5. However, Chinese food chains could do likewise if they would organize themselves as the Western chains do.

A. similarly B. likely C. otherwise D. certainly

Key

1. A 2. B 3. A 4. C 5. A

UNIT 8 Remembrances

Study Focus:

1. Find the best way to reduce stress in modern daily life.
2. Practice using the "The same goes for… " structure.
3. Say something about the positive and negative effects brought about by the communications revolution.
4. Learn how to write Lost Notes.
5. Understand why letter writing is a most effective way to communicate with each other.

Part I Intensive Reading

课文译文

寻找悠闲时刻

弗兰克 H. 贝姆

我是个起早的人。我总是喜欢早早起床，煮一壶咖啡，拿一份报纸，舒舒服服地坐下来享受一小时的清静时光——我称它为悠闲时刻。

我记得小时候母亲把独处作为对我的惩罚，然而，即使那时，我也喜欢到自己的房间里去反省自己的表现，想想需要做些什么事情才能成为一个好孩子。那时我就喜欢这种独处，现在仍然很喜欢，不过现在我认为它不是一种惩罚，而是奖赏。

近几年，我发现我们越来越难留出一点特别的时间，好让自己能从繁杂忙乱的日常生活中脱开身来。然而，找点时间离开繁杂事务，思考些问题，集中注意力或者让思绪自由翱翔对我们的整个身心健康是很重要的。研究已经表明，减少日常生活中的压力能明显降低心脏病发作的风险，降低做心脏手术的几率。

记得以前每天开车上下班的时候是我可以一人独处的时间。现在，腰间别着传呼机和手机，那些时光已经一去不复返了。别人随时随地都会找到我——甚至在我开车时。

人们曾经相信，随着家用电器，如电冰箱、洗衣机、烘干机、洗碗机、微波炉的使用，美国家庭主妇的生活就不会那么紧张忙碌，但他们错了。虽然现代化便利设施的使用可以让许多人暂时提高效率，从而享受宝贵的自由时间，但它也加重了他们的工作负担——因为有了更多的时间后，很多人只会在自己每天的日程中加上更多的琐事。

现代技术已经侵扰了我们的生活。每天上班时间、回家之后阅读、回复电子邮件，虽然它可以使我了解更多的东西，但也占去了我原来用于读书、访友的宝贵时间。同样，传呼机虽然能让我迅速应答别人的需求，但它经常把我拴在附近的电话旁。

我需要什么呢?

记得小时候我们家只有一部电话放在门厅的壁龛里，那是几家合用的——我们称之为同线电话。今天，卧室、书房、客厅、厨房甚至洗澡间里都有电话，经常有两、三条线——当然有时来不及同时接听。

下面就是我为什么喜欢清晨的原因：其他人还没睡醒，家里很安静，没有电话铃声，传真机不在传送，计算机没运行，传呼机还没开，静静的就我一个人，喝喝咖啡、看看报纸、思考思考问题，这就是我每天的悠闲时间。

随着年龄的增长，我发现每天需要更多的闲暇 ，所以从最近开始，我从医院下班回家后，和妻子带上狗一起散步 15 分钟。

我什么现代通讯设备都不带，自由自在地走出大门。我和妻子交流各自的新闻，说说心里话。这就是我和妻子共享的悠闲时刻。

当我们回到家时，发现电话答录机上有三条我们外出散步时发来的新信息，我不由自主地笑了。

悠闲时刻过去了——至少要等到明天一早。

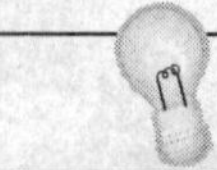

Language Points of the Text

1. I have always enjoyed rising early, making a pot of coffee, getting the newspaper, and settling down for an hour of quiet time—which I call a time-out. (*Para. 1*)

1) rising early, making a pot of coffee, getting the newspaper 和 settling down for an hour of quiet time 为并列关系，都作 enjoyed 的宾语；关系代词 which 指前面整个句子。

2) **settle down:** “舒舒服服地坐下；定居，安顿下来”

a. He settled (himself) down in a chair with a cup of tea, and turned on the TV.

他泡了杯茶，舒舒服服地坐在椅子里，然后打开了电视机。

b. After retiring from service, the old man settled down in his hometown.

退役之后，这位老人在家乡定居。

3) **time-out:** 合成名词，意思是："（工作等活动中的）暂停时间，休息时间，（球类等比赛进行中的）暂停"

a. It's very hot. You'd better take a time-out from work to have a sip of tea.

天气很热，你最好乘工间休息喝口茶。

b. The coach called for a time-out from the match.

教练要求比赛暂停。

2. I enjoyed my time-out then, and I still do, although now I consider a time-out to be a reward rather than a punishment. (*Para. 2*)

1) 此句中，do 是替代词。为避免重复，do 用来替代前一个分句中的 enjoy my time-out。例如：

Paula looks very happy and she always does even when she meets with difficulties.

波拉看起来很快乐，即使在她遇到困难时也总是这样。

2) **reward:** *n.* "奖赏，报酬"

a. The fireman was offered a reward of $100 for saving the child's life, but he declined it.

这位消防员因为救了那孩子的命被奖赏 100 美元，但他谢绝了。

b. The prize was a just reward for all your hard work.

奖品是你辛苦工作应得的报酬。

3) **rather than:** "不是……而是"，往往连接两个完全对等的语法结构，可接名词、代词、形容词、不定式、分词、介词短语等。

a. Since Tom should be responsible for the accident, I think it's him, rather than you, that is to blame.

既然汤姆应该对此事故负责，我认为该受责备的是他，而不是你。

b. She is modest rather than shy.

她是谦虚而不是害羞。

c. Tom decided to stay at home rather than go to the cinema.

汤姆决定不去看电影呆在家里。

d. He insisted on having the old house renovated rather than knocked down.

他坚持把老房子整修一下而不是拆除。

e. She always depends on herself rather than on her parents to overcome difficulties.

她总是依靠自己而不是父母来克服困难。

注意：would rather...than "宁愿，与其……不如……"

I would rather play basketball than football.

我宁愿打篮球而非踢足球。

3. Over the years, I have noticed that it has become more and more difficult to set aside those special moments of the day when we can remove ourselves from the hectic, frenetic pace of everyday life. (*Para. 3*)

1) **over the years:** “在这（或那）几年中”，相当于 these years, in the past few years

2) **set aside:** “留出（时间、金钱）”

a. It’s vital for students to set aside adequate time each day to review and preview their lessons.
对学生来说，每天留出足够的时间复习和预习功课是非常重要的。

b. I’ve set aside some money for the journey.
我为那趟旅行存了一些钱。

3) **remove:** *vt.* “移动；排除”

a. He removed the tea-things from the table after the guests left.
客人离开后他撤去茶具。

b. She removed the books from the table before cleaning it.
她在擦桌子之前搬开了这些书。

c. It’s not easy to remove stains from clothes without special washing-powder.
没有专门的洗衣粉不容易洗去衣服上的油渍。

4) **pace:** *n.* “节奏”

a. They quickened their pace of working to meet the deadline.
为了赶上最后期限，他们加快了工作节奏。

b. He walked at a great pace so as to reach home by dinner time.
他大步走着以便能在吃饭之前赶到家。

4. Yet finding time to get away, to reflect, to concentrate, or to just let the mind wander freely is important for our overall health. (*Para. 3*)

1) **get away:** “离开；脱身”

a. I’m sorry I’m late. I was in class and couldn’t get away.
对不起，我迟到了。我在上课，走不开。

b. The thief was caught stealing, but got away in the dark.
贼偷东西时被抓住，但黑暗中他逃脱了。

2) **reflect:** *v.* “思考；反射/映”

a. The teacher asked him to reflect on possible reasons for his failure.
老师要他思考导致他失败的种种原因。

b. Her face was reflected in the mirror.
她的脸映现在镜子中。

c. Her severe look reflected how she really felt.

她那冷峻的眼神反映出她心中的真正感受。

3) **concentrate:** *v.*“集中（注意力，努力等于……）；专心，专注”

a. Although his son was seriously ill, he concentrated his energies on studying.

尽管儿子病得很严重，他还是把精力集中在研究上。

b. It's very noisy outside. I can't concentrate on my work.

外面太吵，我无法专注于工作。

4) **overall:** *adj.*“全部的；全面的”

a. At the conference they put forward an overall plan for the development of science.

会上他们提出了科学发展的全面规划。

b. The president sized up the overall situation of the university.

校长分析了这所大学的总形势。

5. Studies have shown that reducing stress in daily life significantly reduces the risk of heart attacks or the need for heart surgery. (*Para. 3*)

1) **reduce:** *vt.*“减少，缩小”

a. Small businesses have to reduce costs in order to survive.

小企业不得不减少成本以求生存。

b. This machine can reduce copies of the original page to half size.

这台机器能把复印件缩小到原来尺寸的一半。

2) **stress:** *n.*“压力；强调”

a. He is under great stress because of his new job.

新工作使他感受到沉重的压力。

b. Not all of us can cope with the stress of modern life.

不是我们所有的人都能应付现代生活的压力。

c. In the job interview, the general manager put stress on the importance of cooperation.

求职面试中，总经理强调了协作的重要性。

6. Now, with a beeper strapped to my waist and a cell phone by my side, those days are over. I can be reached anytime, anywhere—even in my car. (*Para. 4*)

1) 此句中 with a beeper strapped to my waist and a cell phone by my side 是独立结构，作状语；a beeper 和 a cell phone 分别是过去分词短语 strapped to my waist 和介词短语 by my side 的逻辑主语。

2) **reach:** *vt.*“与……取得联系”

a. I called but couldn't reach you.

我打电话给你，但没联系上。

b. I can be reached by phone if you want me to help you.

如要我帮忙，打电话能找到我。

7. It was once believed that the American housewife's life would be less hectic and stressful with the introduction of appliances such as refrigerators, washing machines, dryers, dishwashers, and microwave ovens. (*Para. 5*)

1) It 是形式主语，that... 从句是真正的主语。

2) **hectic:** *adj.* "乱哄哄的，激动的"

Everybody was exhausted after a hectic day.

忙乱了一天，大家都筋疲力尽了。

3) **stressful:** *adj.* "紧张的，压力重的"

a. They kept on doing their jobs under stressful conditions, which did harm to their health.

他们一直在紧张的状态下工作，这损害了他们的健康。

b. Life with several children is hard and stressful.

带着几个孩子的生活艰难且负担沉重。

4) **appliance:** *n.* "电器用具；装备"

Vacuum cleaners, washing machines and refrigerators are household appliances.

真空吸尘器、洗衣机和电冰箱都是家用设备。

8. Although the advent of modern conveniences may have made many people temporarily more productive and thereby able to free up valuable time, it also increased their work load—because with the extra time, many individuals merely added more chores to their day. (*Para. 5*)

1) 此句是复合句，主句是 it also increased their work load. Although...; because... 分别是让步状语从句和原因状语从句。

2) **advent:** *n.* "出现，到来"

a. The advent of microwave technology has brought much benefit to people.

微波技术的出现给人们带来了很大益处。

b. With the advent of spring, trees began to sprout new leaves.

春天到了，树木开始长出新叶。

3) **convenience:** *n.* "便利设施；方便"

a. The washing machine is one of the many modern conveniences.

洗衣机是多种现代化设备之一。

b. Shopping bags are provided for the customers' convenience.

为方便顾客备有购物袋。

c. I'm looking forward to a reply at your earliest convenience.

我期望在你方便时尽早给我答复。

4) **productive:** *adj.*“富有成效的；多产的”

a. Your work in the office has not been very productive.

你在办公室的工作业绩不怎么样。

b. He was a productive writer.

他是一位多产作家。

5) **thereby:** *adv.*“因此，从而”

a. He didn't listen to my advice and thereby failed again.

他没听我的忠告，因此又失败了。

b. She became a citizen, thereby gaining the right to vote.

她成为公民，从而取得了选举权。

6) **load:** *n.*“负荷，负担”

a. Her recovery took a load off my mind.

她的康复卸下了我心中的负担。

b. He climbed the hill with a heavy load on his shoulders.

他背着重物登山。

7) **extra:** *adj.*“额外的，外加的”

The employees told the boss that they wouldn't do extra work unless they were paid for it.

雇员们告诉老板，除非给钱否则他们不会加班。

8) **individual:** *n.*“个人”；*adj.*“个别的”

a. The rights of the individual in a free society should be respected.

自由社会中的个人权利应该受到尊重。

b. A teacher cannot give individual attention to his pupils in a large class.

在大班里，老师无法一个一个地去关照学生。

9. Modern technology has invaded our lives. (*Para. 6*)

invade: *vt.*“侵扰；侵入，侵略”

a. Her privacy was invaded by some uncivilized people.

她的个人生活被一些不文明之徒侵扰了。

b. These countries were invaded by Japan during the Second World War.

这些国家在第二次世界大战中受到了日本的侵略。

10. Reading and answering my email at work and later at home each day may keep me better informed, but it also takes away the precious time I used to spend reading a book or visiting friends. (*Para. 6*)

1) **keep me better informed:** 及物动词 + 宾语 + 宾语补足语的结构，有此种结构的常用动词有 keep, find, make 等。

a. You should keep the room clean all the time.

你应该一直保持房间清洁。

b. He found it necessary to reply to the letter.

他感到很有必要回这封信。

c. This portrait makes her (look) very young.

这张画像使她显得很年轻。

2) **informed:** *adj.* “有知识的，见闻广的”

a. He was well informed about all things that happened in the town.

他对镇上发生的大小事儿全都了解得一清二楚。

b. As an alert and informed student, he can cope with the situation.

他是个机灵而有见识的学生，能应付这种局面。

c. Please keep us informed of the new developments.

请告诉我们新的动态。

3) **take away:** “夺去”

Taking part in student activities took away much of his spare time.

参加学生活动花了他许多课余时间。

4) I used to spend reading a book or visiting friends 是定语从句，先行词是 time。

5) used to do something 表示“过去习惯于做某事”

a. He used to get up early and never overslept.

他过去习惯于早起，从不睡过头。

b. I don't smoke these days, but I used to.

我现在不抽烟，但我以前是抽的。

be used to something/doing something 表示“现在习惯于某事/做某事”

a. He is used to the way of life here.

他习惯于这儿的生活。

b. Some young people are not used to getting up early.

有些年轻人不习惯于早起。

11. The same goes for my beeper, which often keeps me tethered to a nearby phone, although it allows me to be rapidly responsive to the needs of others. (*Para. 6*)

1) **go for:** "适用于；去请，去拿"

a. What he said about you goes for me too.

他关于你的一席话对我也适用。

b. His father has gone for a doctor because his mother fell ill.

母亲病了，父亲请医生去了。

比较：go in for "从事；爱好"

a. I thought of going in for teaching.

我想去当老师。

b. As a little boy, he went in for swimming.

小时候他喜欢游泳。

2) **The same goes for...:** "同样适用于"

These rules are made for keeping pets. The same goes for (keeping) poultry.

这些规定是为养宠物定的，同样也适用于饲养家禽。

联想：The same is true of/to... "同样对……适用，符合于"

a. A Western-style conversation between people is like a game of tennis. The same is not true of a Japanese-style conversation.

两人进行的西方式谈话像打网球，日本式谈话就不是这样的了。

b. Teaching well needs love and patience. Possibly the same is true to social work.

教学需要爱心和耐心，做社会福利工作可能也一样吧。

3) **responsive:** *adj.* "（表示）回答的；应答的"

a. He gave her a responsive smile.

他向她报以微笑。

b. It was this policeman who was responsive to his call last night.

昨天夜里是这位警察对他的呼救做出回应的。

联想：respond to "对……做出回答"；be responsible for "对……负责"

a. She didn't respond to my question.

她没有回答我的问题。

b. Being adults, we are responsible for our own actions.

作为成人，我们对自己的行为负责。

12. That one phone was shared by several other families—what we called party lines. (*Para. 8*)

1) **what we called:** "我们所称之为的"

what is called, what we call 和 what you call 表示"所谓的"、"被称之为"，有时略含贬义。

a. He is what is called a genius.

他就是所谓的天才。

b. He is what we call “the Nobel of China”.

他就是被我们称之为“中国的诺贝尔”的那个人。

c. It is what you call democracy.

这就是你们所谓的民主。

2) **party lines:**“合用线，同线电话”

13. This all helps to explain why I love early mornings. No one is awake, the house is quiet, the telephone isn’t ringing, the fax machine isn’t transmitting its messages, and the computer is dormant. (*Para. 9*)

1) **This explains why...:**“这说明了……的原因”

a. This explains why he has chosen teaching as his career.

这就是他为什么选择教书为职业的原因。

b. This explains why it can be so difficult to get a Western-style discussion going with Japanese students of English.

这就说明了为什么让学英语的日本学生展开西方式的讨论会如此困难。

2) 此句中 this 指代下文中的若干句子。

指示代词 this/these 可用于指代上文或下文中整个句子或若干句子；that/those 用于指代上文中整个句子或若干句子。

a. Necessity is the mother of invention. This/That is remarkably true.

需要是发明之母，这是千真万确的。

b. This is what I mean: you should have changed, not deleted that paragraph.

这是我的意思：你本该修改而不是删除那一段内容。

3) **awake:** *adj.*“醒着的”（作表语）

a. She stayed awake to wait for her mother.

她为了等母亲而一直醒着。

b. He was scarcely awake when he heard the knock at the door.

他刚醒来就听见有人敲门。

4) **transmit:** *vt.*“传送；播送”

a. She transmitted his wife’s message to him.

她带了他妻子的口信给他。

b. Some animals can transmit diseases to humans.

有些动物会传播疾病给人类。

c. The World Cup final was transmitted live to over 50 countries.

世界杯决赛向 50 多个国家作了现场直播。

14. I leave all the modern technological and communication devices behind, and walk out my front door a free man. (*Para. 11*)

1) **leave...behind:** “不带，留下；忘带了”

a. It's a fine day, so you can leave your raincoat behind.

天气很好，你不用带雨衣。

b. He went off in a hurry and left behind his watch.

他匆匆离开，忘了把手表带上。

2) **device:** *n.* “器具，仪器”

a. The device for sharpening pencils was invented many years ago.

很多年前就发明了这种削铅笔的器具。

b. He has fitted a device to his car which opens the garage door automatically.

他在车上装了一个能自动开启车库门的装置。

3) **I...walk out my front door a free man.**

我……自由自在地走出大门。

a free man 为主语补足语，说明主语的状况，不修饰动词 walk。在动词后作主语补足语的可以是名词，-ed 分词或形容词等。

a. He left school a good student.

离开学校时他是个好学生。

b. She went home disappointed.

她很失望地回到家。

c. He lay on the floor unconscious.

他躺在地板上，失去了知觉。

d. The sun rises red in the east.

太阳从东方升起，红彤彤的。

15. As we reenter our home, I cannot help but smile as I notice the three new messages on the answering machine that came in while we were out walking. (*Para. 12*)

1) **cannot help but:** “不得不，不会不”；后接原形动词。

I cannot help but admire his courage.

我不得不赞赏他的勇气。

联想：cannot help doing: “禁不住，忍不住”

a. We could not help weeping at the sad news.

听到这悲痛的消息，我们不禁怆然泪下。

b. I can't help thinking that she'd be better off without him.

我不由得认为，没有他她会活得更好。

2) that came in 是定语从句，先行词是 messages。

Part II Text Comprehension (Key)

Reading Analysis

1. A 2. B 3. D 4. D 5. C

Information Recall and Summary

A.

1. He likes getting up early to enjoy some leisure time.
2. Yes, he does. He regards a time-out as a reward.
3. Finding special moments of the day when we can relax without any disturbance. Because stress in daily life does harm to our health, which increases the risks of heart attacks or the need for heart surgery.
4. Because he carries a beeper and a mobile phone with him.
5. Yes. Because people have more work to deal with, such as reading and answering emails, making and answering phone calls, etc.
6. He can do some reading or calling on his friends.
7. He got into the habit of having a daily walk with his wife when he got older. He noticed he needed more time-outs during the day.
8. He needs special moments to be alone with his coffee, newspaper and quiet thoughts; he needs to go for a walk, leaving all the modern technological and communications devices behind; he needs to have more time to communicate with his wife. In short, he needs his daily time-outs to temporarily free himself from the pressures of modern daily life.

B.

In this passage, the author tells us he has always enjoyed his daily time-outs, but these years, with the invasion of modern technology and the quickening pace of everyday life, he has found it more and more difficult to enjoy leisure without any disturbance. However, as he is getting older, he needs more daily time-outs. So recently, besides early mornings, he enjoys taking a walk after work. The author's purpose in writing the article isn't merely to give us an account of how he enjoys his time-outs, but to suggest an effective way to reduce the stress of modern life—finding special moments. (106 words)

Information Organization

Parts	Main Ideas
I (Paras. 1-2)	I have always enjoyed my daily time-outs.
II (Paras. 3-6)	Over the years, with the invasion of modern technology, it has become more and more difficult to enjoy leisure time without any disturbances.
III (Paras. 7-13)	I have reason to love early mornings, and because of the need for more daily time-outs, I've found another special moment.

Part III Skill Building (Key)

Word Forms

A.

1. runner-up 亚军
2. hand-out 讲义/讲座提纲
3. check-out 结账
4. looker-on 旁观者
5. hand-over 移交
6. passer-by 过路人
7. lock-up 拘留所
8. trade-off 交易

B.

1. a. stressed b. stress
2. a. reward b. rewarding
3. a. produce b. productive
4. a. information b. informed

5. a. awake b. awoke

Vocabulary in Context

A.

1. c 2. a 3. f 4. h 5. g 6. b 7. d 8. e

B.

1. He always sets aside some time to preview and review his lessons
2. left all the others behind
3. she couldn't help but cry

C.

1. B 2. A 3. D 4. B 5. C 6. D

D.

1. reward 2. award 3. awarded 4. rewarded

Key Structures

A.

1. The burden of caring for his sick mother is very heavy for him. The same goes for his workload.
2. Everybody has his merits and demerits (优缺点). The same goes for the communications revolution, which has positive and negative effects.
3. The traffic regulations are made for drivers. The same goes for pedestrians.
4. He visited what we called "Ghost House".
5. He is what we call our "fair-weather" friend.
6. He is what we call a "Little Musical Wonder".

B.

1. It was once believed that many patients would have a better chance of recovery with the introduction of advanced medical appliances such as the CT scanner.

2. This explains why she got angry all of a sudden at the party.

Translation

A.

1. 早起的人
2. 特别时刻
3. 散步
4. 工作负担
5. pace of everyday life
6. a cell phone
7. communication devices
8. answer an email

B.

1. A　　　　2. B

Practical Writing

Model 1

译文

遗失启事

2006年7月7日晚上11时，我遗失了我的数码相机，里面有我当天所拍的所有结婚照片。相机有可能是在出租车上遗失的。该相机是一款银色的佳能IXY型数码相机，里面装有一张闪存卡。相机并不重要，但相机内的数码照片对我来说是无价之宝。对归还相机者，必将重谢。若你拾到相机，请拨打电话440-258-0170，或通过电子邮件与我联系，邮箱: singtom33@yahoo.com。

罗伯特 · 贝斯特

Model 2

译文

遗失启事

今天早晨本人遗失了一部银灰色双屏彩显摩托罗拉手机。对归还手机或提供手机信息者，本人将不胜感激！

约翰 · 布莱克

5号宿舍楼205室

2006年9月2日

Writing Exercise

Suggested samples for reference:

1.

Lost

I lost a blue briefcase with a white folder and two vocabulary books from Nanjing University library. I probably lost them at the train station on May 4, 2006. I'd be grateful to anyone who returns these items. If you have any information leading to their recovery, please call 025-3243××××.

Sunny

2.

遗失启事

寻蓝色笔记本，约60-70页，内有用标准意大利文所写的笔记、短语和电话号码，2006年6月26日在寻找公寓时可能遗失在公寓旁的停车场里。我的电子邮件地址：Stevek 70 @hotmail.com，若有该笔记本信息者请随时联系。

Part IV Fast Reading

课文译文

曾记书信时

安东尼·普雷特

我女儿九岁时便承担起一项艰巨的任务，那便是将家里每一张能用上的纸片都涂上字和画。如果特里西或我拿张纸来记个电话号码，我们总会碰到猫咪的故事或马的素描，或花体的单个词。假如我们翻开一本表面看来是空白的笔记本，很快便能感觉到涂鸦者光顾的迹象。

我小时候也喜欢乱涂乱画。但是，只是当我14岁离开家去上学时写作才上了路子并有了明确方向。这要归功于我的母亲，因为她坚持认为每星期写一两封信的要求并不算过分。我出门在外的这些年里——读中学、大学、研究生以及在遥远的城市工作——每周写一到两封信，加上我时常还要给亲戚朋友写便条，这样算起来，所写的信件肯定有几千封。有如此多的练习机会，写作上不可能没有长进。

这段经历在后来特里西和我谈恋爱时派上了用场。尽管俩人相距90英里达半年之久——她在芝加哥教书，我在密尔沃基读书，而且俩人都没有钱经常打电话或乘火车——然而通过鸿雁传书我们的恋爱之花越开越美。婚后，我还给她写信，有时是旅途中在遥远的旅馆写，有时则是闹过别扭后独自坐在厨房的餐桌旁写。

当与我关系密切的人遭遇不幸时，我便写一封信表达我的同情和鼓励，回忆幸福时光，谈论永恒的事物。事后他们都说这封信对他们来说多么重要，我也庆幸自己没有简单地寄张吊唁卡。

这些年我写了傻里傻气的、一本正经的、深思熟虑的、平淡无奇的、诗情画意的、谈天说地的信。如今回想起来，可能正是这众多的信件对我有非常积极的影响，增强了我作为一个作家应具备的各种能力。

现在我不常写私人书信了。自从两年半前母亲去世后我就不怎么写了。现在生活变得更为紧张忙碌，打电话更为省心，别人也不写信——原因很多。事实上，我的最后一封长信是写给弥留之际的母亲的。有太多的事情我想告诉她——是些只有我俩共同经历过的平凡小事，写信是最合适的方式。这封信长达数页，回顾了我们共同经历的欢乐与痛苦，回顾了母亲为我作出的牺牲，表达了我作为一个成年人对她的无私精神是多么感激以及对她的坎坷一生的认同。这封信是我对母亲的赞颂。

她未能读到这封信。我将它带在身边三个星期，等待着适当的时候拿给她看，因为我不想扰乱她的平静，然而她正日渐离我远去。最终，在五月末一个周日的下午，在起居室里，我坐在她的床边，噙着泪水给她念我写的信。我握住她的手，希望她能捏一下我的手以示她已听到我的话，但她却毫无反应，因为为她止痛的麻药已使她失去了知觉。

那天深夜母亲去世了。第二天在灵堂里，当其他亲戚朋友还没到来时，我将这封信放在了她的灵柩里。这似乎是我表达哀思的恰当方式。

Reading Comprehension

Key

1.A 2. C 3. B 4. C 5. D

Part V Extensive Reading

Communications: Easier or More Difficult

Michael Alvear

1 I've got a **mobile phone**, email and **voice mail**. So why am I so lonely?

2 A funny thing happened on the way to the communications revolution: we stopped talking to one another.

3 I was walking in the park with a friend recently, and his mobile phone rang, interrupting our conversation. There we were, walking and talking on a beautiful sunny day and — **poof**! — I became **invisible**, absent from the communication.

4 The park was filled with people talking on their mobile phones. They were passing other people without looking at them, saying hello, noticing their babies or stopping to pet their **puppies**. Evidently, the **untethered electronic** voice is **preferable** to human contact.

5 The telephone used to connect you to the absent. Now it makes people sitting next to you feel absent. Recently I was in a car with three friends. The driver **shushed** the rest of us because he could not hear the person on the other end of his mobile

phone. There we were, four friends **zooming** down the **highway**, unable to talk to one another because of a **gadget designed** to make communication easier.

6 Why is it that the more connected we get the more **disconnected** I feel? Every **advance** in communications technology is a **setback** to the **intimacy** of human **interaction**. With email and **instant** messaging over the Internet, we can now communicate without seeing or talking to one another. With voice mail, you can conduct entire **conversations**.

7 As almost every **conceivable** contact between human beings gets **automated**, the **alienation index** goes up. You can't even call a person to get the phone number of another person anymore. **Directory assistance** is becoming **increasingly** automated.

8 **Pumping petrol** at the station? Why say good morning to the **attendant** when you can **swipe** your credit card at the pump and save yourself the bother of human contact?

9 Making a **deposit** at the bank? Why talk to a **teller** who might live in the neighborhood when you can just **insert** your card into the **ATM**?

10 Pretty soon you won't have the **burden** of making eye contact at the grocery shop. Some supermarket chains are using a **self-scanner** so you can check yourself out, avoiding those check-out people who look at you and ask how you are doing.

11 I am no Luddite. I own a mobile phone, an ATM card, a voice-mail system, and an email account. Giving them up isn't an **option**—they're great for what they're intended to do. It's their unintended **consequences** that make me **cringe**.

12 More and more, I find myself hiding behind email to do a job meant for conversation. Or being **relieved** that voice mail picked up a call because I didn't have time to talk. The communications industry devoted to helping me **keep in touch** is making me lonelier—or at least **facilitating** my **antisocial instincts**.

13 So I've put myself on technology **restriction**: no instant messaging with people who live near me, no talking on the mobile in the presence of friends, no letting the voice mail pick up a call when I'm home.

14 What good is all this **gee-whiz** technology if there's no one in the room to hear you **exclaim**, "Gee whiz"?

(527 words)

NEW WORDS

mobile phone /'məubaılfəun/ *n.* 移动电话，手机

voice mail /'vɔısmeıl/ *n.* ［电脑］话音邮件（系统）

poof /puf/ *int.*（表示轻蔑的）呸，啐

invisible /ın'vızəbl/ *adj.* that cannot be seen 看不见的

puppy /'pʌpi/ *n.* a young dog 小狗，幼犬

untethered /ˌʌn'teðəd/ *adj.* 不受束缚（或限制）的

electronic /ˌelek'trɒnık/ *adj.* 电子的

preferable /'prefərəbl/ *adj.* to be preferred 更合意的，更可取的

shush /ʃuʃ/ *vt.* to tell to be quiet, as by saying "SH" 用"嘘"声要……静下来

zoom /zuːm/ *vi.* to go quickly 疾行，飞驰

highway /'haıweı/ *n.* a wide main road that joints one town to another 公路

gadget /'gædʒıt/ *n.* a small machine or useful apparatus 小装置

design /dı'zaın/ *vt.* to develop for a certain purpose or use 设计

disconnected /ˌdıskə'nektıd/ *adj.* badly connected 分离的，断开的

advance /əd'vɑːns/ *n.* development, improvement 进展

setback /'setbæk/ *n.* going or returning to a less advanced position than at present 阻碍，后退

intimacy /'ıntıməsi/ *n.* the state of being close in relationship 亲密，密切

interaction /ˌıntəræk∫ən/ *n.* the state or activity of working together (or with something else) to produce an effect on each other 相互作用，相互影响，互动

instant /'ınstənt/ *adj.* happening at once 立刻的，即刻的

conceivable /kə'siː vəbl/ *adj.* that can be thought of, imaginable 可想到的，可想象的

automated /'ɔːtəmeıtıd/ *adj.* 自动化的

alienation /ˌeılıə'neı∫ən/ *n.* （情感上的）疏远，离间

index /'ındeks/ *n.* measure of prices or wages compared with a previous month, year, etc. 指数；索引

directory /dı'rektəri/ *n.* a book or a list of names, facts etc., usually arranged in alphabetical order 号码簿；索引簿

assistance /ə'sıstəns/ *n.* help, support 帮助，援助

increasingly /ın'kriːsıŋli/ *adv.* more and more all the time 日益；越来越多地

pump /pʌmp/ *vt.* to fill (something) with a liquid, or gas by means of a pump 泵送；打气

petrol /'petrəl/ *n.* （英）汽油

attendant /ə'tendənt/ *n.* a person who goes with and serves or looks after another 服务员，侍者

swipe /swaıp/ *vt.* 刷（卡）

deposit /dı'pɒzıt/ *n.* money in a bank account 存款 *vt.* 1) to place in a bank or safe 储蓄；2) store or entrust for keeping 存放

teller /'telə(r)/ *n.* a person employed to receive and pay out money in a bank （银行的）出纳员

insert /ın'sɜːt/ *vt.* to put something inside (something else) 插入，嵌入

New Words

ATM /ˌeɪtiː ˈem/ *n.* automatic/automated teller machine 自动出纳机，自动柜员机

burden /ˈbɜːdən/ *n.* a heavy load 担子，负担

self-scanner /ˌselfˈskænə(r)/ *n.* 自动刷卡系统

option /ˈɒpʃən/ *n.* something chosen or offered for choice 选择

consequence /ˈkɒnsɪkwəns/ *n.* something that follows from an action or condition; result 后果，结果

cringe /krɪndʒ/ *vi.* 退缩，畏缩

relieve /rɪˈliː v/ *vt.* to lessen (pain or trouble) 减轻，解除

facilitate /fəˈsɪlɪteɪt/ *vt.* to help 有助于

antisocial /ˌæntɪˈsəʊʃəl/ *adj.* not liking to mix with other people 不喜欢社交的，不合群的

instinct /ˈɪnstɪŋkt/ *n.* 天性；本能，直觉

restrict /rɪˈstrɪkt/ *vt.* to keep within limits 限制，约束

restriction /rɪˈstrɪkʃən/ *n.* the act of restricting or state of being restricted 限制，约束

gee-whiz /ˌdʒiːˈhwɪz/ *int.*（俚语）哎呀，哎哟（表示惊奇、兴奋或失望等）

exclaim /ɪksˈkleɪm/ *vt.* to say loudly because of strong feelings 惊叫，大声说

Phrases & Expressions

keep in touch 保持联系

Proper Names

Luddite /ˈlʌdaɪt/ 卢德分子

Cultural Background

Luddite

卢德分子，英国历史上 1811 年至 1816 年间，英国手工业工人中参加捣毁机器的人。这些人把机器看成是贫困的根源，通过捣毁机器来反对企业主。本文中代指反对机械化、自动化的人。

课文译文

沟通：更加容易还是更加困难了

迈克尔·阿尔韦亚尔

我已有了手机、电子邮件及语音邮件，却为什么还如此孤独寂寞？

通讯革命的大道上，出现了一桩滑稽的事：我们没有了相互交谈。

最近，我和一位朋友在公园散步时，他的手机响了，打断了我们的谈话。那是一个阳光明媚的日子，我俩在那儿边走边聊。可是，啪！一下子我倒成为对方视而不见的人，被摒弃在谈话圈之外了。

公园里满是打手机的人。他们对与他们擦肩而过的人们不看一眼，不打招呼，不逗逗他们的婴儿，也不停下来抚弄一下他们的小狗。显然，和人与人的接触相比，人们更喜欢不受限制的电子声音。

电话本是用来和不在场的人联系的，现在却让坐在你身旁的人感觉好像不在场似的。最近，我和三个朋友坐车出行。开车人因听不清手机里的话而示意我们其余的人不要出声。这样，坐在疾驰在高速公路上的车里的四个朋友，就因为那个专为方便交流而设计的小玩意儿而不能交谈。

为什么我们联系得越密切，我却感到越有隔膜？通讯技术的每一个进步都是人类交往亲密程度上的一种倒退。有了因特网上的电子邮件和快捷信息，我们现在可以彼此不见面或彼此不面谈而进行交流。有了语音邮件，你可以不必与人会面，就能进行交谈。

随着几乎所能想象得到的人际间的接触与联系都可以自动进行，感情疏远指数在上升。你甚至不会再跟一个人打电话询问另外一个人的电话号码。电话号码查询系统的自动化程度在日益提高。

在加油站加油情况又是如何？当你可以在油泵前刷信用卡而不用劳神去跟他人打交道时，干吗还要跟服务员打招呼问好呢？

到银行存钱又会怎样？你只要把磁卡插入自动出纳机就可以了，何必还要跟某个也许就是邻居的职员说话呢？

很快，你到食品杂货店买东西结账时就不必与人四目相对了。有些连锁超市正在启动自动刷卡系统，因此，你可以自行付费，避开那些又是打量又是和你寒暄的收银员。

我决不是个反对自动化的人。我有手机，有自动柜员机卡，有语音信箱以及电子邮件账号。放弃它们不是我的选择。它们在履行设计者初衷方面做得很好，只是它们产生的并非人们本意的后果令我畏缩。

我发觉自己越来越埋头于阅读电子邮件，去做本应通过与人谈话来进行的工作；或者感到自己如释重负，因为虽然我没有时间与人谈话，但有自动语音系统帮助接电话。竭诚帮助人们更好地相互联系的通讯工业，却使我比以往更感孤独——或者说至少助长了我不爱交际的天性。

因此，我对自己实施了技术限制：对住在附近的人不使用快速信息传递方式；在朋友面前不用手机和别人交谈；只要我在家就不启用自动语音系统接电话。

如果没有人在房间里听你激动地叫喊“啊，真奇妙！”，那么这些惊人的技术又有什么用呢？

Notes to the Text

1. A funny thing happened on the way to the communications revolution: we stopped talking to one another. (*Para. 2*)

   the communications revolution: “通讯革命”

2. I became invisible, absent from the communication. (*Para. 3*)

   absent from 原意是“缺席”，此句中表示“被摒弃在……之外”。

   absent from the communication 是形容词短语作状语，说明主语的状态。在英语中，形容词（短语）可作状语，置于句首、句中或句末，表示时间、方式、原因、伴随等，或说明主语的状态。如：

   a. Ripe, the oranges will sell at a good price.
   橘子熟了能卖个好价钱。（时间）

   b. Alice tiptoed to the bed, careful not to wake the baby.
   为了不吵醒孩子，爱丽丝小心翼翼地踮着脚上床。（目的）

   c. Afraid of being late, she got up at five in the morning.
   因为害怕迟到，她早晨五点钟就起床了。（原因）

   d. Breathless , she rushed in through the back door.
   她从后门冲了进来，气喘吁吁。（伴随）

   e. Energetic and enthusiastic, he plunged into the new work.
   他以充沛的精力、满腔的热情投入了新的工作。（说明主语的状态）

3. The park was filled with people talking on their mobile phones. They were passing

other people without looking at them, saying hello, noticing their babies or stopping to pet their puppies. (*Para. 4*)

第一句中的 talking on their mobile phones 是现在分词短语作定语，意思是："对着手机讲话（或打手机）"。

第二句中 without looking at them, saying hello, noticing their babies or stopping to pet their puppies 包含几个并列的动名词短语，因为他们跟在具有否定意义的词 without 后，所以并列连词用的是 or，而不是 and，如果用 and 则表示"停下来……"；另外，此句遵循了平行结构准则，为使句子前后保持平衡和协调，句中的并列成分用的是相同词性的词，在结构上保持了一致。如：

Her job is washing, cleaning and taking care of the children.

她的工作是洗衣服、打扫卫生和看孩子。

4. Why is it that the more connected we get, the more disconnected I feel? (*Para. 6*)

   it 是形式主语，指代 that 后的内容。如：Why is it that he hasn't received the admission notice? 为什么他还没有接到录取通知书?

5. Pumping petrol at the station? (*Para. 8*)

   此句是省略句，相当于 What about pumping petrol at the station?，用以引出有关自动化设施在加油站的运用。本文中同样结构的句子还有：Making a deposit at the bank? (*Para. 9*)

6. Why say good morning to the attendant when you can swipe your credit card at the pump and save yourself the bother of human contact? (*Para. 8*)

   此句是修辞性问句，不需要回答，相当于陈述句，表示建议，具有否定意义。Why…? 相当于"何必……呢?"如：Why ask him for advice? 何必征求他的建议呢? 如果是否定结构则表示肯定意义，如：Why not try again? 为何不再试试呢? 此外，修辞性问句还可以表示强调、悔恨、赞赏、惊讶、暗示等。

   a. Isn't it silly to do such things?

      做这种事不是太愚蠢了吗?

   b. Why didn't I take his advice?

      我当时为什么不接受他的建议呀?

   c. Wasn't it a wonderful evening?

      多么美好的夜晚啊!

   d. Who would have written the poem but her?

      除了她，谁还会写那首诗!

e. Who doesn't know this?

这个谁不知道?

7. I am no Luddite. (*Para. 11*)

我绝不是个反对自动化的人。

此句中含有 no + 名词结构，no 是形容词，用来否定名词。no 否定名词时往往带有感情色彩，用在表示职业或人物的名词前常含贬义，意为“无资格，外行，不会”等。

a. He is no artist.

他绝不是个艺术家。

b. They are no friends of ours.

他们绝非我们的朋友。

c. He is no fool.

他很精明/绝不是个傻子。

8. Or being relieved that voice mail picked up a call because I didn't have time to talk. (*Para. 12*)

本句承接上一句，语法结构不完整，完整句应为：I find myself relieved that voice mail picked up the call because I didn't have time to talk. 或：I was relieved that voice mail picked up the call because I didn't have time to talk.

9. The communications industry devoted to helping me keep in touch is making me lonelier—or at least facilitating my antisocial instinct. (*Para. 12*)

主句部分是：The communications industry…is making me lonelier.

make me lonelier 是动词 + 宾语 + 宾语补足语结构。

例如：The news that her mother had fallen ill made her sad.

母亲病了的消息使她很难过。

devoted to helping me keep in touch 是过去分词短语作定语，to 是介词，接名词或 -ing 分词，破折号后的内容起补充说明的作用。

10. What good is all this gee-whiz technology if there's no-one in the room to hear you exclaim, "Gee whiz"? (*Para. 14*)

句型 What good is…? 相当于 What is the good of…?/What's the use of…? 译成：……有什么用呢? 如：What good is it to talk with him again since he won't take your advice? 既然他不会接受你的建议，再跟他谈有什么用呢?

= What is the good of talking with him again since he won't take your advice?

= What's the use of talking with him again since he won't take your advice?

hear you exclaim 中，hear 后的动词不定式不带 to。

Reading Comprehension

Choose the best option to complete each of the following statements.

1. According to the article, a great number of people prefer __________.

   A. walking in the park to talking to each other

   B. talking on their mobile phones to sending emails

   C. talking on their mobile phones to having a face-to-face conversation

   D. human contact to an electronic voice

2. The reason why the more modern communication devices there are the lonelier the author feels is that __________.

   A. people can communicate on their mobile phones without seeing one another

   B. people can carry on entire conversations without ever reaching anyone

   C. people can leave messages on an answering machine

   D. every advance in communications technology has a negative effect on the intimacy of human interaction

3. The phone number of another person can be got __________.

   A. by calling a person to ask for it

   B. with the help of automated directory assistance

   C. by sending an email

   D. by writing a letter

4. All the following statements are not true EXCEPT __________.

   A. The communications industry is meant to contribute to convenient communication

   B. The author doubts about the benefits brought about by the communications industry

   C. The communications industry is meant to make people disconnected

   D. The author always communicates with others by email or mobile phone

5. The author writes the article mainly to tell the readers __________.

   A. the benefits brought about by communications technology

   B. the introduction of modern technological and communication devices

   C. the negative effects brought about by communications technology

   D. both the positive and negative effects brought about by communications technology

Key

1. C 2. D 3. B 4. A 5. C

Vocabulary Study

Replace each of the underlined parts with the best choice given.

1. I was walking in the park with a friend recently, and his mobile phone rang, interrupting our conversation.
   A. interfering B. breaking C. involving D. entering
2. Every advance in communications technology is a setback to the intimacy of human interaction.
   A. reversal B. limitation C. restriction D. defeat
3. With voice mail, you can conduct entire conversations without ever reaching anyone.
   A. direct B. guide C. carry on D. carry out
4. As almost every conceivable contact between human beings gets automated, the alienation index goes up.
   A. convinced B. workable C. believable D. imaginable
5. Giving them up isn't an option—they're great for what they're intended to do.
   A. a choice B. an object C. an aim D. an offer
6. It's their unintended consequences that make me cringe.
   A. requests B. chains C. results D. checks

Key

1. B 2. A 3. C 4. D 5. A 6. C

Expressing Disappointment or Regret

Study Focus:

1. 字母组合 ig, igh, ai, ind 以及 wa 的发音
2. 如何表示失望或后悔以及回答

Part I Listening

Section A Phonetics

Key

1. C 2. B 3. A 4. B 5. D

Section B Short Conversations

Tapescript

1. W: Are you ready for the math test tomorrow?

   M: Not yet. Do you know what it's going to cover?

   W: The professor said it will be a comprehensive test.

   M: Oh no, I bombed the final test last semester and I felt very frustrated. How am I going to pass this new exam!

   Q: What is the conversation about?

2. W: You must come to our party. Allan will really be disappointed if you don't.

   M: But I've got my exams all next week. And also we don't have a car. It's too far away.

   W: Come on, just one night. Don't worry about the car. My brother said I can borrow his car as long as I get it back to him first thing tomorrow.

   M: All right.

   Q: When is the party?

3. M: Well, here we are.

W: Do you mean this is a scenic spot? But there's nothing here.

M: Oh, come on, the view isn't bad at all.

W: Why, there's nothing but a bare mountain. What a disappointment!

Q: Which of the following is TRUE?

4. M: Did you know that Harry was going to take Kathy on a Caribbean cruise?

W: Yes, I did. He was planning on surprising her with the tickets for their anniversary, but someone spilled the beans.

M: What a shame! That was supposed to have been a surprise.

W: Yes, it's too bad that someone told her about the trip beforehand and ruined Harry's surprise.

Q: What can we learn from the conversation?

5. W: I regretted very much having bought that designer dress.

M: Why? Did you pay too much?

W: No. I spilled some wine on it and can never wear it again.

M: Oh, what a shame.

Q: Why does the woman regret having bought her dress?

Key

1. C　　2. B　　3. D　　4. D　　5. A

Section C Passages

Exercise One

Tapescript

My mother has a pair of keen eyes which can speak. With her eyes, she observed my mood, gave me courage and made me strong. Therefore, I could face difficulties.

When I was a baby learning to walk, my mother always lent me a hand and encouraged me to get up when I fell down. As I finally threw myself into her arms, her eyes smiled with praise. Later as I grew up, I met with more difficulties. But whenever I was frustrated, my mother's eyes always gave me hope and encouragement. Once when I failed in a math exam, my mother encouraged me to find out the reasons. Instead of blaming me she pushed me to do better. At last I overcame the difficulty. Now I have grown up and become more independent, but whenever I come across setbacks, my mother's eyes are always with me encouraging me wherever I go.

Key

1) gave me　　2) face difficulties　　3) a hand　　4) fell down

5) grew up　　6) mother's eyes　　7) math exam　　8) come across

Exercise Two

Tapescript

Although I am not very athletic-looking, it doesn't prevent me from being a sports fan. Though a good table tennis player, I failed to enter the school's table tennis team. Feeling very disappointed, I shifted my interest to basketball. It's taken for granted that a boy of my stature should be a born basketball player. Because of my height, I'm envied by many of my playmates. Unfortunately, tall as I am, I'm no match for those short but bulky guys in body contact. Being aware of this vital drawback of mine I have to look for amusement in other fields, especially pop music. A collector of tapes, I find light music more appealing than those noisy Rock 'n' Roll ones. Of all pop song singers, Carpenter is my favorite. That doesn't suggest that I don't like fast songs. Sometimes, after a hard day's studying, I love to listen to some disco music with the radio turned up full blast.

By and large, I'm a person of many contrasts and one of few words, yet, behind this quiet and mediocre appearance, there is a warm heart (做好准备) and a desire to learn.

Questions:

1. How does the author describe himself?
2. Why did he feel disappointed?
3. What makes him change his interest?
4. Who is his favorite of all pop song singers?
5. What does the passage imply?

Key

1. A   2. B   3. B   4. D   5. D

Notes

1. designer

意思是"设计师品牌"。20 世纪 80 年代，这个词指那些以设计师为商标或品名的商品。通常这类商品与大规模市场上的同类产品没有很大区别，但相比之下它们要贵得多。这个词最先用于服装，尤其是牛仔裤，其后扩展到箱包类商品。现在许多商品都这样命名，所以这个词实际上也就没什么意义了。

2. Rock 'n' Roll

意思是"摇滚"。20 世纪 50 年代后期出现的一种流行乐，其特征是强音、重节奏和简单反复的词句，实质上是节奏布鲁斯的商业化版本。它是首次成为青年叛逆和父辈恐慌焦点的一种流行乐形式。伴以这种音乐而跳得极为疯狂的摇摆舞，也称为摇滚。该词大约在1953年由美国电台音乐节目主持人艾伦·弗里德（Alan Freed）首先使用。他发现节奏布鲁斯音乐上带有的种族烙印阻碍了白人听众对它的接受。

Part II Speaking

Section A Functional Language

➡ ***How to express disappointment or regret:***

Suggested expressions

I felt very frustrated.

Allan will really be disappointed if you don't.

What a disappointment!

I regretted very much having bought that designer dress.

➡ ***How to respond to disappointment or regret:***

Suggested expressions

Don't worry about…

Yes, it's too bad that someone…

Oh, what a shame!

Section B Dialogue

Key

1. D 2. A 3. A 4. C 5. C

Section C Situational Communication

Phase 1

Suggested sample

1. — How is the cafeteria service on our campus?

— Well, I must say I'm greatly disappointed in it.

— Yes, it's too bad that the dishes are not quite tasty, and the price is too high.

— I don't think I can stand it.

2. — I regret very much having bought that pair of shoes.

— Anything wrong? Did you pay too much?

— Yes, you know they are on sale these days.

— I see. Why not go there to exchange them?

Phase 2

Possible disappointment or regret and replies for reference

1. — I think today's lecture is dull. I regret having attended it.

   — Was it that bad?

2. — I must say I'm disappointed in the room. There's no air conditioning or TV.

   — Why not change to another hotel/why not change hotels?

3. — Hey, Susan, I'm pretty depressed when I learned that I failed the exam.

   — Don't lose heart. Just learn a lesson from it.

4. — I'm disappointed about the bus. I'm afraid I won't be able to attend the class on time.

   — Don't worry about that.

5. — I regret to tell you that our neighbor Mrs. Chen has already gone on vacation. She can't come to get the kids.

   — It's a pity. Oh well, I suppose I'll just have to put up with it.

UNIT 10 Campus Cheats

Study Focus:

1. Understand how campus cheats have been surging.
2. Grasp the “catch somebody doing something” structure in this sentence: He once caught one student using his cell phone to send answers to a friend’s pager.
3. Explain why cheating students are missing the point of education.
4. Illustrate the importance of academic integrity.

Part I Intensive Reading

课文译文

让我们谴责校园作弊

斯蒂芬·巴尔

亚利桑那州大学的 James Taylor 发现其历史课上学生作弊十分猖獗，这让他惊诧不已。学生们你看我的，我看你的，设计各种咳嗽暗号传送给朋友，还把答案写在手背上，在假装伸懒腰的时候迅速透露出去。

有一次他抓住一个学生正用手机往朋友的传呼机上发答案。比如，代号“54*2”意味着第 54 题的答案是 B。Taylor 把他们轰出教室，判他们两个都不及格。

爱荷华州苏城规模较小的 Morningside 学院哲学教授 Heather Reid 在她的伦理学入门课上发现有学生作假。两名学生交上来的家庭作业几乎一模一样。Reid 将此事报告教务主任，于是校方作了调查。其中一名学生被勒令停学，此门课也作不及格处理。

诸如此类的事情司空见惯。近几年来，许多大学均报告剽窃、未经许可的串通作业和考试作弊现象迅猛增长。

Rutgers 大学的 Donald McCabe 教授在过去的 10 年中，对 31 所学校进行了一项研究，发现几乎 70% 的学生承认大学期间的某个时候有过作弊，15% 以上的学生自曝是，用 McCabe 的话说，“严重型、反复型作弊者”。

虽然作弊的迅猛增长可归咎于许多方面的因素，包括家庭和学校对道德价值观的重视程度下降，但毫无疑问，现在要作弊比以往任何时候都来得容易是原因之一。有了因特网，学生们可以进入一个信息的宝库，随心所欲地各取所需而不说明出处。“关于因特网，人们存在着一种无赖心理，认为那里的信息任人利用，只要他们觉得恰当，”宾西法尼亚州大学学生操守办公室主任 Michele Goldfarb 如是说。

得克萨斯州大学讲师 Sharan Daniel 在一堂作文课上曾要求学生写一篇评论性议论文，可以包括当代电影影评。有位学生选择 Bruce Willis 的电影。

文章交上来时发现与该生以往风格不同，Daniel 怀疑是剽窃。她在因特网上进行了搜查，结果显示该影评属全文照搬。

互联网上像 schoolsucks. com 和 CollegeTermPapers.com 这样的网址数以百计，可以提供从字母 A（如 anthropology 人类学）到字母 Z（如 zoology 动物学）涵盖各种话题的现成论文。 部分网址免费，只要你提交一篇自己的文章，而其他的则收取从很少的会员费到每篇 100 多美元不等的费用。

学生们也可以从同学处直接抄袭。随着学期临近结束，许多网上公告栏和聊天室充斥着情急学生征求论文的帖子。

某个名叫“作弊魔窟”的网址每天拥有 2,000 名访问者，这里你可以找到考试作弊诀窍，也可以看到来自某些被描写成“心满意足的用户”所作出的评论，有位学生声称付了 9.95 美元年费后，平均分从 D⁻ 提高到 B⁺。

许多有关学期论文的网址都声明他们的服务仅适用于研究工作，但此类免责声明均被视为玩笑而已。

专家认为大学生作弊早在初中便已开始，到了高中已成陋习。根据《美国高中生名人录》最近对 3,100 名优秀学生所进行的一项调查，美国 80%最优秀、最聪明的高中生承认在校作弊，比前一年增加了 5 个百分点。

有些人辩解说，如果这门课程不是主修课，而考试纯粹是为了毕业，那么作弊无可厚非。也有人认为作弊是无害过错。 在一个关于作弊的网上论坛中，得克萨斯大学的一名学生甚至还在邮件中替作弊辩护，声称作弊是一种合理的学习方法。“我个人从不作弊，除非我能从中学到东西，”这位学生写到，“如果作弊意味着看一下小测验的答案，我认为作弊者能把答案记得更牢，因为答案是无奈之下通过作弊手段获得的。

Language Points of the Text

1. Let's Put the Heat on Campus Cheats. (*Title*)

the heat （非正式）表示 pressure, criticism“压力，批评”，故本文题目译成“让我们谴责校园作弊”。

2. James Taylor was astonished at the rampant cheating taking place in his history class at the University of Arizona. (*Para. 1*)

astonish 与 startle, shock, stun, amaze, alarm 均含 surprise“令人惊讶”的意思,稍有不同的是: astonish 和 startle 是指“令人非常惊讶”，如：

a. What astonishes me most is his complete lack of fear.
令我非常惊讶的是他毫无畏惧。

b. We were astonished to find the temple still in its original condition.
发现寺庙完好如初，我们感到十分惊讶。

c. His words had a startling effect on the children.
他的话在孩子们身上产生的作用令人惊讶不已。

shock:“使人震惊，骇人，令人怵目惊心”；stun:“使人发愣，目瞪口呆，不知所措”。shock 和 stun 都有“使人休克，昏迷”的意思。如：

a. I was shocked to hear the news of his sudden death.
听到他猝死的噩耗，我十分震惊。

b. She was standing stunned and in tears.
她站在那里，目瞪口呆，泪流满面。

amaze 通常指“(好的事情)令人惊奇”；alarm“使人惊慌，不安”

a. She has an amazing talent for music.
她在音乐方面有着惊人的才华。

b. I was amazed that he had made such rapid progress in English.
他的英语进步迅速，令我惊讶。

这些词的 ing 形式 +ly 都具有“非常，极度”的意思，例如：

astonishingly beautiful, startlingly pale, shockingly short stories, a surprisingly easy exam

需要指出的是，使用这类词汇常有三种句型：

a. I was surprised/amazed, etc. at.../that.../to learn that...

b. It is shocking/surprising, etc. to think that...

c. To my surprise, amazement, astonishment, etc., I learned that...

3. Students looked over each other's shoulders, devised coughing codes to communicate to friends, and flashed answers on the backs of their hands while pretending to stretch. (*Para. 1*)

1) 句中 looked..., devised..., and flashed... 是并列结构。两个或两个以上用 and, or, but 等互相连接又属于同一层次具有相同句法功能的语言结构叫做并列结构，可作主语、谓语、宾语、主语补语、状语等。如：

a. I'd like a sandwich, an ice-cream, and a cup of coffee.
我要一块三明治，一个冰淇淋，还有一杯咖啡。

b. He is tall, dark, and lean.

他又高又黑又瘦。

c. They sat down to dinner, drinking, eating, and smoking merrily.

他们坐下来吃饭，愉快地喝着，吃着，还抽起烟来。

d. He skipped my class partly because he was ill and partly because he was lazy.

他逃我的课部分原因是因为他病了，部分原因是因为他懒。

e. He said that he was busy today but that he would be free tomorrow.

他说他今天很忙，但明天会有空。

2) communicate 的宾语是 coughing codes，即 communicate coughing codes to friends，注意与 communicate with 不同，后者指“与……联系，沟通”，如：

We communicate with each other by letter (telephone/email).

我们通过书信（电话/电邮）相互联系。

3) while pretending to stretch 是状语从句的省略，连词后省略 they were，又如：

a. If (it is) carefully done, the experiment will be successful.

如果小心，试验会成功的。

b. Don't speak until (you are) spoken to.

别人不跟你讲话，你就不要跟别人讲话。

c. He will work hard wherever (he is) sent by his company.

无论公司派他去哪里，他都会努力工作。

d. The old lady was looking well although (she was) living alone.

尽管老太太一个人生活，但看起来状况不错。

e. While (he is) respected, he is not liked by us.

我们虽然尊重他，但并不喜欢他。

f. He will die soon unless (he is) treated at once.

如不马上治疗，他很快会死的。

4. He once caught one student using his cell phone to send answers to a friend's pager. (*Para.* 2)

catch 是表示感觉的动词，所以用作宾语补语的 use，由于 one student 是其逻辑主语，须用 -ing 形式。还有更多的例句：

a. I felt somebody patting me on the shoulder.

我感到有人拍我的肩膀。

b. Listen to the birds singing.

倾听鸟的鸣叫。

c. Can you smell anything burning?

你闻见什么烧起来了吗？

两点值得注意：

1) 上述现在分词表示动作的进行，如若表示全过程，则用不带 to 的不定式，如：

a. I didn't see the ball break the window.

我没看到球砸坏窗户。

b. I watched her cross the street.

我看着她穿过马路。

2) 如句中宾语是其后宾语补语的逻辑宾语，则用过去分词，如：

a. He felt his eyes dazzled by the bright light.

他感到明亮的光线使得他眼花目眩。

b. We found her greatly changed.

我们发现她的变化很大。

5. The code "54 * 2," for instance, meant the answer to question 54 was B. (*Para. 2*)

answer 后的介词是 to 而不是 of，类似的还有：

a solution to that problem, the key to a door, notes to the text, a witness to the murder, the preface to a book, a brief introduction to Nanjing Medical University (但是，the introduction of a new product from abroad 是指外国新产品的引进)

6. Taylor kicked them out of his classroom and gave both an F. (*Para. 2*)

F 发元音，故前面的冠词是 an，同理，an MA 是指 a master of arts。

7. Two students turned in homework assignments that were almost identical. (*Para. 3*)

英语中 almost 使用频率较高。almost 常用于 all, always, nothing, everyone 等词前，意思同 nearly, virtually, practically, just about。

Almost all the people in Nanjing were mobilized to serve the 10th National Games held in that city.

几乎所有的南京人都被动员起来为在这座城市举行的十运会服务。

8. Incidents such as these are all too common. (*Para. 4*)

all too: "（遗憾地）太过于……"，例如：

The trip ended all too soon.

这次旅行结束得太早了。

关于 too 还有一些词和句子需要记住：

a. I'm **only too** pleased to be able to get back home.

能回到家，我真高兴。

b. This musical is **none too** appealing to the audience.

这部音乐剧对观众一点吸引力也没有。

c. I'm afraid that this cap is **much too** big for me.

这顶帽子我戴恐怕太大了。

d. That is **rather too** much for me.

那对我来说稍微多了一点。

e. It's never **too** late **to** learn.

活到老，学到老。

f. You **cannot** be **too** careful.

你再小心也不为过。

9. In research conducted at 31 schools over the past decade, Rutgers University professor Donald McCabe has found that nearly 70 percent of students admit to cheating at some point during college, with over 15 percent reporting that they were, in McCabe's words, "serious, repetitive cheaters." (*Para. 5*)

1) admit to doing something 同 confess to doing something，作"坦白"讲，to 可以省略。to 用作介词而非不定式符号，故后跟 -ing 形式，而不是动词原形。这样的短语很多，如：

look forward to, be used to, be accustomed to, take to, when it comes to, resort to, consent to

2) with over 15 percent reporting... 是独立主格结构

10. While this surge has been blamed on many factors, including a declining emphasis on moral values in the home and school, without question it's never been easier to cheat. (*Para. 6*)

1) **while:** *conj.* although"虽然"，如：

While she is a likeable girl, she can be extremely difficult to work with.

虽然她是个可爱的姑娘，但有可能很难相处。

2) **be blamed on:** to be caused by, to be the result of, to be attributed to, to be due to"归咎于，由……引起"。blame 的常见搭配是：

a. You're not to **blame for** what happened.

所发生的事情不怪你。

b. The report **blames** poor safety standards **for** the accident.

报告把这起事故归咎于安全水平低。

c. The other driver kept trying to **put/lay the blame on** me.

另一位司机一直怪罪于我。

3) **decline:** *v.* to become less or worse, to decrease "减少，下降，衰退"

declining prices 价格下降；declining health 健康每况愈下

介宾短语为 on the decline

decline 还指 politely refuse to accept or do something "婉言谢绝"

decline an invitation/an offer/a proposal, etc. 婉言谢绝邀请/馈赠/建议等

4) **without question:** without any doubt, beyond question 和 out of question （过时）"毫无疑问"

Marilyn was, without question, a very beautiful woman.

毫无疑问，玛丽琳是个非常漂亮的女人。

不同于 out of the question: not possible, not allowed "不可能的，不允许的"

You can't go to the wedding in that old shirt—it's quite out of the question.

你不能穿那件旧衬衫去参加婚礼，那是绝对不允许的。

11. With the Internet, students have access to a treasure-trove of information they can pinch without proper attribution. (*Para. 6*)

1) **have/gain access to:** 1) to have the right to see official documents "有权得到"；2) to have the right to enter a place "有权进入"

a. Access to the papers is restricted to Defense Department personnel only.

能接触到这些文件的仅限国防部人员。

b. Growing numbers of young people in China can have access to higher education.

越来越多的中国年轻人可以上大学。

2) **treasure-trove:** *n.* "贵重的发现（物）"，句中是单位词 (unit noun)，用作隐语 (metaphor)，如：

a rain of bullets 枪林弹雨；a sea of trouble 满腹烦恼；a river of blood 血流成河

3) **pinch:** *vt.* 本文为（口语）偷，骗取，据此可以大概猜出 attribution 的含义："（古）职权，权限"。

attribution 还是 attribute 的名词形式，所以又可解释为"归因"。如：

He was said to have caused the accident, but the attribution proved to be wrong.

据说那起事故是他引起的，但该指责证实是错的。

12. "There's a cowboy feeling about the Internet that the information is out there for everybody to use as they see fit," says Michele Goldfarb, director of the Office of Student Conduct at the University of Pennsylvania. (*Para. 6*)

1) **cowboy:** *n.* "牛仔"，在此可意译为"无赖"。

2) **conduct:** *v. & n.* 多义词，通常用作动词，重音在第二个音节：表示 perform, do, carry out, 如：

conduct an operation/a survey/an experiment/an inquiry

本句中是不可数名词，重音在第一音节，表示 the way someone behaves“品行，操守”，如：a man of good conduct 品行端正的人；the rules of conduct 行为准则；shameful conduct 可耻的行为。同一单词常因词性不同而重读音节也不同，本课这样的词还有：survey, suspect。

13. Daniel suspected plagiarism when the paper turned in was different in style from the student's previous work. (*Para. 8*)

句中 in style 插入 was different from 中间，是插入成分。为了寻求句子结构平衡，有时一些修饰附加词语会强行插入到原应紧密连接的成分中。如：

a. the leading provider, **worldwide**, of software for personal computer

世界范围内的个人计算机软件主要供货商

b. He was—**to me at least, if not to you**—a figure that was worth having pity on.

至少我觉得如此，即使你不这样认为，他是一个值得同情的人。

c. This desk is superior **in color** to that one.

这张桌子的颜色比那张好。

d. His laziness has contributed **at least in part** to his failure in the final examination.

他期末考试不及格部分原因是他懒惰。

e. Government should place few, **if any**, restrictions on scientific research.

就算政府对科学研究有限制，也应该很少。

f. Some other Asian countries are similar **in many respects** to China.

一些其他亚洲国家在许多方面与中国相似。

14. She did a search on the Internet and found the review the student had lifted in its entirety. (*Para. 8*)

in its/their entirety: as a whole and including every part “整个地”

If published, it must be published in its entirety.

要出版，就要全部出版。

15. There are hundreds of websites, with names like Schoolsucks. Com and CollegeTermPapers. com, which offer readymade essays on topics ranging from anthropology to zoology. (*Para. 9*)

range from... to...: “从……到……不等”

a. The shoes range in price from $25 to $100.

这些鞋子的价格从 25 美元到 100 美元不等。

b. The patients admitted to this ward ranged in age from six months to 88.

这个病房收治的病人从半岁到 88 岁不等。

c. There were 120 students whose ages ranged from 10 to 18.

有 120 名学生，其年龄从 10 岁到 18 岁不等。

16. The website of the Evil House of Cheat boasts 2000 daily visitors. (*Para. 11*)

boast: *v.* “以拥有……而自豪”

a. Few teams can boast such a good record in European football.

在欧洲足球史上很少有球队能有如此辉煌的记录。

b. The hotels boast the finest view in Wales.

这些旅馆拥有威尔士最好的风景。

17. A recent survey of 3100 high-achieving students by Who's Who Among American High School Students revealed that 80 percent of the nation's best and brightest admitted cheating in school, up five percent from the year before. (*Para. 13*)

这一句型常见于科技论文等书面语，如：

A brief review of medical literature now available suggests/reveals/indicates/shows that...

我们对现有的医学文献进行了简要的综述，结果发现……

18. “If that involves looking at one answer on a quiz, I think the person is more likely to remember that one answer since they had to resort to cheating to obtain it.” (*Para. 14*)

1) **involve:** *v.* to mean, to include something as a necessary part or result “需要，意味着，涉及到”，后应跟动词的 -ing 形式

a. To be a nurse involves working on the night shift.

做护士就得上夜班。

b. To accept the job involves moving to London.

接受这份工作就意味着要去伦敦。

2) **resort to:** to use something or do something that is bad, in order to succeed or deal with a problem “诉诸，凭借（通常不好的东西）”；短语为 as a last resort “作为最后一招”

a. Sally resorted to stealing when her money ran out.

钱用完了，萨利就去偷。

b. Drug treatment should only be used as a last resort.

药物治疗应该只是到最后才使用。

Part II Text Comprehension (Key)

Reading Analysis

1. C 2. C 3. D 4. C 5. B

Information Recall and Summary

A.

1. James Taylor at the University of Arizona.
2. Introductory ethics.
3. 70%, and over 15% were serious, repetitive cheaters.
4. Cowboys.
5. The paper turned in was different in style from the student's previous work.
6. As early as middle school.

B.

In this text, the author reveals a severe phenomenon of campus cheats popular in the United States. Apart from a declining emphasis on moral values, the author claims, the surge of academic cheating should be mainly attributed to the easy access to the Internet, where students can get whatever they need in terms of assignments or exams. Finally, he points out that the bad habit begins even at middle school and that few students have realized its gravity. (78 words)

Information Organization

Topics	Supporting Details
Surge in Campus Cheats (Paras. 1-5)	James Taylor was astonished at <u>the rampant cheating in his history class</u>. Heather Reid discovered <u>two students turned in almost identical assignments</u>. Donald McCabe found <u>nearly 70% of students at 31 schools admitted cheating during college</u>.

(*to be continued*)

(*continued*)

Topics	Supporting Details
Blame on the Internet (Paras. 6-12)	Michele Goldfarb says that there is a cowboy feeling about the Internet. Sharan Daniel suspected plagiarism when the paper handed in was different in style from the student's previous work. There are hundreds of websites, which offer ready-made essays on many topics. Online message boards and chat rooms fill with requests for papers from desperate students. The Evil House of Cheat boasts 2000 daily visitors who can pick up tips on campus cheats. Disclaimers of many websites are regarded as a joke.
Well-honed Habit (Para. 13)	Academic cheating begins as early as middle school and often becomes a well-honed habit by high school. An example: a recent survey of 3,100 high-achieving students.
Wrong Attitude Towards Campus Cheats (Para. 14)	Some rationalize that cheating is acceptable if the course is not in their major but is required for graduating. Others assume cheating is a victimless offense. One student's opinion: Cheating helps remember the answers.

Part III Skill Building (Key)

Word Forms

A.

1. integrity 2. hardships 3. criticism 4. terrorism 5. membership 6. certainty

B.

1. a. identical b. identified
2. a. repeatedly b. repetitive
3. a. suspect b. suspicion

Vocabulary in Context

A.

1. h 2. e 3. a 4. g 5. b 6. f 7. d 8. c

B.

1. can be blamed on my addiction to TV.
2. went so far as to threaten to kill herself.
3. ranged in color from red to blue.

C.

1. B 2. B 3. C 4. B 5. C

D.

a. 1) doubt 2) doubt 3) suspected 4) suspect 5) suspect
b. 1) concluded 2) cease 3) suspended 4) suspended 5) pause

Key Structures

A.

1. I caught a boy stealing apples from the garden.
2. The traffic policemen caught a driver doing 63 mph in a 60 zone.
3. Gemma turned round and caught a stranger looking at her intently.
4. I can't help you unless you tell me what's wrong.
5. He didn't devote much of his time to studying anything unless he liked it.
6. She won't go to sleep unless you tell her a story.

B.

1. Some people rationalize that it's okay to tell lies if they are not ill-natured but white lies.
2. If to be a nurse involves working on the night shift, I think she is more likely to quit the job since she hates it.

Translation

A.

1. 家庭作业 2. 完全，整个儿

3. 长期养成的习惯 4. high-achieving students
5. annual membership fee 6. cheat on tests/exams

B.

1. B 2. A

Writing

A.

1. both 2. Another similarity 3. too 4. In the same way 5. likewise

B.

Writing personal letters is more enjoyable than writing compositions. It is fun to write letters to friends and family, as you don't have to worry about topic sentences, supporting details, or your grammar. You can write about anything you want. There is no deadline or word limit, so you can do it whenever you are in the mood and write as much as you like. In contrast, writing a composition is not so much fun. A paragraph must begin with a topic sentence and you must rack your brains to find details to support it. Also you must be careful not to make serious grammar mistakes. There is always a deadline to meet and you are restricted by the word limit. All this makes composition writing much less enjoyable than letter writing.

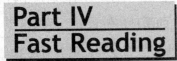

Part IV Fast Reading

课文译文

校园诚信：全凭自觉，无关校规

格雷格·斯诺

想象一下，今天你所害怕的那门课要举行期末考试，可能是物理（课程代码 PH1111），抑或是数学（课程代码 MA1024），这无关紧要。你走进诺大的报告厅，收拾好所有的笔记，坐到一排座位号是奇数的椅子上，在你和下一位之间还要留出一个空位。时钟敲响十点，某件非同寻常的事情发生了：走进来的不是教授和她那支助教队伍，而是她一个人！接着你听到她说，“我注意到下节课你们中的许多人还有另一场考试，因此，为了不让你们过于匆忙，你们可以把这份卷子带回家考。只要求三件事：不要参考任何资料，包括不要咨询你的同学或其他人；答卷时间仅为一个小时，明天上午 10 点之前把做完的试卷送回我的信箱。”她把一摞试卷放在讲台上就离开了。请将这一情景在脑海中留住片刻。

现在让我言归正传：校园诚信。仅诚信一词便有着深刻的内涵。《美国文化遗产大词典》将其定义为“坚定不移地恪守严格的伦理道德准则”。当与学校一词合用时，我便想起萨米尔 · 约翰逊说过的一句话：“没有诚信的知识是危险可怕的。”

如果说教育机构的宗旨是培养学生产生求学和探索的欲望，那么学习的地方居然没有诚信在我看来似乎令人费解，而这恰恰好像在全国业已成为一个趋势。你只要看看晚间新闻，就会理解大学校园的不诚实现象已升级到多么严重的程度了。

一定有一种办法可以阻挡这种越演越烈的趋势。今后几个月里，我们学校将探索建立学术界所必须具备的诚信之路。在此寻求过程中，或许我们应当回忆一下过去。20 年前，WPI 计划（WPI, Worcester Polytechnic Institute 伍斯特理工学院的简称，位于美国马萨诸塞州的 Worcester，由 John Boynton, Ichabod Washburn, and Stephen Salisbury II 等人创立）的先驱们就写到：“应当鼓励学生养成学术诚信的习惯，以便一些惯常的设想和理念可以经得起严格的检验。”

他们还暗示要营造一种轻松舒适、有生活气息的校园环境，以使通常的校园伦理道德转化为人们的自觉行为，而不再是校规校纪。

我不清楚他们这部分憧憬在 WPI 是否曾经具体落实，但现在尝试为时也不算晚。

如果校园有了发自内心的诚信，生活在那里将会感受到怎样的一种解放啊！老师不再为学生考试会作弊而忧心忡忡，学生也可摆脱参加考试时存在的那种仿佛置身于要求极严的军事重地的感觉。我们大家可以不再那么担心被利用，可以更多专注于共同的教育体验。这真的将是一次大解放！

最后，还是回到教授离开报告大厅的情景——卷子上依旧一片空白。不过，除非我们能够建立一种充满诚信的校园环境，否则上述局面永远不可能实现；然而，通过最近一次关于学术诚信的对话，我深信希望还在。

Reading Comprehension (Skimming and Scanning)

Key

1. Y	2. N	3. N	4. Y	5. N	6. Y
7. NG	8. escalated	9. in an academic community		10. trust and honesty reign	

Part V Extensive Reading

Plagiarism for Dummies: Why Cheating Students Are Missing the Point of Education

Paula Stiles

1 To hear college professors tell it, the current wave of student cheating and plagiarism is **brand-new** to higher education. **Alas**, student plagiarism, especially of the "Can I use your paper for my **assignment**?" variety, has probably been around since there has been organized schooling, **let alone** colleges or universities. Fortunately, this problem **has** never completely **taken over** colleges and universities for the same reason that college professors **crack down on** it **in the first place**. That reason is simple and **has been summed up** best by the great early 20th century artist Pablo Picasso: "Bad artists copy. Great artists steal."

2 Picasso may have been a **jerk** in his personal life, but he was a smart guy **when it came to** being a student of his art. He grasped young the basic point of education in anything – you're there to learn. When you use a source, examine the information, see how you can make it work to support your own piece of writing, then reshape and refit it to make it **evidence** for your argument (using **quotes** where appropriate). Then, **cite** it in your paper to show where you found your evidence, so that the reader can follow your research and also learn. Learning is the point, especially in college.

3 College students who cheat or plagiarize don't get this. The grade may seem the most important thing, but that's not why students, or their parents, paid all that money to get into a college or university. It's not why you get a college degree and it's not why employers will hire a college graduate. A student goes to college for one reason: to get an education. In this education, students learn skills that will help them in life and help them get a job. Grades are meant to show both the student and others who may hire a graduate or accept one into higher education what students have learned and how well they learned it—**in other words**, the quality of the education. But beyond that, grades don't mean very much. This also

holds true for SATs, GREs, MATs and every other general or subject test out there. They test how much you've learned.

4 Cheating and plagiarizing don't help you learn these skills. This means that the higher up cheating students go, the less **competent** they are in their studies and the less comfortable they feel. In other words, cheating students cheat themselves out of their own education. The college or university **goes after** them, not just because their behavior cheapens college degrees in general and **tarnishes** the **reputation** of any **institution** that gives them a degree, but because cheating students are not getting what they paid for. And they're doing it all **to themselves**.

5 It's become popular to blame students solely for this situation in higher education, but other reasons and actors **come into play**. Anyone even considering cheating on an exam or plagiarizing a paper needs to know about these reasons to make a smarter decision. Grading is more of an art than a science among college professors, which means that college level grades can mean wildly different things for different classes. Life isn't fair and college professors are not good at their jobs. However, if students cheat, they **miss out on** an opportunity to learn how to **deal with** a **tough** situation that they will encounter in life again and again. Failure is a part of life and every student must learn to deal with it. Also, **ironically**, many of the professors who grade the hardest will also teach a student the most. In cheating or plagiarizing a paper to get a good grade, you can miss out on the entire point of taking a really hard class. **Varied** grading **criteria** wouldn't be such a problem if college departments, **particularly** in the hard sciences, didn't use grades to **weed out** students they don't want.

6 So, the next time you think about plagiarizing, think about how you're cheating yourself. Think about the long-term skills and life lessons you won't be learning as a student. And when you're done weighing the **options**, just say no. (685 words)

NEW WORDS

dummy /'dʌmi/ *n.* 1) a layperson 初学者，外行；2) ［美口语］a stupid person 笨蛋，傻瓜

brand-new /ˌbrænd'nju:/ *adj.* completely new 全新的

alas /ə'læs/ *adv.* unfortunately 不幸的是 *int.* used to express sadness, shame, or fear 哎呀！（表示悲哀，惋惜，不安等）

assignment /ə'saɪnmənt/ *n.* 1) homework 作业；2) task, duty 任务

NEW WORDS

jerk /dʒɜːk/ *n.* 1) [美俚语] a stupid man who does not care about the effects of his actions 做事不顾后果的蠢蛋；2) a sudden quick movement 猛的一拉

evidence /'evɪdəns/ *n.* words or things that prove something 根据，证据

quote /kwəʊt/ *n.* 引用，援引

cite /saɪt/ *vt.* to mention something as an example, esp. one that supports, proves, or explains an idea or situation 引用，引证

competent /'kɒmpɪtənt/ *adj.* having enough skill or knowledge to do something to a satisfactory standard 有能力的，胜任的

tarnish /'tɑːnɪʃ/ *vt.* 1) to stain 玷污，败坏，使（名誉）蒙上污点；2) to become dull and lose color 使（金属）失去光泽

reputation /ˌrepjə'teɪʃən/ *n.* fame 名气，名声，名望

institution /ˌɪnstɪ'tjuːʃən/ *n.*1) a large organization such as a school, a hospital or a bank（学校，医院等）公共机构；2) an established system or custom in society 制度，习俗

tough /tʌf/ *adj.* 1) difficult 困难的，艰苦的；2) (someone) strong 强壮的，坚强的，能吃苦耐劳的

ironically /aɪ'rɒnɪkəli/ *adv.* used when talking about a situation that seems strange, unexpected, and often amusing 有讽刺意味的是

varied /'veərɪd/ *adj.* including many different kinds of things or people 种种的，各种形式的

criteria /kraɪ'tɪəriə/ *n.* （单：criterion）standard 衡量标准，尺度

particularly /pə'tɪkjələli/ *adv.* especially 特别，尤其

option /'ɒpʃən/ *n.* choice 选择

PHRASES & EXPRESSIONS

miss the point of 未能理解……的意义

let alone 更不用说

take over 占据

crack down on 严加取缔，严厉处罚，斥责

in the first place 最初，首先

sum up 概括

when it comes to 说到……

in other words 换言之

go after 追赶

to oneself 对自己

come into play 开始行动，开始起作用

miss out on 错过

deal with 处理，应对

weed out 将……除去

Cultural Background

1. SAT

SAT（赛达）为 Scholastic Assessment Test 的缩写，是美国高中生进入大学必须参加的考试，其重要性相当于中国的高考，也是世界各国高中生申请进入美国名校学习能否被录取及能否得到奖学金的重要参考。

2. GRE

Graduate Record Exam，由美国教育考试服务处 (Educational Testing Service，简称 ETS) 主办，1937 年首次由美国哈佛、耶鲁、哥伦比亚、普林斯顿四所大学联合举办，初期由卡耐基基金会（Carnegie Foundation）承办，1948 年交由新成立的教育测试中心 ETS 负责。之后每年在世界许多地方举行。中国国外考试协调处负责中国归口管理和承办 GRE 等国外考试。GRE 是美国、加拿大大学各类研究生院（除管理类学院、法学院）要求申请者所必须参加的一种考试，其成绩也是教授对申请者是否授予奖学金所依据的最重要的标准。GRE 考试分两种：一是一般能力或称倾向性测验 (General Test 或 Aptitude Test)。二是专业测验或称高级测验 (Subject Test 或 Advanced Test)。

3. MAT

Miller Analogies Test, 米勒类推测验。 MAT 被一些美国研究生院作为入学考试普遍接受。MAT 测试英语知识和分辨两种思想之间关系的能力。它同时也测试文学、历史和科学的知识。

4. dummies

近来美国流行书名带有 ... for Dummies 的 DIY 系列丛书，读者群为外行、初学者，如 *Excel for Dummies, Windows for Dummies, Wines for Dummies, Breadfeeding for Dummies*, 等等。

5. Pablo Picasso

毕加索（1881-1973），西班牙著名画家、雕刻家。

课文译文

为何说作弊生正在错失教育的真谛
——给剽窃新手

保拉 · 斯泰尔斯

听许多大学教授说，时下高等教育中学生作弊和剽窃之风是新近才出现的。不幸的是，学生剽窃，尤其是诸如“我的作业能用一下你的文章吗？”之类，自有正式学校以来，可能早已有之，遑论大学。幸运的是，也正因为大学教授遇到作弊首先就会严加制裁，这一问题才从未在高校中完全蔓延开来。原因简单，诚如20世纪早期伟大的艺术家毕加索所概述的一样，“糟糕的艺术家剽窃，伟大的艺术家偷窃”。

毕加索在其个人生活中或许是个蠢蛋，但说起学艺术，则是个聪明的家伙。年轻时无论学什么他都掌握了教育的真谛——你来是学习的。在利用某一资源时，要认真研读其中信息，先看看可以怎样使其发挥作用来佐证自己的写作，再加以修改，使之成为自己文章的论据（即适当引用）。然后文中注明出处，说明你的论据来源，如此读者可以根据你的研究也学到东西。学习才是根本，尤其在高校。

作弊或剽窃的大学生们没能理解这一道理。分数固然至为重要，但这并非是学生（或家长）花那么一大笔钱进大学的目的，也不是你拿到大学学历和用人单位雇用大学毕业生的原因。学生进大学只有一个原因，那就是接受教育，这种教育使其学会生活中有用的技能，并且助其找到工作。而分数则旨在告诉学生本人和可能雇佣学生或接受学生进一步深造的他人该生学到了些什么，学得怎么样，换言之，教育质量如何。除此之外，分数的意义并不很大。SAT, GRE, MAT，包括所有其他一般能力考试和专业考试在内都是如此，是要测试你学到多少。

作弊或剽窃无法帮你学到这些技能。这就意味着学生作弊陷得越深，学习便越差，他们感觉也就越不自在。换句话说，作弊生自欺欺人，从而失去受教育的机会。高校追究他们，并不仅仅是因为其行为从一般意义上贬低了大学学历的价值并玷污了学历授予院校的声誉，而是因为作弊生没有学到与其所付学费等值的东西。而这一切都是自找的。

面对高等教育的这一局面，普遍的做法是仅仅责怪学生，其实这是多方面原因和参与者共同作用的结果。任何人，哪怕只是动了一下考试作弊或剽窃文章的念头，均需了解这些原因，以便做出较为明智的决定。大学教授们的打分与其说是一门科学，还不如说只是一种技艺，这就意味着同等的大学成绩，因为来自不同的班级有可能代表迥然不同的意义。生活并非总是公平的，而且大学教授并非都擅长其工作。然而，倘若学生作弊，他们就错过了学习如何应对困境的机会，而这种困境在他们未来的生活中还可能遭遇不止一次。失败是生活的一个部分，每位同学都要学会应对。再者，具有讽刺意义的是，许多打分最为严格的教授，教授给学生的也是最多的。如果你为了拿到高分不惜作弊或剽窃论文，便失去了辛苦上课所具备的完整意义。如果各个院系，特别是那些较难的学科，不去凭借分数淘汰他们不喜欢的学生，那么打分标准不一终将不再是个问题了。

所以，下次想到剽窃文章时，想想你在欺骗你自己，想想作为学生你将因此学不到长期受用的技能和生活经验。权衡利弊后，对剽窃说不吧！

Notes to the Text

1. To hear college professors tell it, the current wave of student cheating and plagiarism is brand new to higher education. Alas, student plagiarism, especially of the "Can I use your paper for my assignment?" variety, has probably been around since there has been organized schooling, let alone colleges or universities. (*Para. 1*)
   1) 文章一开始提到有人说作弊和剽窃 brand new to higher education，与题目中 Plagiarism for Dummies 产生联系，转而又说 Plagiarism has probably been around since... 根据上下文可以猜出 around 的含义。
   2) let alone 表示"更不用说"，其后可以跟名词和动词，注意后面的动词形式：
      a. The baby can't crawl yet, let alone <u>walk</u>.
      这孩子还不会爬，更不用说走路了。
      b. I had never seen him, let alone <u>spoken</u> to him.
      我从未见过他，更不用说跟他说话了。
      c. The story was not worth reading, let alone <u>filming</u>.
      该故事不值一读，更甭说拍成电影了。

2. "Bad artists copy. Great artists steal." (*Para. 1*)
   作者借用毕加索的话提出自己的观点，但没有明说，让读者先去思考，然后在第二段亮出全文中心思想句 (thesis statement) : Learning is the point, especially in college.
   the point: the purpose, the main meaning "目的，意义，根本"
   另外还有一些带有 point 的短语需要记住：to the point "切题"；off/beside the point "走题"；a good case in point "适当的例子"；on the point of "将要，快要"；in point of "关于"

3. College students who cheat or plagiarize don't get this. (*Para. 3*)
   1) 代词 this，指代文章中心思想句，与上文衔接，此句又起到引起下文的作用，第三段（及第四段）从作弊和剽窃学生的角度谈他们的问题所在。
   2) 本段中有两处语言点值得注意：
      be meant to = be intended to = be designed to = be aimed to "旨在，打算"（用于表示研究的目的、书籍的编写目的、宗旨时常用被动语态）
   This book is meant to help students lay a sound foundation in English. = The purpose/objective/aim/goal of this book is to help students lay a sound foundation in English.
   本书旨在帮助学生打下扎实的英语基础。
   beyond 通常是指 out of , outside the limits of someone or something "超越"

a. Most people do not choose to work beyond the normal retirement age.

大多数人都不愿意超过退休年龄还上班。

b. Medicine should be placed beyond the reach of kids.

药品要放在孩子们够不着的地方。

c. Mathematics is always beyond me.

数学我总是学不会。

d. Nanjing has changed beyond my recognition.

南京已经变得我不认识了。

e. What changes await us in the year 2008 and beyond?

2008 年及其以后会有什么样的变化等着我们?

但本课中该词特殊，指 "except" used in negative sentences, "除非"，用于否定句，又如：

I can't tell you anything beyond what you know already.

除了你已经知道的外，别的我没有什么能告诉你的了。

4. The college or university goes after them, not just because their behavior cheapens college degrees in general and tarnishes the reputation of any institution that gives them a degree, but because cheating students are not getting what they paid for. (*Para. 4*)

not just because…but because… 相当于 not only because…but also because…

5. It's become popular to blame students solely for this situation in higher education, but other reasons and actors come into play. (*Para. 5*)

此句也起承上启下的作用，议论角度从学生转向老师和院系。

6. Grading is more of an art than a science among college professors, which means that college level grades can mean wildly different things for different classes. (*Para. 5*)

more…than… "与其……不如……"

This scholarship is more spiritual inspiration than material incentive.

该奖学金不仅是物质上的鼓励，更是一种精神上的感召。

7. Varied grading criteria wouldn't be such a problem if college departments, particularly in the hard sciences, didn't use grades to weed out students they don't want. (*Para. 5*)

此句是虚拟句，可见作者觉得不大容易实现。

8. So, the next time you think about plagiarizing, think about how you're cheating yourself. Think about the long-term skills and life lessons you won't be learning as a

student. And when you're done weighing the options, just say no. (*Para. 6*)

最后一段以 so 开头，提示读者这是全文的结论之处。其中 long-term skills and life lessons 再次点明这是高等教育之本，与题目和中心思想句形成呼应。文章以 learn/the point of education 贯串始终。语言简洁，条理清晰，说服力强。

Reading Comprehension

Choose the best option to complete each statement and answer each question.

1. What did Picasso mean by saying: "Bad artists copy. Great artists steal."?

   A. To be great, an artist should not only copy but also steal some masterpieces.

   B. To be great, an artist should steal masterpieces instead of copying them.

   C. An artist should try to learn from others before achieving success.

   D. Great artists, good or bad, should neither copy nor steal.

2. According to the author, all the following factors EXCEPT __________ have contributed to the popularity of cheating and plagiarism in higher education.

   A. college students　　B. college professors

   C. the authorities concerned　　D. parents

3. The word "around" in Line 4, Paragraph 1 means __________.

   A. nearby　　B. present

   C. noticeable　　D. severe

4. The author writes about plagiarism in order to __________.

   A. remind students of the real meaning of education

   B. accuse cheating and plagiarizing students

   C. criticize the university authorities and faculty

   D. complain about the poor quality of higher education

5. Another possible title for this passage is __________.

   A. Say No to Declining Quality of Higher Education

   B. Say No to University Authorities and Teachers

   C. Say No to Campus Cheats

   D. Say No to Hiking Tuition

Key

1. C　2. D　3. B　4. A　5. C

Vocabulary Study

Replace each of the underlined parts with the best choice given.

1. The <u>current</u> wave of student cheating and plagiarism is brand new to higher education.

   A. present　　B. fashionable

   C. popular　　D. serious

2. Picasso may have been a jerk in his personal life, but he was a <u>smart</u> guy when it came to being a student of his art.

   A. clever　　B. well-dressed

   C. cute　　D. quick

3. But <u>beyond</u> that, grades don't mean very much.

   A. out of　　B. prior to

   C. besides　　D. except

4. Their behavior cheapens college degrees in general and <u>tarnishes</u> the reputation of any institution that gives them a degree.

   A. stains　　B. polishes

   C. diminishes　　D. strengthens

5. They miss out on an opportunity to learn how to deal with a <u>tough</u> situation.

   A. violent　　B. strong

   C. determined　　D. difficult

1. A　2. A　3. D　4. A　5. D

UNIT 11 The Future

Study Focus:

1. Find out what our life will be like in the future.
2. Grasp the structure of "have something done".
3. Imagine the future which is controlled by robots and computers.
4. Learn how to write Found Notes.
5. Understand various ways of reading in the future.

Part I Intensive Reading

课文译文

展望未来

你的未来

未来不由其自身所决定。今天的行动决定未来。

你的大脑

你的脑波也许会被用来检查你是否很忙、很累或者工作是否正常。

伊利诺斯大学心理学家阿瑟·费·克雷默对正在做算术题的志愿者进行过测试。他发现可以通过脑电波活动的情况预测志愿者的成绩。脑电波可以通过头皮进行测量。

未来会怎么样呢？老板可以通过测量大脑活动来判断工人的工作状况：表现良好，积极努力，或是疲劳得无法正常工作。通过持续的电脑分析能够判断工作人员，比如飞行调度员，是否在很仔细地照看所有必须监控的情况。

你的医生

医生们将越来越多地使用电脑进行诊断和治疗。

你去看病时会发现医生不再依靠教科书，而是使用电脑屏幕上提供的有关你病情的直观信息进行诊治。

家用电脑可以让你通过人机交互方式回答有关你健康的问题并告诉你你的某种行为会

带来不同的结果。

你的汽车

汽车将几乎完全被电脑所控制。

为了支付道路建设和交通成本，使用高速收费公路的汽车将要付费。电脑将记录车辆通过的情况并从车主电脑银行账户上自动扣除费用。

电脑会通过车上的小显示屏显示出车所经地区的地图，告诉车主所处位置。

电脑将会诊断汽车发动机出现的任何问题。电脑网络会列出最近的修理点，所需新零件的价格及购买地点。

电脑家庭

近年来美国所售个人电脑的一大半成了家庭用品。这一现象带来的结果是电脑将成为西方家庭的生活必需品。电脑已在家庭中发挥的功能有：

电脑在人们下班回家前打开电灯、暖气和其他基本的家庭服务设备。电脑还控制负责做饭、烧热水和提供安全保障的系统。

有了电脑，人们完成家庭作业可以利用全世界的资源，比如世界各地的博物馆和科学设施。做家庭作业时既可以查询本地的图书馆以及远在纽约和伦敦这些地方的图书馆和数据库，也可以向全球的老师和同学请教。

许多购物者通过网上供应商在家里订购食品杂货，并且要求送货上门。他们压根不用走进商店。

工作场所

在西方社会，工作及工作场所的不断变化是最为广泛的影响之一。

妇女现在占劳动人口的半数以上，而且这个百分比还在上升。妇女们继续自己开办小型公司企业，她们通常在家里上班。

人们现在平均每十年更换一次工作，而不是一辈子只做一种。

以信息和知识为基础的行业的增加减少了中间管理层。高级管理者拥有和一线员工合作所需的一切信息。

公司把更多的业务交给外来承包商。专家正变得比普通工人更为重要。

Language Points of the Text

1. Looking to the Future (*Title*)

look to: to regard with expectation and anticipation “展望”

a. We look to the future and greater advances in science and technology.

我们展望未来及科技上的更大进步。

b. The economist advised us to look to the future with optimism and hope.

这个经济学家建议我们要对未来乐观且有信心。

比较：**look to somebody:** to hope or expect to get some help, advice, etc. from somebody“指望，依赖”

a. As freshmen, we looked to our teachers for guidance.

作为大学新生，我们依赖老师的指导。

b. They are looking to me to take care of their son.

他们指望我照顾他们的儿子。

2. Your brainwaves may be used to check out whether you are busy, tired or doing your work properly. (*Para. 2*)

1) **brainwave:** *n.* “脑波”

Brainwaves are electrical impulses generated by different parts of the brain.

脑波是大脑中不同部位产生的电脉冲。

与 brain 组成的复合词和短语还有 brainstorm“头脑风暴，自由讨论；专家对重大问题的献计献策”；brainwash“对……进行洗脑”；brain teasers“智力测验题”；brain trust“智囊团”；brain drain“人才流失”。

a. China must take effective measures to check the third wave of **brain drain**.

中国必须采取有效措施阻止第三次人才流失的浪潮。

b. We **brainstormed** a list of behaviors we didn't want in the classroom.

我们进行了自由讨论，列出了一些不良课堂行为。

c. The **brain teasers** are meant to build problem-solving skills, so they may take a little while to solve.

智力测验题用于培养解决问题的技能，因此做这些题目需要一定的时间。

d. Michael Deaver, a member of the **brain trust** of US ex-president Ronald Reagan, has paid several visits to China.

美国前总统罗纳德·里根智囊团成员迈克尔·迪佛已几度访问中国。

e. Some Americans have been **brainwashed** into believing that all the terrorists are Arabs or Palestinians.

有些美国人被灌输了这样的思想：所有的恐怖分子都是阿拉伯人或巴勒斯坦人。

2) **check out:** to examine somebody or something in order to be certain that everything is correct, true, satisfactory, etc.“检查，查看”

Can anyone help me check out whether the translation is correct or not?

有人能帮我检查一下这个翻译对不对吗?

比较:

a. John had already **checked out** of the hotel. 约翰已经结完账离开宾馆了。(办手续离开)

b. He said he **checked in** to hotels using his real name and made no attempt to conceal his identity. 他说他用真名登记住饭店，不想掩盖自己的身份。(登记入住)

3. Psychologist Arthur F. Kramer, at the University of Illinois, tested volunteers working on arithmetic problems. (*Para. 3*)

1) **psycho- :** connected with one's brain "心理的，精神的"，与某些动词、名词和形容词组成复合词，如:

psychoanalyze 用心理分析法治疗；psychoanalysis 心理分析（疗法）；

psychoanalyst 心理医生，精神分析学家；psychology 心理学

psychologist 心理学家

-ist: "……主义者；有……特性的"，如:

feminist 女权主义者；女权主义的；sexist 主张性别歧视者；主张性别歧视的；socialist 社会主义者；社会主义的

也可指"……家，……操作者"，如:

scientist 科学家；linguist 语言学家；novelist 小说家；machinist 机工，机械师

2) **volunteer:** *n.* "志愿者；自愿"；*v.* "做义工"

a. It was reported that the Beijing Volunteer Association was the first of its kind in China, set up in 1993.

据报道，北京志愿者协会是中国第一个志愿者组织，成立于 1993 年。

b. The students volunteered to take part in the community service activities.

学生们自愿参加社区的各种服务活动。

3) **work on something:** to spend time producing or improving something "从事，致力于"

His grandmother pays extra so he can work on his pronunciation with foreigners.

他的祖母另外付钱让他和外国人练习提高发音水平。

work on somebody: to try to influence somebody "试图影响，努力说服"

We'll have to work on Mary to find out what's going on.

我们必须努力从玛丽那里弄清楚发生了什么事。

work at something: to try hard to develop or improve something "在……上下功夫，致力于"

You'll have to work at the weak points in your English if you want to pass the examination.

如果你要通过这个考试就必须多在你的英语弱项上下功夫。

4. This is measured through the scalp. (*Para. 3*)

1) this 指前文中的 the strength of the brain's electrical activity。

2) **measure:** *v.* to discover the exact size, amount, etc. of (something), or be of a particular size "测量，计量；尺寸（规格）为……"

a. This machine measures your heart rate.
这台机器测量你的心率。

b. The kitchen, measuring 5 meters by 3 meters, has a small dining area.
厨房长 5 米宽 3 米，有个小小的就餐区。

measure out/off: "量出，量取"

c. I measured out 10 grams of sugar and added it to the mixture.
我称出 10 克糖掺了进去。

measure up: to have good enough qualities "合格，够得上"

d. Will he measure up to the challenges that lie ahead of him?
他能应付摆在他面前的那些挑战吗?

measure one's length "全身跌倒躺在地上"

take measures to do something "采取措施来做……"

take somebody's measure/get the measure of somebody "估量某人，掂某人的分量"

beyond measure "无可估量的，非常大的"

take/make measurements "测量"

5. Ongoing computer analysis could tell whether a worker, such as an air traffic controller, is seeing all the activity clearly enough to monitor it well. (*Para. 4*)

1) **ongoing:** *adj.* "持续的；进行中的"

a. As part of our ongoing effort to improve customer satisfaction, we are conducting a short survey.
作为我们不断努力提高顾客满意度活动的一部分，我们正在进行一个简短调查。

b. Work to improve this situation is ongoing.
人们正在努力改变这种状况。

2) **analysis:** *n.* "分析"

a. There is no discussion of how data analysis was undertaken.
关于数据分析没有进行任何讨论。

b. I accepted her analysis of the situation.
我同意她对形势所作的分析。

in the final/last/ultimate analysis "归根结底，总之"; make an initial diagnosis "做初步诊断"。
analysis 的复数是 analyses; analyze/analyse *v.* "分析"；analyst *n.* "分析者"；analytic/analytical *adj.* "分析的"。

3) **tell:** *v.* to show or reveal, to make known “显露，显示”

a. Your expression tells me everything.

你的表情向我表明了一切。

b. This test can tell whether you’re pregnant or not.

这个测试可以看出你是否怀孕了。

6. More and more, doctors will use computers for medical diagnosis and treatment. (*Para. 5*)

1) **more and more:** “日益，越来越……；越来越多的”

a. More and more, we are seeing an increase in viruses attacking the Internet.

我们看到袭击因特网的病毒在日益增加。

b. More and more, people are choosing to spend their holidays abroad.

人们越来越多地选择到国外度假。

2) **treatment:** *n.* “治疗”

Early diagnosis and treatment can prevent serious problems.

早期诊断和治疗可以防止出现严重问题。

其他相关词汇：examine “检查”；diagnose “诊断”；cure “治愈”；prescribe “开处方”；discharge “使……出院”

7. You will visit your doctor, and find that he uses a computer screen and visual information about your condition, instead of his textbooks. (*Para. 6*)

1) **visual:** *adj.* relating to sight or seeing “视觉的，视力的”

Television news brings us visual images from around the world.

电视新闻给我们带来了世界各地的视觉图像。

visual arts 视觉艺术；visual aid 直观教具；visual examination 视力检查

2) **condition:** *n.* an illness or health problem “病”

David has a severe heart condition.

戴维有严重心脏病。

3) **instead of:** rather than “代替，而不是”

Their children go to school in boats instead of on foot.

孩子们坐船而不是步行去上学。

比较：

She never studies. Instead, she plays tennis all day.

她从不学习。相反，她整天打网球。

If I can’t cope with the gym, I go swimming instead.

如果做不了室内健美操，我就去游泳。

8. Computers in your home will enable you to answer interactive questions about your health and show the alternative results which will affect you if you act in a certain way. (*Para. 7*)

alternative: *adj.* different from something else and able to be used instead of it "供选择的，供替代的"

What are alternative explanations for this phenomenon?

关于这个现象的其他解释是什么？

alternative 另外一个意思是"非传统的"，"另类的"，如：

alternative lifestyle 另类的生活方式；alternative energy sources 非传统能源；

alternative medicine 非传统西医疗法

9. To pay for roads and transport costs, cars will be billed for using high-speed toll roads. (*Para. 9*)

1) **bill:** *vt.* "开账单给……"；*n.* "账单"

We were billed for three nights when we were only there for two nights.

我们只在那里住了两晚，却被要求付三个晚上的费用。

electricity/gas/phone bill 电费 / 煤气 / 电话单

搭配：foot/pay the bill "付款"

Who will foot the bill for tonight's dinner?

谁来付今晚的餐费？

2) **toll:** *n.* an amount of money one pays to use a bridge, road, etc. "通行费"

They examined goods and collected tolls on roads and bridges.

他们检查货物，并收取过路费和过桥费。

tollgate/tollbooth 收费处；a national toll-free hotline 国内免费热线

10. Computers turn on the lights, heating and essential household services before people arrive home from work. (*Para. 13*)

household: *adj.* used in homes or relating to homes or all the people in one family "家庭的，家用的；全家人的"

a. Research shows those most likely to upgrade household appliances are households with children, married couples and consumers with income over $50,000.

研究发现最有可能更新家用器具的是有孩子的家庭，已婚夫妇以及收入超过 50,000 美元的消费者。

b. It is estimated that average annual household income is between $10,000 and $15,000.

据估计年均家庭收入在 10,000 到 15,000 美元。

c. Microsoft has become a household name/word.

微软已成为家喻户晓的名字。

d. a four-person household 四口之家

11. Computers enable homework assignments to be done with worldwide resources, using sources such as museums and science facilities all around the world. (*Para. 14*)

1) **worldwide:** *adj.* throughout the world “全世界的；在世界各地”

a. Our company employs 1,500 staff worldwide.

我们公司在世界各地雇佣了 1,500 名职员。

b. The United Nations Educational Scientific and Cultural Organization, UNESCO, released a report in April projecting a worldwide shortage of 18 million teachers over the next decade.

联合国科教文组织四月份发布的一份报告中预计在未来 10 年中全世界教师缺口达 1,800 万。

-wide: throughout 与名词构成形容词或副词，表示“在……范围内的/地”，如：nationwide, citywide, schoolwide

2) **resource:** *n.* a source of supply, support, wealth of a country “资源；（信息等的）来源”

a. Internet has become a valuable resource in schools.

因特网已成为学校里一个非常有用的教育资源。

b. African countries are very rich in natural resources.

非洲国家的自然资源非常丰富。

c. The school has a resource room where video and audio equipment is stored.

学校有个储放录像和音响设备的资料室。

resourced: *adj.*“资财充裕的”

The police are massively under-staffed and under-resourced.

警方的警力和资金都严重不足。

3) 句中 using sources such as...around the world 部分是现在分词作方式状语，说明利用世界各地资源的方式。

4) **facility:** *n.* something such as a room or a piece of equipment that is provided at a place for people to use（通常用复数）“设施，设备”

a. We chose that hotel because of its facilities for conferences.

我们选择这家饭店是因为它有会议设施。

b. A temporary ten-bed facility will open next month.

一个有十张床位的临时诊所下月开张。

facility: *n.* a natural ability to do something well （用单数）“天赋，技能”

Does he have a facility for languages?

他有学习语言的天赋吗？

12. Homework assistance can come equally from the local library, libraries and databases in places as far apart as New York and London, or from teachers and fellow students around the globe. (*Para. 14*)

1) **far:** *adv.* very much “很，极”

a. There are more than 75 signatures, which is far above the required number.

有超过 75 人签名，远远超过要求的数量。

b. Stimulating young people to learn is far too important to leave entirely to the schools.

激励年轻人学习非常重要，不能完全依赖学校。

c. That sociology teacher is far more boring than I would be if I were teaching that class.

那个社会学老师上课无聊透了，要是我上也比他强多了。

2) **apart:** *adv.* separately in place, time, motion, etc. “相隔的，隔开的”

a. New York and Tokyo are thousands of miles apart.

纽约和东京相隔数千英里。

b. Our birthdays are three days apart.

我们的生日相差三天。

相关的词组：

fall apart “崩溃，破裂，解体”

John lost his job, and soon afterwards his marriage fell apart.

约翰丢了工作，不久之后他的婚姻也破裂了。

tell/know...apart “分清，区别开来”

I can’t tell the twins apart. 我分不清这对双胞胎。

apart from “除……之外（还）”

a. Apart from other considerations, time is a factor.

除了其他考虑之外，时间也是一个因素。

b. Apart from a few scratches, the car was undamaged.

除了几处刮痕外，汽车没有什么损坏。

3) **globe:** *n.* the world “世界”

In the 1840s, the news that there was gold in California circled the globe.

19 世纪 40 年代加利福尼亚发现金子的消息传遍了全世界。

global *adj*. “全球的”；globalized *adj*. “全球化的”；globalization *n*. “全球化”

the global village 地球村；global warming 全球变暖

13. Women now form more than half of the workforce, and the percentage is rising. (*Para. 17*)

percentage: *n*. a rate per hundred “百分比，百分率”

a. A high percentage of our students go on to college.

我们很大部分学生上大学深造。

b. What percentage of your income do you spend on food?

你收入的百分之几花在食物上?

c. Interest rates have risen by two percentage points.

利息率上涨了两个百分点。

14. Women continue to start up small businesses of their own, often working from home. (*Para. 17*)

1) **start up:** to bring a business, organization or project into existence “创办，发起，创建”

She left the company last year to start up her own business.

去年她离开公司创办了自己的企业。

相关短语：

a. It's time we **started on** the packing.

我们该动手准备行李了。

b. Having missed the last bus, we had to **start out** walking.

因为错过了最后一班车，我们只好步行出发。

c. I **started out** to make the dress myself, but in the end I had to ask for help.

我原打算自己做这件衣服，但最后不得不请人帮忙。

d. It was fine **to start with**, and then it began to rain。

刚开始天还不错，但后来开始下雨了。

e. We will now hear the students read their poems, **starting with** Tom.

我们下面来听学生们朗诵他们的诗，从汤姆开始。

2) **business:** *n*. an organization that buys or sells products or services for money “工商企业，商店，公司”

Sheryl's parents run a small clothing business.

谢利尔的父母经营着一家小服装店。

注意 business 用于此词义时是可数名词，用于“生意、事务”等词义时为不可数名词。

相关词组：

a. We'd better stop chatting and **get down to business**.

我们别再闲聊，干正经事吧。

b. You **have no business** going through my private papers.

你无权查看我的私人文件。

c. This is not a game. We **mean business**.

这不是开玩笑，我们是认真的。

business card 名片；business class 商务舱；business day 工作日；

business hours 营业时间；business park 工业园区

15. People are changing careers on average every ten years now, instead of staying in a job for life. (*Para. 18*)

on (an/the) average: usually, typically "按平均值，通常"

On the average, your car was moving at a speed of 25 miles per hour.

你的车速平均为每小时 25 英里。

16. The increase in information and knowledge-based business is reducing the levels of middle management. (*Para. 19*)

information and knowledge-based: "以信息和知识为基础的"

-based 与名词构成形容词，有两种意思：1) making use of "以……为基础的，利用……的"（如文中）；2) operating or working from "总部在……的，设在……的"，如：

logic-based artificial intelligence 逻辑人工智能

computer-based accountancy 使用计算机进行的会计工作

the agency's New York-based press officer 该机构驻纽约的新闻官员

17. Top managers get all the information they need to work together with front-line staff. (*Para. 19*)

staff: *n.* the people working for a company, organization or institution（谓语动词用单复数皆可）"员工，全体职工"

a. It is a small hospital with a staff of just over a hundred.

这是家小医院，只有 100 多名员工。

b. She joined the staff of the *Journal of Neurosurgery* in 1997.

1997 年她成了《神经外科学》杂志的工作人员。

c. Ms. Smith is on the teaching staff at the University of St. Thomas.

史密斯女士是圣 · 托马斯大学的教师。

part-time staff 兼职人员；full-time staff 专职人员

注意和美语中 faculty 区别，后者指"全体教员"，如：

We are planning a meeting for students, faculty and administrators.

我们正计划召开学生、教师和行政人员的全体会议。

staff 可以作动词，表示"为……配备人员"，如：

Local schools will be fully staffed for the start of the new school year.

地方学校将为新学年的开始配备足够的人员。

Part II Text Comprehension (Key)

Reading Analysis

1. B 2. B 3. A 4. C 5. B

Information Recall and Summary

A.

1. The future will be determined by the actions of the present day.
2. He found he could predict the performance of the volunteers in his experiment from the strength of the brain's electrical activity.
3. The person's brainwaves.
4. Medical diagnosis and treatment will be done with the help of computers.
5. They will enable people to answer interactive questions about their health and show the alternative results which will affect them if they act in a certain way.
6. Computers will record the passage of the car and automatically take the money from the car owner's computerized bank accounts.
7. Because computers will help people with their housework, homework assignments, shopping and so on.
8. Some of the changes that will take place at the workplace are: More and more women will join the workforce; people will change their jobs more often than before; the levels of middle management will be reduced; more work in the corporate field will be given to contractors outside the company; specialists will be more important than general workers.

B.

The passage presents a comparatively comprehensive picture of our life in the future. The author first points out that our future is determined by what we do now, then he describes our future in the following aspects: 1. brain activity will be measured to find out how a person is doing his job; 2. much of a person's healthcare is provided with the help of computers; 3. cars will be controlled by computers; 4. homes will be computerized; 5. a lot of changes will take place at the workplace. (91 words)

Information Organization

Topics	Supporting Details
Introduction (Para. 1)	The future is determined by the actions of the present day.
Brain (Paras. 2-4)	1. Brainwaves may be used to check out whether one is busy, tired or doing his or her work properly. 2. Psychologist Arthur F. Kramer found that he could predict the performance of the volunteers in his experiment from the strength of the brain's electrical activity. 3. Bosses will be able to tell whether a worker is performing well, working hard or too tired to do the job properly with the help of brain activity.
Doctor (Paras. 5-7)	1. Doctors will use computers for medical diagnosis and treatment. 2. Computers in people's home will enable them to answer interactive questions about their health and show the alternative results which will affect them if they act in a certain way.
Car (Paras. 8-11)	1. Computers will record a car's passage on high-speed toll roads and automatically take the money from the car owner's computerized bank accounts. 2. Computers will tell drivers where they are by showing maps of districts the car is traveling through on a small screen in the car. 3. Computers will diagnose any problems with a car engine, list the nearest places of repair, and tell the driver the cost of the new parts and where they can be bought.

(*to be continued*)

(*continued*)

Home (Paras. 12-15)	1. Computers at home can turn on the lights and heating, control cooking and security. 2. Computers can help people with homework assignments. 3. People can buy things/do the shopping without leaving their house with the help of a computer.
Workplace (Paras. 16-20)	1. Women now form more than half of the workforce, and the percentage is rising. 2. People are changing careers on average every ten years. 3. The levels of middle management are being reduced. 4. Specialists are becoming more important than general workers.

Part III
Skill Building (Key)

Word Forms

A.

1. hardened 2. enriched 3. Lengthened
4. embodies 5. lessen 6. emboldened
7. broken 8. woolen 9. Enrooted

B.

1. a. measurements b. measuring 2. a. prediction b. predicted
3. a. analysis b. analyzing 4. a. enables b. disabled
5. a. interaction b. have interacted

Vocabulary in Context

A.

1. e 2. c 3. f 4. g 5. h 6. b 7. d 8. a

B.

1. check out whether your Internet connection is active

2. On average, spend six hours per week on this course
3. start up a rock band

C.

1. A 2. B 3. C 4. D 5. D 6. D

D.

a. 1) effect 2) affect 3) effected 4) effect

b. 1) traffic, transport/transportation 2) transported
3) traffic 4) Transportation, transportation

Key Structures

A.

1. The woman went to a computer shop to have her computer repaired.
2. The student appealed to his teacher to have his assignment re-marked.
3. I telephoned my sister yesterday to have my letter posted.
4. The clinical examination video enabled the students to experience the ways in which they could diagnose illnesses through clinical examinations.
5. The program enabled my parents to understand such computer terminologies as mouse and virus.
6. The successful completion of the course will enable the teachers to teach in both Catholic and non-Catholic schools.

B.

1. More than half of the old furniture has gone into his study. The result is that there is hardly any standing room for him.
2. Men formed 10% of all the students in graduate programs in this nursing school in 1992, and the percentage jumped to 18% five years later.

Translation

A.

1. 修理部/处 2. 家用设施
3. 信息和知识为基础的行业 4. top managers
5. stay in a job for life 6. around the world/globe

B.

1. C　　2. B

Practical Writing

Model 1

译文

招领启事

本人于6月18日晚在曼哈顿百老汇的一家星巴克咖啡馆捡到一个蓝色的Nike牌背包，内有一本驾照，一张El Camino学院的身份证件和一件价值不菲的物品。我欲将此物归还失主或其家人。请来电认领。

联系人：约翰・史密斯

联系电话：909-260-9591

2007年6月19日

Model 2

译文

招领启事

本人拣到一个钱包，内有现金若干和银行卡。请失主速到105教室来认领。

琳达

06级英语2班

2006年10月15日

Writing Exercises

Suggested samples for reference:

1

Found

On June 18, 2005, I found a small Sony video camera in a taxicab in Chicago. It has CTTADEI written on it and contains a tape of a baby's first Halloween. My email address is ydsch998@aol.com. Please contact me.

Roger

2.

Found

Large fluffy tiger cat. Brown with black stripes. Brown feet. Very friendly. Found around Brown Deer Road, Aug. 24. Email chelebell@wi.rr.com to identify.

Diane

Part IV Fast Reading

课文译文

未来阅读

马莎·门多萨

科技进步不会使我们的书面语言变得过时，只是让字脱离书页而已。在过去的两年中，里奇·戈尔德率领一支由科学家、艺术家、工程师和设计师组成的队伍在Xerox Palo Alto研究中心研究“未来阅读”，他说道：“不但不是集中一种阅读方式，而是将会出现令人难以置信的不同阅读方式。”

想象一下敲击图示，倾听声音效果，或观看文字在眼前闪烁，而不是用眼睛整页地注视单词，或轻按一种新型标点符号（也许是三角型的）以使脚注或关于主题的更多信息在屏幕上跳出来。

“阅读的形式没有消失，但是阅读的内容以及阅读的方式将变得更加广泛，”设在圣何赛被电子出版商们广泛使用的软件制造商Adobe系统的主席约翰·沃诺克说道。

一些未来阅读方式的典范在圣何赛的技术革新博物馆被展出：

——“阅读眼狗”，是一条面对放置阅读材料的书架，眼部装有摄像机的金属狗。使用根据课文说话的软件，阅读眼狗大声朗读书、商业卡片、报纸或其他任何东西。

——步入式连环漫画书，让参观者漫步其中，阅读插图大如房间的故事，其精彩细节隐藏在窥视镜之后。

——倾斜的台子上有不断闪烁的荧屏，屏幕上覆盖着单词和图像。移动台子使得图像滚动或滑动，这样就可以浏览文件，而如果把文件打印出来的话，则会铺满一间大屋的地板。

圣弗朗西斯科书本研究中心主任史蒂夫·伍戴尔说，未来阅读既强调阅读重要性，又强调在这个领域创作空间的重要性。

他说："科技进步正为我们的阅读方式创造令人难以置信的机会。"

书本研究中心专门研究手工制作书本的八位艺术家将使用传统手工艺和先进的数字工具在工作室中设计创造书本，人们建立此工作室用以展示艺术和科学的创造性结合。

技术学院院长彼得·贾尔斯说，对以未来科学为中心的硅谷博物馆来说，有着8,000年发展历程的阅读是个极佳的主题。

"我们的目的是激励人们的创新精神，与参观者们一起分享触及他们日常生活的科技方法，"他说，"的确，阅读是个历史悠久的过程，但它是个不断演变的过程。我们在此展望未来。"

Reading Comprehension

Key

1. C　2. A　3. B　4. A　5. D

The Last Letter

By Ken Beatty

June 1, 2050

Anyone

Anywhere

Dear Anyone,

1 As the last of the **Homo sapiens** on Earth—and an old human at that—I've decided to write the last letter. Perhaps someone, somewhere, sometime will be able to read it. Perhaps only **robots** and computers will **peruse** it and have a good

laugh. How did I come to be the last living person? Let me explain.

2 People have dreamed about robots and thinking machines for thousands of years. The ancient Greeks talked about Talos, a giant metal robot that **supposedly** walked around the island of Crete three times each day. It was a slave that helped the King of Crete fight his enemies. And this has always been the problem. People have always thought of robots as slaves; they never thought these powerful tools might one day become the masters and make people the slaves.

3 At first, people didn't think about how they were being surrounded by thinking machines. But they were soon everywhere. Some of the earliest thinking machines controlled the temperature—when it was too cold, they **turned up** the heat and when it was too warm, they turned on the **air conditioner**. This doesn't sound too dangerous, but once people got used to temperatures and then lights being controlled, they started having machines control the doors of buildings, fire **sprinkler**s and many **household** appliances. Robot **vacuum** cleaners started **roam**ing around the inside of people's homes and machines programmed to **tend** the gardens worked outside. It was great! People had more free time! Well, actually, only rich people had more free time. The humans who used to do a lot of the robots' jobs had to find other work. Suddenly, the world was breaking into two classes: technology haves and technology **have-nots**.

4 Of course, it was only natural that technology have-nots would want more. Soon, they started stealing from and rebelling against humans with technology. Something had to be done. Again, machines seemed to be the answer. People **installed** security systems in their homes and businesses. Computers used **video cameras** to watch everything and everyone. When security **deteriorated**, people started thinking about having robot guards. Of course, the robot guards **were** just **supposed to** stop and **detain** criminals, not hurt them. But when robot guards started being destroyed, people insisted that the robots be **armed**.

5 While all this was going on, two other **lines** of research were being pursued in **artificial** intelligence laboratories. One area of interest was robots that could recreate themselves. The plan was to send them to a new planet, like Mars, and let them start building cities for **colonists** who would come after. No one ever thought of what would happen if they escaped their labs on Earth. Another research

direction was in **parallel** processing. Rather than just create a supercomputer, scientists realized that several ordinary computers **networked** together could think in the same way. Soon, computers connected over the Internet were talking to each other and solving problems. But they could also create problems.

6 One of the real problems was the whole idea of **remote** control. In Finland, people started using their mobile phones to control all kinds of things in their homes. They wanted their rooms warm when they got home from work and wanted the stoves cooking their dinners and the **bathtubs** full of hot water. But what if someone or something else could control these same things? What if your rooms could be turned ice cold while you slept, your **oven** set on fire and your bathtub made to overflow? When my old **wind-up** radio still worked, the first news reports blamed have-not computer **hackers** for spreading computer **viruses** that made robots and computers do everything they could to kill humans, starting with interrupting food, water, electricity and **fuel** supplies. I don't know if that's true.

7 But I did see the end coming. Forty years ago, I left the city, moved into a **cave** high in the mountains and started growing my own food and making everything I needed by hand. When the first robot wars started, they didn't even notice I was up here, without electricity or a single machine. **Eventually**, of course, the robots **ruled** the world. And what did they need humans for?

8 Well, I better finish this now. The robot mailman will be here in a few minutes.

Yours sincerely and good luck,

Eve Last (728 words)

New Words

Homo sapiens /ˌhəʊməʊˈsæpienz/ *n.* the kind or species of human being that exists now 现代人，智人

robot /ˈrəʊbɒt/ *n.* 机器人

peruse /pəˈruːz/ *vt.* to read something, esp. in a careful way 细读

supposedly /səˈpəʊzɪdli/ *adv.* according to what is generally thought or believed but not known for certain 假定地，被信以为真地

air conditioner /ˈeəkənˌdɪʃənə(r)/ *n.* 空调

sprinkler /ˈsprɪŋklə(r)/ *n.* 洒水灭火装置

household /ˈhaʊshəʊld/ *adj.* 家用的

vacuum /ˈvækjuːm/ *adj.* 真空的

roam /rəʊm/ *vi.* to wander with no clear aim (没有目的地）走来走去

tend /tend/ *vt.* to take care of 照料

NEW WORDS

have-not /'hævnɒt/ *n.* people who do not have money or possessions 穷人

install /ɪn'stɔːl/ *vt.* to set up 安装

video camera /'vɪdiəʊ'kæmərə/ *n.* 摄像机

deteriorate /dɪ'tɪəriəreɪt/ *vi.* to become worse 恶化

detain /dɪ'teɪn/ *vt.* to officially prevent someone from leaving 拘留

arm /ɑːm/ *vt.* to supply with weapons 武装，装备

line /laɪn/ *n.* an area of interest 兴趣领域

artificial /ˌɑːtɪ'fɪʃəl/ *adj.* made by man; not natural 人工的

colonist /'kɒlənɪst/ *n.* 殖民主义者

parallel /'pærəlel/ *adj.* 平行的

network /'netwɜːk/ *vt.* (使计算机)联网

remote /rɪ'məʊt/ *adj.* distant in space or time 遥远的

bathtub /'bɑːθtʌb/ *n.* 浴缸

oven /'ʌvən/ *n.* 炉子

wind-up /'waɪndʌp/ *adj.* 上发条的

hacker /'hækə(r)/ *n.* a person who spends a lot of time using computers for a hobby, esp. to look at data without permission 黑客

virus /'vaɪərəs/ *n.* instructions that are hidden within a computer program and are designed to cause faults or destroy data 病毒

fuel /'fjuːəl/ *n.* any material that produces heat or power, usu. when it is burnt 燃料

cave /keɪv/ *n.* 洞穴

eventually /ɪ'ventʃuəli/ *adv.* in the end, at last 最后，终于

rule /ruːl/ *vt.* 统治

PHRASES & EXPRESSIONS

turn up 调高

be supposed to 应该，被认为

Cultural Background

1. Talos

   [希神] 铜人太洛斯：指宙斯制造的巨型铜人，职责是在克里特岛守卫着希腊神话中的米洛斯王（Minos）的宝藏，但最后被寻找金羊皮的众英雄所毁。

2. Crete

   克里特岛，希腊东南沿海的一个岛屿，位于地中海东部。克里特岛是希腊最大岛屿、古老文化中心、地中海著名旅游地，它也是地中海文明的发祥地之一。

课文译文

最后的信

任何人

任何地方

亲爱的任何人：

作为地球上最后一个现代人，一个年老的人，我决定写这最后一封信。也许某人某天在某地将读到这封信，也许只有机器人和计算机仔细研读，然后开怀大笑。我是怎么成为最后一个活着的人呢？让我来解释。

数千年来人们一直梦想着机器人和思维机。古希腊人谈论过太洛斯 —— 一个巨大的金属机器人，据称围着克里特岛每天走三次。帮助克里特国王作战的只不过是一个奴隶，而这一直是问题所在。人们总是把机器人当成奴隶，从来没有想过这些强大的工具可能有一天成为主人，把人们变成奴隶。

起初人们没有想过他们如何被思维机包围，但很快到处都是思维机。最早的一些思维机控制着温度——太冷时它们调高暖气温度，太热时打开空调。这听起来并不太危险，可一旦人们习惯了温度、灯光由机器控制，他们就开始用机器控制建筑的大门、洒水灭火装置和很多家用电器。自动真空吸尘器开始在人们家里走动，安装了修整花园程序的机器在户外工作。这太棒了！人们有了更多自由时间！不过事实上只有富人有了更多的自由时间。那些过去从事机器人所干的活的人，现在只能另寻其他的工作。突然之间，这个世界分成了两个阶层：技术富人和技术穷人。

那些技术穷人自然想得到更多。很快，他们开始偷窃和反抗技术富人。必须要采取措施。机器再次成了人们的答案。人们在家里和公司安装了安全系统，电脑用摄像头监视所有的事和人。当安全恶化了，人们开始考虑使用机器人保安。当然，机器人保安的作用应该是制止和拘留罪犯，而不是伤害他们。但是当机器人保安被毁坏时，人们坚持机器人应该武装起来。

在所有这一切进行的同时，人工智能实验室里还进行着另两个领域的研究。一是研究可以复制自身的机器人，计划把它们送到外星球，如火星，让它们为以后可能前往的殖民者建造城市。没人想过如果这些机器人逃离了地球上的实验室会发生什么。另一个研究方向是平行处理。科学家们意识到几个普通计算机联网也能发挥相同的思维作用而不只是创建一个超级计算机。很快，经互联网连接的计算机开始对话，一起解决问题，但它们同样可以制造许多问题。

其中真正的问题是关于遥控的想法。在芬兰，人们开始用手机控制家里各种各样的东西。他们希望下班回家后房间里是温暖的，炉子上做着晚餐，浴缸里盛满了热水。但是倘使别人或别的事物也可以控制这些东西会怎样呢？如果你睡了之后房间被调得冰冷，炉子起火，浴缸里的水溢出来，怎么办？当我的老式发条收音机还能用时，第一条新闻报导批评了贫穷的电脑黑客们传播计算机病毒，使得机器人和计算机想方设法地，从阻断食物、水电和燃料供应开始来扼杀人类。我不知道这一切是否是真的。

但我的确看到末日来临。40 年前，我离开了城市，搬进了山里高处的一个山洞里，自己种食物，用双手制造一切需要的东西。当第一场机器人大战开始时，它们甚至没有注意到我住在这儿,没有电和任何电器。当然,最终机器人统治了世界。它们需要人类干什么?

好吧，我最好就此结束。几分钟后，机器人邮差就会来了。

真诚地祝好运!

夏娃 · 拉斯特

2050 年 6 月 1 日

Notes to the Text

1. 书信的格式方面，英文信与中文信不完全相同，一般英文书信有以下几部分组成，其格式如下图：

Heading (写信人地址及写信日期)

Inside address (收信人姓名及地址)

Salutation (称呼)

Body (正文) ____________________

____

____

Complimentary close (结束语)

Signature (署名)

Postscript (附加语)

Enclosure (附件)

2. It was a slave that helped the King of Crete fight his enemies. (*Para. 2*)

这句是强调句型，It is/was + 被强调部分 + that...。该句型可用来强调主语、宾语、状语部分。一般不强调谓语动词，需要时可用 do 来强调谓语，如文中第 7 段 But I did see the end coming.

注意强调句型和定语从句的区别：

a. It is a question that needs careful consideration.
   这是个需要仔细考虑的问题。

b. It is novels that Miss White enjoys reading.
   怀特小姐最喜欢读小说。

句 a 是个含定语从句的句子，在这里 it 是指示代词，It is a question 是个主语 + 系动词 + 表语结构。而 b 句是个强调句型，在这里 it 是个引词，没有具体含义。

3. Of course, the robot guards were just supposed to stop and detain criminals, not hurt them. (*Para. 4*)

be supposed to do："应该，表示期待，义务，预定"等，有时表示间接的命令。

a. Every student is supposed to know the school regulation.
   每个学生都应该知道校规。

b. You're supposed to prepare the lesson.
   你应该准备功课。

c. You are not supposed to smoke here.
   你不该在这儿抽烟。

4. But when robot guards started being destroyed, people insisted that the robots be armed. (*Para. 4*)

insist 表示"坚持，坚持要求时"，that 从句用虚拟语气 should + 动词原形或直接用动词原形。如：

He insisted that I (should) go with him.

他坚持要求我跟他一起去。

但当 insist 作"坚持认为，坚持说"解时，其宾语从句要用陈述语气。如：

She insisted that she heard somebody in the house.

她坚持认为她听见有人在屋子里。

5. What if your rooms could be turned ice cold while you slept, ... (*Para. 6*)

What if... 是 What will (would) happen if...? 的缩略形式，译为"如果……将会怎么样？"从句中多用虚拟语气。

a. What if a storm should come up?
   如果暴风雨来了怎么办？

b. What if I should lose my passport?

万一我遗失了护照怎么办?

What if 还可以引出一个建议，邀请或要求，它引出的从句大多使用一般现在时，但也可以使用过去时，使用过去时是为了使建议变得委婉一些，显得不那么肯定。

c. What if you join us for lunch?

跟我们一起吃午饭怎么样?

d. What if we move the picture over there? Do you think it'll look better?

把画移到那儿怎么样? 你看会不会好看一点?

6. When my old wind-up radio still worked, the first news reports blamed have-not computer hackers for spreading computer viruses that made robots and computers do everything they could to kill humans, starting with interrupting food, water, electricity and fuel supplies. (*Para. 6*)

句中 that 引导的是一个定语从句，修饰 viruses; ... they could 是作 everything 的后置定语。

7. Well, I better finish this now. (*Para. 8*)

I better 是 I had better 的省略形式。

8. Eve Last

作者的名字带有讽刺意味,《圣经》关于世界起源的故事中，夏娃 (Eve) 是第一个女人，Last (最后一个) 表明后面再也没有人了。

Reading Comprehension

Choose the best option to complete each statement or answer each question according to the text.

1. Homo Sapiens are __________.

A. human beings B. robots C. computers D. the Earth

2. In this passage, robots and computers are described __________.

A. in a negative way

B. as geniuses

C. as world leaders

D. as inconvenient

3. According to the letter, in the future __________.

A. some people will become poorer

B. everyone will have free time

C. everyone will be safer

D. people can enjoy a comfortable life

4. Which of the following is NOT an interest of the computer research?

A. Artificial intelligence.

B. Robots recreating themselves.

C. Parallel processing.

D. Turning men into robots.

5. Which of the following statements is NOT true according to the passage?

A. Robots will control the world.

B. Computers will one day be smarter than humans.

C. Computers can think independently.

D. Robots may make people their slaves.

Key

1. A 2. A 3. A 4. D 5. C

Vocabulary Study

Replace each of the underlined parts with the best choice given.

1. People <u>installed</u> security systems in their homes and businesses.

A. set up B. founded C. established D. mounted

2. When security <u>deteriorated</u>, people started thinking about having robot guards.

A. became better B. came C. became worse D. declined

3. But when robot guards started being destroyed, people insisted that the robots be <u>armed</u>.

A. supported by us B. supplied with weapons C. lent a hand D. defeated by us

4. <u>Eventually</u>, of course, the robots ruled the world.

A. Undoubtedly B. Inevitably C. Equally D. At last

Key

1. A 2. C 3. B 4. D

UNIT 12 Giving Praise and Expressing Admiration

Study Focus:

1. 字母组合 ou, al, ia, ie 以及 io 的发音
2. 如何表示赞扬、羡慕

Part I Listening

Section A Phonetics

Key

1. D 2. A 3. B 4. C 5. C

Section B Short Conversations

Tapescripts

1. M: You look amazing. What's the occasion?

   W: I really want to look my best for my scholarship interview this afternoon.

   M: Well you look great. I hope it goes well.

   W: Thanks a lot.

   Q: Which of the following statements is true?

2. W: We have stayed six nights at the Grand Hotel.

   M: I hear that's a great hotel.

   W: Yes, but I'm ready to go back home.

   M: Oh, there's no place like home.

   Q: What is the conversation about?

3. W: Jenny is good at tennis.

   M: Speaking of tennis, John is the best.

   W: That's for sure. All sports are right up his alley. Actually, nobody has gotten a better hand over him yet.

M: He'll make a successful sportsman, I think.

Q: What does the man imply?

4. W: Mr. White, May I tell you what a nice suit that is you're wearing today?

M: Why, thank you, Lucy. Congratulations on your high sales figures this month.

W: With a product as good as yours, it practically sells itself!

M: Yes, well, I'm sure you and your team put in a lot of extra effort.

Q: For what reason does the man praise Lucy?

5. M: I really admire Mr. Brown.

W: For what?

M: Mr. Brown showed that he was worth his salt as a salesman when he got the highest sales record for the year.

W: Yes, you're right.

Q: Which of the following words is used to describe Mr. Brown as a salesman?

Key

1. C 2. C 3. B 4. A 5. D

Section C Passages

Exercise One

Tapescript

For centuries, Paris has attracted the admiration of the world. The charm of Paris impresses all who visit it.

Where can you discover the charm of Paris for yourself? Is it in the legacy of all the French rulers who worked to beautify their beloved city? Is it in the famous castles, palaces, statues and monuments, such as the Eiffel Tower? Can you find it in the world-class museums, such as the Louvre? Perhaps the charm of Paris lies in the zest and style of the Parisians.

Key

1) has attracted 2) who visit 3) for yourself 4) French rulers
5) the famous 6) such as 7) find it 8) lies in

Exercise Two

Tapescript

Do you enjoy being admired? Of course you do. We all do. After all, we have an innate desire to be admired. We want to be respected and held in high regard. Since we all feel that way, my statement comes as no surprise. However, what we may overlook is that we have an equally strong desire to admire and respect others. How can we have such a desire and be unaware of it?

Well, before we can love, appreciate, and admire others, we have to love, appreciate, and admire ourselves. But how can those who were brought up with frequent criticism admire themselves? For they feel defective. If they are often criticized, something must be wrong with them, they reason. If they are not respected by others, how can they have self-respect? And because they do not admire themselves, they do not learn how to admire others.

The admiration of others is a mark of maturity. When we are free of emotional baggage and in control of our lives, we come to accept, appreciate, and admire others. That's what I mean by saying, "We don't grow up until we look up to someone."

Questions:

1. What is the best title for the passage?
2. Which of the following statements is NOT true?
3. What will happen if people don't admire themselves?
4. What does the author mean by saying "We don't grow up until we look up to someone."?
5. Which of the following words is NOT mentioned in the passage?

Key

1. A 2. D 3. B 4. C 5. A

Notes

1. look amazing

意思是"看起来真棒！"。amazing"令人惊异的；了不起的"，例如：The new car goes at an amazing speed. 新车跑起来快得惊人。

2. … there's no place like home.

翻译为"金窝银窝不如自家狗窝"，这是由一部歌剧中的歌词演化而来，广为流传后渐渐成为谚语。这句话还有一个浓缩版："No place like home."

3. make a successful sportsman

意思是"成为一个成功的运动员"。make"（因有某特点、品质等而）足以成为，可发展为"，例如：He will make an excellent singer. 他将成为一名优秀的歌手。She will make a fine teacher. 她将来可以成为一个好教师。

Part II Speaking

Section A Functional Language

➡ ***How to give praise:***

Suggested expressions

You look amazing.

Very good.

I hear that's a great hotel.

Speaking of tennis, John is the best.

Nobody has gotten a better hand over him yet.

What a nice suit you're wearing today!

He was worth his salt as…

➡ ***How to express admiration:***

Suggested expressions

I really admire Mr. Brown.

➡ ***How to respond to praise or admiration:***

Suggested expressions

Thanks a lot.

That's for sure.

For what?

Section B Dialogue

Key

1. C 2. C 3. B 4. B 5. D

Section C Situational Communication

Phase 1

Suggested expressions

1. — This is really a nice restaurant.

— Yes. The environment is pleasant and the food looks great, too.

— Everything tastes great.

— Yeah. I enjoy the food here.

2. — I really admire Liu Xiang.

— For what?

— He has set a new world record in the men's 110-metre hurdles.

— You're right. Speaking of hurdlers, he is the best.

— That's for sure. I'm so proud of him.

Phase 2

Possible praise or admiration and replies for reference

1. — Nice going! That's how to get ahead.

— Thanks a lot.

2. — Shelley, what a nice hat (that is) you're wearing today!

— Thanks. My sister bought it for me.

3. — I'm so envious that you are flying/going to Australia. I want to go, too.

— That's nice to hear, thank you.

4. — Hi, Jean. Your new hairstyle is just perfect.

— What? Are you kidding?

5. — Wow, Lily. Your English is incredible.

— Thank you! It's nice of you to say so.